Pacific
WITHDRAWN
University

PACIFIC UNIVERSITY LIBRARY
FOREST GROVE. OREGON

Milton and the Paradoxes of Renaissance Heroism

JOHN M. STEADMAN

Milton and the Paradoxes of Renaissance Heroism

Louisiana State University Press
Baton Rouge and London

PACIFIC UNIVERSITY LIBRARY
FOREST GROVE, OREGON

Copyright © 1987 by Louisiana State University Press
ALL RIGHTS RESERVED
Manufactured in the United States of America

Designer: Laura Roubique
Typeface: Palatino
Typesetter: G & S Typesetters, Inc.
Printer: Thomson-Shore, Inc.
Binder: John H. Dekker & Sons, Inc.

10 9 8 7 6 5 4 3 2 1

LIBRARY OF CONGRESS CATALOGING-IN-PUBLICATION DATA

Steadman, John M.
    Milton and the paradoxes of renaissance heroism.

    Includes index.
    1. Milton, John, 1608–1674—Characters—Heroes.
    2. Milton, John, 1608–1674—Criticism and interpretation.
    3. Heroes in literature.   4. Courage in literature.
    5. Heroic virtue in literature.   6. Epic poetry—History
    and criticism.   I. Title.
    PR3592.H47S74   1987   821'.4   86-20080
    ISBN 0-8071-1332-8

The author is grateful to the editors of the following journals, monographs, and festschrifts for permission to reprint (with revisions) the essays that appear here as Chapters 1 through 5 and that were originally published in their pages: "The Arming of an Archetype: Heroic Virtue and the Conventions of Literary Epic," in Norman T. Burns and Christoper Reagan (eds.), *Concepts of the Hero in the Middle Ages and the Renaissance* (Albany, N.Y., 1975), 147–96; "Achilles and Renaissance Epic: Moral Criticism and Literary Tradition," in Horst Meller and H.-J. Zimmermann (eds.), *Lebende Antike: Symposion für Rudolf Sühnel* (Berlin, 1967), 139–54; "Beyond Hercules: Bacon and the Scientist as Hero," *Studies in the Literary Imagination*, IV (April, 1971), 3–47; "Milton's Rhetoric: Satan and the 'Unjust Discourse,'" *Milton Studies*, I (1969), 67–92; "*Ethos* and *Dianoia*: Character and Rhetoric in *Paradise Lost*," in R. D. Emma and J. T. Shawcross (eds.), *Language and Style in Milton* (New York, 1967), 193–232. Portions of Chapter 9 were presented as lectures at McMaster University in Hamilton, Ontario, and the University of Illinois at Urbana.

Contents

Preface and Acknowledgments

THE ESSAYS in this volume are focused primarily on the representation of spiritual combat in Milton's major poetry. They reexamine the theological presuppositions and rhetorical implications of the central temptation ordeals, and explore some of the ways in which the poet adapts rhetoric and theology alike to the demands of epic or dramatic structure and the image of the hero.

The first section of this study reconsiders the representation of heroic virtue in the Renaissance epic, contemporary reassessments of the Achilles-type hero, and Baconian idealizations of the scientist as a type of the hero. The second section reexamines Satan's command of rhetoric and his mastery of the techniques of the sophistic "unjust discourse." The third section considers aspects of magnanimity in *Samson Agonistes* and *Paradise Regained*: dialectical process in Milton's major poetry; the motif of Hercules at the crossroads as an element in the ordeal of initial choice; the Satanic exploitation of humanistic *topoi* in proposing the temptation of Athenian wisdom; and the paradoxes of heroic action and inaction in *Samson Agonistes*. The complexity of the Renaissance heroic tradition offered Milton ample opportunity for originality and variety in forming his epic and tragic characters and in structuring his epic and tragic plots. In particular, the close associations between heroic virtue and magnanimity gave him sanction for centering his poems on the ordeal of the spirit as the basis for testing and illustrating true "greatness of mind."

vii

A fellowship from the John Simon Guggenheim Memorial Foundation and subsequently a sabbatical leave from the University of California at Riverside were helpful in assisting me to organize this volume. To my friends and colleagues at the University of California, Riverside, and at the Henry E. Huntington Library, I am grateful for encouragement in planning this book. I am indebted to the editors and publishers of the journals and monographs in which several of these essays first appeared for permission to reprint.

PART I

Renaissance Heroic Paradigms
Action and Contemplation

Since neither wealth, nor honour, arms nor arts,
Kingdom nor Empire pleases thee, nor aught
By me propos'd in life contemplative,
Or active, tended on by glory, or fame,
What dost thou in this World?

—*Milton*, Paradise Regained

CHAPTER 1

The Arming of an Archetype: Heroic Virtue in Renaissance Epic

THE ARMING of the hero is a favorite epic motif. Prominent in medieval romance, in the oral tradition of the Slavs, and in the heroic poems of Homer, Virgil, and their imitators, it can be traced back—by those who like to extend the frontiers of literary history into prehistory—to the archaic poetry of the Middle East, to the Babylonian creation epic and to the Canaanite epic of Baal. The metaphorical variants of this motif are almost as familiar: the "moral rearmament" of the virtues and vices in the *Psychomachia* and the spiritual rearming of the warfaring Christian by Erasmus and Spenser and Saint Paul. Taking this trope as a point of departure, let us examine a few of the literary and ethical dilemmas that confronted the Renaissance poet in his attempts to invest his pattern hero not only with the martial arms of classical and romantic worthies but also with the moral and theological virtues of the Christian knight. Like the divine smith who had forged the arms of Achilles and Aeneas, the heroic poet was an armorer. His task was a double one: to endow the conventional military hero with the panoply of the higher virtues, and to equip an ethical abstraction with the material weapons of the warrior-prince. Teaching delightfully by force of example, he would on occasion employ the example of force. His labor (and it was a labor of Vulcan if not of Hercules) was to arm an archetype.

An Alexandrian poem, *The Argonauts*, has been called "an epic in search of a hero."[1] In Renaissance epic we may observe a compa-

1. Charles Rowan Beye, *The "Iliad," the "Odyssey," and the Epic Tradition* (Garden City, N.Y., 1966), 210.

3

rable quest—the search of the martial hero for the norms of a higher heroism and, conversely, the quest of the heroic ideals for a champion worthy of bearing their image and their name. Inherent in the epic tradition was a series of inner contradictions that seemed almost impossible to resolve: the tension between the customary matter of the virtues and the subject matter of epic poetry; the tension between the ideal form of the epic and the ideal forms of the heroic virtues; the tension between the form and matter of the poem; and, finally, the tension between the aims of pleasure and instruction. Poetry was simultaneously the imitation of an action and the imitation of moral archetypes. While Neo-Aristotelian poetics emphasized the plot as the very soul of the poem, the apologists for poetry as a moral discipline stressed its ability to imitate the ideas of virtue and vice. This dual emphasis on plot-as-pattern and hero-as-pattern sometimes confronted the poet with divergent, though not irreconcilable, imperatives. Even though he might be theoretically committed to entertaining his audience through a narrative fable and to edifying them through moral exemplars, he found it difficult at times to pursue both of these objectives simultaneously.

In the first place, it was hard to excite interest in the fortunes of an abstract idea. To the historian of ideas, the adventures of an archetype may indeed be the fabric of romance, the clash of concepts in a dialectical battle a far more absorbing encounter than the clatter of lance against shield or sword against sword. The duel of intellects in formal disputation and debate, or the struggle of self against self in meditative combat, may appear far more engaging than an ordeal by arms in the lists. To unhorse an idea in learned controversy may seem a greater and far more praiseworthy exploit than to unseat an antagonist at a joust or tournament. But a Renaissance epic poet and his audience might view the matter differently. It is easier to become involved in the fortunes of Orlando and Angelica or Scudamour and Amoret than in the hopes and perils of an abstraction. In a battle scene, one can muster up little sympathy for the wounds, however deadly, of a bloodless and fleshless idea.

Second, even though the poet might recognize the close relationships between logic and poetry, he was usually compelled to acknowledge that their methods were by no means the same. Although Milton's *Fuller Institution of the Art of Logic, Arranged after the Method of Peter Ramus* quoted passages from poets and orators to illustrate the principal *topoi* for argument, he was fully aware that the method of the poet—simple, sensuous, and passionate—differed as significantly from that of the dialectician as the open palm of rhetoric from the logician's clenched fist. As he observed near the end of his treatise, poets and orators may follow the analytic method when they set out to teach an auditor easily and clearly, but *"they do not always move in it and insist on it."* When the audience is to be *"allured with pleasure or some stronger impulse by an orator or a poet . . . a crypsis of method will usually be employed,"* and the *"order of things will be inverted."* Their *"*own doctrine of method," Milton concludes, "is to be turned over to the orators and poets" themselves—"or at least to those who teach oratory and poetics."[2]

Similarly, though Tasso regarded poetry as subordinate to dialectics (insofar as the poet aimed at probability and verisimilitude) or to logic, he was equally conscious of the difference between arguing a proposition and imitating an action.[3] As most Renaissance poets would have acknowledged, the movement of a formal syllogism from premises to conclusion through manipulation of a middle term is a different sort of progression from the movement of a poetic fable through its beginning and middle to its probable or necessary end. The structure of logical thought and the structure of narrative action remain fundamentally distinct even when they are employing the same concepts.

Among the outstanding features of the Renaissance heroic tradition are: first, the proliferation not only of epic poems but (more notably) of epic theories; second, the tension between classical ideals of the heroic poem and the conventions of the flourishing vernacular romance; third, the ambiguous and controversial relationship between the aesthetic aims of heroic poetry and its moral or religious ends; fourth, a predominantly normative and idealistic approach to the definition of the epic genre and the character of the epic person; and, finally, the variety of alternative norms or archetypes available both for the hero and for the heroic poem. The range and diversity of Renaissance heroic ideals aggravated the problem of accommodating them to an epic action. Not all

2. John Milton, *Artis Logicae Plenior Institutio*, ed. and trans. Allan H. Gilbert, in Frank Allen Patterson (ed.), *The Works of John Milton* (18 vols.; New York, 1931–38), XI, 481–85. The Patterson edition is hereinafter cited as *Works*.

3. Torquato Tasso, *Le prose diverse di Torquato Tasso*, ed. Cesare Guasti (2 vols.; Florence, 1875), I, 98–99.

modes of heroism lent themselves with equal facility to the requirements of narrative structure or the traditional techniques of epic presentation. In varying degrees the conventions of literary epic itself tended (paradoxically) to screen out the values of the higher heroism.

By definition, the heroic poem was devoted to the imitation of heroic action and heroic virtue, and to the praise of "godlike men." Traditionally, these were men of war—military leaders and princes. Their characteristic virtues were martial valor joined with tactical cunning or strategic prudence; and the actions in which they displayed these qualities were military enterprises. They belonged to a warlike (and frequently a courtly) culture, and the poetry dedicated to their exploits was often addressed to a similar society—to an aristocratic audience upon whose favor the poet himself might be dependent for patronage.

This conception of the epic as an aristocratic genre portraying the *ethos* of a military elite and directed to a ruling class of warriors is common to both oral and literary epic, though this distinction would not have held the same meaning for a Renaissance critic as for a twentieth-century scholar familiar with the researches of Milman Parry and Albert B. Lord. In a society where poet and audience shared the same heroic values as those of the epic protagonists themselves, there would have been little real tension between epic and heroic traditions: the poetic image would have tended to coincide with the cultural ideal of the hero. The epic poem could serve as mirror, vehicle, and norm for values that were not only traditional in the society, but were still widely accepted and commonly believed.

Nevertheless, like all other sublunary things, the epic tradition was subject to change—to generation and corruption—and inevitably, to revaluation. The Homeric poems themselves reflect a reconception of more primitive heroic tales—and, perhaps, an implicit critique of the older epic heroism.[4] Virgil's epic, in turn, represents a revaluation of the Homeric *ethos*. At the hands of Milton and Tasso, both Virgilian and Homeric ideals underwent a further revaluation. Once committed safely to paper, the oral epic had become a part of the literary tradition, serving as a potential

4. Cedric H. Whitman, *Homer and the Heroic Tradition* (New York, 1965), 154–55, 220.

model for poems composed under radically different circumstances and addressed to audiences reared in very different cul-
tures. Surviving the society that had created it, the Homeric epic
had become the cultural heritage of less martial classes in more
literate societies; it belonged to an audience of philologists and
antiquarians, philosophers and rhetoricians, who might treasure
it for meanings the poet himself had never intended and for values alien to its original audience.

Even in classical antiquity Homer's poetry had been reinterpreted by Stoics and Neoplatonists repelled by the violence of an
earlier heroic age; in their hands it became a vehicle for natural
and moral philosophy and for the values of a philosophical heroism. The heroic concept had outgrown the heroic song; the epic
itself needed to be transformed from within, reinterpreted and
thoroughly moralized in order to accommodate newer and more
spiritual ideals.

In many Renaissance epics one encounters significant dis-
parities between the heroic values conventional in the epic tradition and those of the poet's own society—tensions between the
traditional *ethos* of the epic hero and the norms of the "higher
heroism."[5] Epic and heroic traditions were manifestly at odds,
and the task of reconciling them—the problem of harmonizing
their conflicting values within a unified poetic structure—was
rather like trying to square the circle.

It is one of the ironies of heroic poetry that it should sometimes
obscure the very concept that it professes to illustrate. In attempting to subject a heroic action to the requirements of epic form, the
poet might feel compelled to modify his own conceptions of heroic virtue; he could distort his idea of the hero in the actual process of embodying it in a heroic image. However lofty or however
brutal the writer's ideas of heroic virtue might be, he must somehow present them within the framework of an intelligible story,
and he must also accommodate them to the tastes of his audience.
If his readers expected entertainment, he could not afford to bore
them with excessive moralizing. If they expected high serious-
ness, he could not satiate them with frivolities. If Achilles seemed
too savage for their tastes, and Odysseus too crafty, he must tem-

5. See *Times* (London) *Literary Supplement*, February 8, 1968, p. 134.

per his images of Homeric types with Renaissance chivalric ideas and the values of a spiritual aristocracy—a *Christiana nobilitas.*

Although the epic hero might sometimes defy human and divine ordinances, he could not consistently violate the principles of epic poetry. His character and actions alike must inevitably be conditioned by the demands of the narrative mode. Let us suppose, however, that the poet (and perhaps his audience as well) actually regards martial fortitude as inferior to Stoic and Christian patience, and that he really prefers the speculative wisdom of the philosopher or the intuitive vision of the saint to the warlord's strategic cunning. Let us assume that he really esteems the intellectual and theological virtues as proper to a higher heroism than physical valor. How is he to portray these loftier virtues in poetic form? As a narrative poet, he is committed to depicting them in and through an epic action. If he celebrates the "better fortitude" of patience and heroic martyrdom—an inner strength manifested in passion rather than action and through suffering rather than doing—he must organize his plot around heroes who do not primarily act, but are acted upon. If he portrays a contemplative heroism, tested through intellectual exercise rather than in deeds, he must nevertheless construct his narrative fable as an *imitatio actionis*, the imitation of an action. Moreover, unless he deliberately breaks with the established epic tradition and rejects a martial subject, he must depict these higher virtues in a predominantly military context.

At this stage, however, another difficulty arises. Although wars may be the conventional subject matter of heroic poetry, they are not necessarily the most suitable matter for heroic virtue. According to both classical and Christian ethics, the various categories of virtue and vice possessed their own appropriate subject matter, in which they were properly tested, perfected, and exercised. The most suitable matter for illustrating one virtue was not necessarily the matter best fitted for exhibiting a different virtue. One did not normally test temperance on a battlefield, for instance, or valor at a banquet. Similarly, though martial combat could exercise fortitude and even a certain kind of prudence, it was by no means the most appropriate vehicle for the majority of the higher virtues.

Nevertheless, as long as the poet retained a martial argument, this could profoundly influence his portrait of the higher heroism. Whatever spiritual excellencies he might wish to attribute to his hero, the actual victory must be won on the battlefield through force of arms; it would usually appear to have been achieved less by superior faith or charity or righteousness than by superior tactical skill, agility, and physical strength.

To portray effectively the values of the higher heroism, the poet must somehow introduce the actual matter of these virtues into the framework of his epic plot, contriving narrative situations that could adequately and appropriately test these qualities—manipulating incidents and arranging circumstances in order to emphasize loftier motives than wrath, ambition, and lust for glory. In such instances the hero's moral decisions, in some hermit's cell or lady's bower, could conceivably rival or even outweigh his *aristeia* on the battlefield. His inner motivation could become as significant as the external proofs of his valor, and the ends for which he fought more notable than his actual skill in combat. Moral crisis could thus become more decisive than the crisis of battle, and the hero's self-mastery more important than his mastery of arms. For Virgil, Aeneas' piety was more significant than his martial fortitude; and for the modern reader his encounters with Dido and the Cumaean Sibyl overshadow his duel with Turnus. In Renaissance epic, likewise, the divinely ordained ends for which the hero contended and the ethical motives underlying his commitment to his enterprise could divert emphasis from the physical means whereby he secured his victory—his "gorgeous arms" and his mastery of the techniques of dissection—to his spiritual arms and moral prowess, to the valor and heroism of the mind.

The inherent tensions within the Renaissance heroic tradition—between active and contemplative virtues, acquired and infused virtues, moral and theological virtues; between ideals of the hero as destroyer and benefactor, philosopher and conqueror, inventor and orator, ascetic and lover, martyr and Machiavellian prince—tended to heighten the technical problems that confronted the epic poet in choosing an argument, in adapting it to the formal demands of a narrative plot, and in finding a protagonist strong enough and wise enough to sustain the ethical burden of a pattern hero. Although Renaissance authors were not equally sensitive to these tensions between conflicting conceptions of the heroic *ethos*, and though some were content to ignore them altogether, Milton and the more "sage and serious" poets among his precursors were acutely aware of these problems and attempted in various ways to resolve them.

Allegorical interpretation had been a convenient and customary refuge for classical moralists dissatisfied with the brutish and sensual *ethos* of the older epic heroes; among Renaissance poets and critics it was still a standard technique for converting the heroic poem into a vehicle for a moral philosophy. By this means Sophists and Stoics, Neoplatonists—and even Christian bishops like Eustathius—had rendered Homer's heroic images acceptable to a more fastidious age.[6] Other exegetes had performed a comparable charity for Virgil, moralizing the egregiously moral *Aeneid* and accentuating the piety of its notoriously pious hero. In Renaissance epic and romance, lapses from moral decorum or from probability had been rationalized as allegory and justified on the grounds of their hidden meaning. In editions of Ariosto, Tasso, Graziani, and other Renaissance poets, allegorical commentaries became, not surprisingly, a standard bibliographical feature. Gratifying the contemporary taste for mysteries and enigmas, they could also help to forestall hostile criticism.

For the poet who desired to adapt epic conventions to higher ethical norms, the allegorical method offered distinct advantages. Although poetic conceptions of the traditional subject matter of epic narrative and philosophical doctrines concerning the appropriate matter of the virtues remained separate and distinct in theory, they could nevertheless be made to coincide in poetic allegory by superimposing one meaning upon the other. By exploiting the imagery of the *Psychomachia*, the epic narrator could effectively portray the combat of the virtues and vices (or the struggle of the soul against world, flesh, and devil) through the traditional symbol of a military enterprise. Martial combat could function symbolically as an extended metaphor for spiritual combat; the crisis on the battlefield could serve as a concrete image for the crisis in the human soul. Through the double vision of the allegorist, the values of the warrior could be transformed into those of the moral philosopher; and the essential outlines

6. For Renaissance allegorical interpretations of Homer and Virgil, see Don Cameron Allen, *Mysteriously Meant: The Rediscovery of Pagan Symbolism and Allegorical Interpretation in the Renaissance* (Baltimore, 1970), 83–105, 135–62.

of an ethical system could be compressed into a poetic fable. Through the process of poetic hermeneutics both levels of meaning—physical and spiritual conflict—could be firmly integrated within the framework of a single poem.

Recent criticism has wisely alerted us to the hazards of anticipating a one-to-one correspondence between events on the literal and the allegorical level. The coincidence of meanings, like the coincidence of contraries, is occasional rather than systematic. On occasion the narrative fiction becomes translucent, like the glaze on a Chinese bowl; the ideal meaning under the surface becomes visible, like the ideogram incised by the potter or the design in underglaze blue. As an instrument of moral philosophy (as in theory it claimed to be), the allegorical method could be eminently successful in communicating abstract ideas through concrete forms, in giving definition and focus to a single isolated concept, in emphasizing its interrelationships with allied concepts, and in clarifying its meaning by opposing it to its logical contrary. In scholastic logic it was axiomatic that the meaning of a given term could be made more evident by juxtaposing it with its opposite, and both poet and rhetorician were equally conscious of the persuasive force of contrary examples. For writers who desired to retain the conventional epic argument of warfare, the allegorical method permitted a sharper and more systematic concentration on the idea of heroic virtue and on the dialectical conflict with its contraries.

Although the allegorical mode might enable the poet to overcome the disparity between martial and ethical content and to present the trial of virtue in and through the trial at arms, it did not provide an easy solution to problems of structure. It was difficult to present the scholastic subtleties of formal ethics through heroic poetry, through a medium that was not only simple, sensuous, and passionate, but also demanded a special kind of structure inherited from classical epic, from medieval romance, or from both. Despite the popularity of moral allegory during the Renaissance, it rarely influenced epic structure to the extent that it had affected the structure of medieval poetry. Even though allegorical episodes are fairly common not only in the chivalric epics on Orlando but also in classicizing epics like Trissino's *Italia Liberata*, they remain, as a rule, isolated episodes in an action conceived rather as fictionalized history or fable than as a sustained metaphor. Parts of the Renaissance epic are conceived allegorically, but rarely the poem as a whole. Although Tasso and Graziani offered allegorical explanations that comprehended the entire poetic fable—interpreting the principal actions of *Jerusalem Delivered* and *The Conquest of Granada* as symbolic images of the pursuit of felicity—neither allegory is truly organic or intrinsic to the poem itself. To the contrary, both allegories appear to be ex post facto rationalizations, like earlier attempts to moralize the *Iliad*, the *Odyssey*, and the *Aeneid*. Formally and structurally, both of these Renaissance poems are essentially classical epics; both have adapted the argument of a holy war and the magical and erotic paraphernalia of the romance to a formal structure based on Homer and Virgil.

Spenser's epic reflects a rather different treatment of the allegorical mode. Unlike the epics of Tasso and Graziani, *The Faerie Queene* is conceived and executed virtually throughout as allegory; it requires an allegorical interpretation for the full appreciation of the story. Nor are its allegorical patterns merely episodic, like Trissino's allegory of Acratia or Tasso's allegory of Fortuna. In varying degrees and with varying success, Spenser has attempted to organize each book around a particular virtue associated with a particular champion, contriving the various episodes within that book in such a way as to exhibit the attributes of that virtue, its association with related virtues and their goals, and its opposition to its contrary vice or vices. Moreover, the comprehensive nature of Magnanimity—a virtue that, like *virtus heroica* and *caritas*, includes the totality of the virtues—is concretely demonstrated through the role of Prince Arthur (or Magnificence) and his intervention in the actions of the various books devoted to more specialized virtues. In linking together the separate books of his epic through the person of Arthur, through the Order of the Knights of Maidenhead, and through the final, unwritten, scene at Gloriana's court (where all of the principal champions set out on their respective quests), Spenser not only endeavored to combine the variety of the romantic fable with the unified plot structure of classical epic; he also succeeded, in large part, in fusing ethical structure with narrative structure, in accommodating a pattern of ideas to the pattern of incidents and a pattern of incidents to a pattern of ideas.

Nevertheless, there were major limitations to the exploitation of allegory in heroic poetry. Even in the lifetime of Spenser and Tasso, the allegorist was being steadily forced upon the defensive;

and this attack was based on moral grounds as well as on grounds of poetic theory. Tasso had argued that the poet ought to delight through his imitation and instruct through his allegorical content; other writers had similarly exhorted the reader to look beneath the veil of the poetic fable to the latent moral sense. Underlying these exhortations was a *topos* that could be traced back to Lucretius and beyond—the conception of the poet as a physician of the soul, and of poetry itself as a honeyed medicine or sugared pill. To these arguments a churlish moralist might reply that the poet was not a licensed pharmacist and that his apothecary's shop was crammed with strange and even monstrous remedies— dragon's bones, Chimaera's skins, and even the manifold scalps of the Hydra. Moreover, in compounding his medicines, he usually mixed his ingredients wrongly. Instead of mingling profit and pleasure in equal proportions, he often neglected the *utile* for the *dulce*, the useful for the sweet. The medicinal element was minimal, and the sugarcoating infected with vice. Instead of a wholesome pill, he offered his feverish patient an envenomed sweetmeat, a poisoned bonbon.

As the allegorical method had been closely associated with the romance, it inevitably became an issue in the critical controversies of the period. The moral justification of the romance—and perhaps its chief defense—rested largely on the value of pleasing fictions as a vehicle for wholesome truths. Beneath the amours of cavaliers and ladies and the mutual dissections of fabled knights in battles feigned, the reader was encouraged to search for a hidden moral; even the improbabilities of the romantic plot could be rationalized as allegory. On the literal level, however, the martial and amorous adventures of chivalric epic and romance—their images "of dames, of knights, of arms, of love's delight, / Of courtesies, of high attempts"—were vulnerable to the same accusations that Ascham leveled against Malory's romance, charges of "open mans slaughter and bold bawdrye." Ariosto might identify Angelica's ring with reason and suggest that to a judicious reader, capable of penetrating beneath the surface of the fiction to its hidden meaning, much that seemed "brutto e rio" would appear "bello e buono"—but this assertion did not protect him against accusations of immorality and improbability. Although Tasso professed to "Anoint with sweets the vessel's foremost parts" and thus beguile his audience into swallowing its "potions sharp," he did not manage to deceive all of his readers, and some of them protested violently against this mixture of "fictions light . . . with truth divine." In the eyes of "Stoicke censours," the "Fierce warres and faithfull loves" of Spenser's epic definitely did not "moralize his song." On the contrary, to hostile critics they were dangerous frivolities, meretricious baits that could seduce his younger and frailer readers from the arduous trail of virtue into the smoother ways of dalliance. The opening stanza of Book IV of *The Faerie Queene* shows Spenser's concern about such critics:

> The rugged forhead that with grave foresight
> Welds kingdomes causes, and affaires of state,
> My looser rimes (I wote) doth sharply wite,
> For praising love, as I have done of late,
> And magnifying lovers deare debate;
> By which fraile youth is oft to follie led,
> Through false allurement of that pleasing baite,
> That better were in vertues discipled,
> Then with vaine poemes weeds to have their fancies fed.

In the long run, however, the censures of literary critics and the changing tastes of the poet's audience were largely responsible for undermining the allegory. The romance itself was under attack for disregarding unity of action, for basing its arguments on fables rather than on history, for violating decorum in persons and style, and for failing to observe verisimilitude and probability. Its apologists protested in vain that it was legally exempt from the laws governing the epic; that fiction could be more instructive than history; that variety gave more pleasure than formal unity; and that the romantic poet addressed his fantasies to the imagination, and their allegorical meaning to the reason. One of the crucial points at issue was whether violations of probability and verisimilitude could be justified on the grounds of allegory. In defending Dante's *Commedia*, Jacopo Mazzoni maintained that they could; the "impossible" might nonetheless be perfectly "credible" by virtue of its allegorical content.[7] Tasso's theory permitted

---

7. See Robert L. Montgomery, Jr., "Allegory and the Incredible Fable: The Italian View from Dante to Tasso," *PMLA*, LXXXI (1966), 45–55; Allan H. Gilbert, *Literary Criticism: Plato to Dryden* (2nd ed.; Detroit, 1962), 365–88; Murray Krieger, "Jacopo Mazzoni, Repository of Diverse Traditions or Source of a New One?" in Rosario P. Armato and John M. Spalek (eds.), *Medieval Epic to the "Epic Theater" of Brecht* (Los Angeles, 1968), 97–107; Irene Samuel, *Dante and Milton: The "Commedia" and "Paradise Lost"* (Ithaca, N.Y., 1966); and John M. Steadman, "Allegory and Verisimilitude in *Paradise Lost*: The Problem of the 'Impossible Credible,'" *PMLA*, LXXVIII (1963), 36–39. In his *Della difesa della Commedia di Dante*, Mazzoni

ample scope for allegory, but nevertheless demanded verisimilitude and probability in the poet's imitation.[8] A taste for "Tour-
neys" and "Trophies" and "enchantments drear, / Where more is
meant than meets the ear" persisted well into the seventeenth
century; but the climate in which it struggled to survive became
progressively colder and more inclement. Neo-Aristotelian and
Horatian criticism left little room for allegory, and it was the ra-
tionalistic approach to poetic imitation—the demand for probability and verisimilitude—that eventually triumphed.

The allegorical mode was better suited to the narrative method
of the romances than to the plot structure of epics composed
on classical models. Its value as a vehicle for ethical concepts
depended largely on carefully contrived situations: particular
scenes and episodes in which the personified virtue (or its champion) formed alliances with related virtues or decisively defeated
a contrary vice. As an imitator of abstract ideas in concrete forms,
the allegorist achieved the ethical intent of his art most effectively by sharply differentiating a single concept and subsequently tracing its operation through various situations that
could systematically analyze and symbolically clarify its logical
relationships to other moral categories. This mode of presentation could be employed to best advantage in a loosely organized
plot allowing a variety of individual scenes and episodes, rather
than in a tightly structured narrative. It enabled the poet, from
time to time, to isolate an idea and bring it temporarily into
sharper focus through a visual tableau or verbal emblem. We see
it at its best in such episodes as Scudamour's vigil in the House
of Care and the metamorphosis of Malbecco from jealous husband into Jealousy itself. In the House of Care, Spenser combines a wide variety of mythological and musicological themes

---

had elaborated Plato's distinction between icastic and fantastic imitation (in the
Sophist) and Aristotle's distinction between dramatic and narrative modes of imitation into a complex poetic theory that classified poetry as a "subdivision of . . .
sophistic," inasmuch as it paid "more attention to the credible than to the true." In
his *Discorsi del poema eroico*, Tasso challenged this classification, arguing that poetry (or at least the most perfect poetry) belongs not to sophistic but to dialectic or
logic. *Cf.* Tasso, *Prose diverse*, I, 98–100. The most perfect poetry is not fantastic
imitation, as Mazzoni had asserted, but the imitation of things that are or were or
can be, like the Trojan War and Achilles' wrath and Aeneas' piety and the battles
between Trojans and Latins.

8. See Tasso, "Allegoria della *Gerusalemme Liberata*," in *Prose diverse*, I, 301;
Tasso, *Discorsi del poema eroico, ibid.*, I, 88, 98.

in a single emblematic tableau of the jealousy of the lover; in the Malbecco episode he begins with a narrative exemplum of marital jealousy and ends with a personification. The vice is no longer merely an adjunct of the man, but the man himself.

Although Milton would subsequently introduce allegorical episodes into a neoclassical epic, the fortunes of the allegorical method were too closely interlinked with those of the romance to flourish in the latter's decay. Critical attacks on the multiple actions of the romance, on its interwoven plots, and on its episodic structure thus worked indirectly to the disadvantage of the allegorist. And, indeed, Milton himself would incur the censure of later critics for his allegory of Sin and Death.

The allegorical mode, then, might enable the poet to display the higher virtues within a martial context, but on the literal level it left him vulnerable to hostile criticism; the overt moral content of his story and his manner of developing it had been attacked by moralists and literary theorists alike. There remained, however, still another alternative. The epic poet might reject a martial argument altogether and select a subject matter more appropriate for exercising the virtues of a perfect hero. To illustrate chastity, for instance, he might recast the stories of Susanna and Joseph in epic form. For the trial of heroic patience he already possessed a divinely inspired—and divinely dictated—model in the biblical epic (or tragedy) of Job, as well as a successful neo-Latin epic on the Passion of Christ.[9] Significantly, one of Milton's juvenilia, an incomplete ode on the Passion, specifically commends Vida's heroic poem on this subject ("Loud o'er the rest *Cremona's* Trump doth sound"). The young Englishman still regarded himself as a novice; his powers were not yet adequate for Calliope's trumpet, and for the present he must confine himself to lyric modes, the "softer strings of Lute, or Viol." Nevertheless, his "softer airs" are devoted to the same "Most perfect *Hero*" and the same heroic trial in "heaviest plight / Of labors huge and hard, too hard for human wight." From Milton's point of view—and probably from Vida's— the Passion might seem to be an inevitable subject for sacred epic. It could represent, in a degree that no other argument could, the

9. On the Book of Job as epic, see Barbara Kiefer Lewalski, *Milton's Brief Epic: The Genre, Meaning, and Art of "Paradise Regained"* (Providence, R.I., 1966); Charles W. Jones, "Milton's Brief Epic," *Studies in Philology*, XLIV (1947), 209–27.

aristeia of the godlike man, for its protagonist was no less than the Logos itself in human form, the divine archetype embodied in a pattern hero. It contained the traditional heroic motifs of deliverance and public safety (*salus*), but transferred from the physical plane to the spiritual, and from the national dimension to the universal. It exhibited the norm of spiritual warfare and victory— combat against demonic principalities and dominions and triumph over Satan's monstrous vicegerents, Sin and Death. It illustrated the conventional heroic pattern of superlative merits acquired through arduous labors and rewarded with apotheosis or glorification. Finally, in the image of the Suffering Servant it exhibited the norm of heroic patience and the fortitude of the martyr. In a culture theoretically dedicated to the *imitatio Christi*, the epic quest for a perfect hero, embodying the heroic archetype in its perfection, would seem to point to the Passion itself as the epic argument par excellence. From a somewhat narrower viewpoint, indeed, this might appear to be virtually the only heroic argument. By one definition of the hero—as the son of a deity and a mortal—the epic person of Vida's *Christiad* and Milton's *Paradise Regained* would, in the strictest sense, be the *only* hero.

In this case the problem of finding a subject matter and an epic protagonist capable of sustaining the weight of the heroic virtues would appear to be largely resolved. As an incarnation of the divine image, the epic person would be more than a symbolic representative of the heroic archetype, more than a personification of an abstract moral ideal, more than an idealized substratum for the virtues—more than an artificial hero created by the poet himself and crushed under the weight of the virtues with which the poet had invested him. In an epic on the Passion, the epic hero would actually be the heroic archetype. Instead of merely embodying the ideal of *virtus heroica* or possessing the heroic virtues as adjuncts, he would *be* heroic virtue; in the language of the Neoplatonists, he would be the "exemplary virtues."

By taking the incarnate Logos as his epic person, the *poeta Christianus* was thus able to circumvent one of the major obstacles that confronted his contemporaries in their search for a pattern hero. On the other hand, he faced other difficulties that might prove equally embarrassing. Although these obstacles did not deter Diego de Hojeda, Robert Clarke, and later poets from essaying a *Christiad*, or discourage Rapin from writing a short heroic poem on *Christus Patiens*, they may perhaps have deterred John

Milton from writing an epic on the Passion. It is significant that though in both of his epics he extolled the Passion as the supreme heroic exploit—the *aristeia* of the most perfect hero—and though he once considered it as a subject for tragedy, he did not elect it as an epic argument. In *Paradise Lost* he centered his plot on the contrary pole of the Adam-Christ parallel—the disobedience of the first man and his expulsion from Paradise. In *Paradise Regained* he chose as his argument the temptation of Christ. Although both arguments were proleptic and derived their full significance from their relationship to the Passion, this event actually lay beyond the scope of his epic fable; the Passion was not the actual subject of either epic; nor did it fall within the time span of the principal action. It could only be indirectly foreshadowed or directly prophesied. In a sense *Paradise Lost* is the *Iliad* of the "celestial cycle"; it points forward to the saga of redemption in roughly the same way that (for a Renaissance audience reading Homer in the light of Virgil) the action of the *Iliad* points forward to that of the *Aeneid* and to the foundation of new and greater dominions in the West by Brutus, Francus, and other exiled Trojan heroes.[10] (Indeed Milton himself, in his description of Eve, introduced an allusion to the Judgment of Paris.) Just as the destruction of Troy prepares the way for the foundation of Rome and the establishment of Troynovant (British Troy), Adam's exile from Paradise through disobedience sets the stage for Christ's establishment of a new and happier Paradise within and the triumph of the Church, the *regnum Dei* or kingdom of Heaven. *Paradise Regained,* in turn, as an ordeal of initial choice confronting the youthful hero at the commencement of his heroic career, bears essentially the same relationship to Christ's ministry and Passion that Hercules' Choice and Scipio's Dream bear to the future exploits of these classical worthies.

Perhaps the chief disadvantage of the Passion as an epic subject was the fact that the detailed narratives of the Evangelists afforded the poet comparatively little scope for invention. In the opinion of many Renaissance critics, poetic imitation resided in the invention of probable circumstances—fictional incidents and details that would enable the poet to construct a well-made plot

10. See Watson Kirkconnell, *The Celestial Cycle: The Theme of Paradise Lost in World Literature* (Toronto, 1952), for this phrase. On analogies between the epics of Milton and Homer, see Martin E. Mueller, "The Tragic Epic, *Paradise Lost* and the *Iliad*" (Ph.D. dissertation, Indiana University, 1966).

and to develop his narrative with verisimilitude and probability. Elaborating the suggestions he had found in Aristotle's poetic and logical treatises, Tasso had advised the poet to select a subject matter capable of receiving the form or idea of the heroic poem. Ideally, this would be some history remote and obscure enough to allow the poet ample license to invent or feign, though Tasso foresaw practical difficulties in a very ancient theme.[11] Although Milton based his epic arguments on scriptural authority (despite Tasso's admonition against a biblical theme), in both cases the textual accounts were sufficiently brief and obscure to allow him full scope for inventing details and organizing his material according to the formal rules of the epic genre and the example of the ancients.[12]

Early readers of *Paradise Lost* were sometimes perplexed as to its genre, whether it might "be called an heroic poem," while others were merely irritated by the question. Addison preferred to "waive the discussion of that point," declaring that nothing was "more irksome" than "general discourses, especially when they turn chiefly upon words." Those who denied Milton's epic the title of heroic poem might "call it (if they please) a divine poem." In Jonathan Richardson's opinion, the question was insignificant ("'tis of no great importance whether this be called an heroic or a divine poem, or only, as the author himself has called it in his title-page, a poem"). All the same, *Paradise Lost* was, in fact, heroic

11. See Tasso, *Prose diverse*, I, 86–87, 111–13. After observing that the history of a very remote period or nation would be a suitable subject for a heroic poem, Tasso points out the technical difficulties inherent in a subject derived from ancient or modern history. If the poet chooses an argument based on antiquity, he must run the risk of boring his readers by describing the customs and mores of antiquity— its methods of warfare, its banquets and ceremonies, and other usages of some remote period. If he introduces modern usages into ancient times, he will resemble an injudicious painter who invests his portrait of Cato or Cincinnatus with the fashions of the Milanese or Neapolitan youth. Modern histories, in turn, take away the license to feign and imitate, which is very necessary to poets, especially to writers of epics. Finally Tasso appeals to the authority of Aristotle, who had explained in his *Problems* why the narration of things neither too new nor too ancient is pleasing. Milton's epic argument would not be vulnerable to the objection against matters too remote inasmuch as it rested on the authority of Scripture. At the same time the biblical account of the Fall was sufficiently brief and obscure to permit the poet to add the probable or necessary circumstances that would give verisimilitude, plausibility, and structural unity to his plot.

12. Tasso, *Prose diverse*, I, 110–11.

poetry—"properly and strictly heroic, and such Milton intended it, as he has intimated in his short discourse concerning the kind of verse, . . . as also in his entrance on the ninth book." Samuel Johnson similarly dismissed the problem as irrelevant; the questions "whether the poem can be properly termed *heroick,* and who is the hero, are raised by such readers as draw their principles of judgement rather from books than from reason." Like Richardson, he observed that though Milton entitled *Paradise Lost* "only a *poem,*" he "calls it himself *heroic song.*"[13]

Nevertheless, from the point of view of the literary historian, the question of genre cannot be dismissed so lightly. In an age when literary criticism was still a captive of its own inherited categories, still shackled within the theory of literary kinds and formal rules, this issue was more than a verbal quibble. Unless Milton had altogether outgrown his earlier respect for generic distinctions and the principles underlying the various literary species, the question of the genre of *Paradise Lost* would have seemed far from insignificant to him. A full awareness of his innovations in heroic tradition—his variations on the heroic image and his revaluations of epic heroism—would depend, in large part, on his audience's recognition of the genre of his epic on the Fall. It is simultaneously (and perhaps paradoxically) heroic poetry and divine poetry: heroic inasmuch as its protagonist is a man initially perfect, though capable of marring his perfection; and divine inasmuch as it draws its argument from Scripture and consistently orders its plot *ad majorem gloriam Dei.* Insofar as Milton's epic achieves a critique and partial reorientation of the heroic tradition, it does so within the framework of heroic poetry and through the conscious juxtaposition of human and divine merits.

Why the title pages of the first and second editions of *Paradise Lost* identified it simply as "A Poem" without further specifying its genre, and why *Paradise Regained* bore the same innocuous and noncommittal designation, remains uncertain. Although Milton must have given his consent, the suggestion could conceivably have come from someone else (possibly the publisher) aware of what a contemporary audience expected a heroic poem to be and reluctant to provoke critical attacks if they could be avoided. To an

13. James Thorpe (ed.), *Milton Criticism: Selections from Four Centuries* (2nd ed.; New York, 1969), 23, 56–57, 75–76.

audience nurtured on cavalier epics and heroic plays, the fall of man might seem, of all arguments, the least promising for heroic poetry; a title like "Paradise Lost. An Heroick Poem" might appear self-contradictory. Some of them might admire it as an ingenious paradox or an audacious oxymoron; but others might greet it as churlishly as that earlier generation of browsers who had encountered *Tetrachordon* on the bookstalls: "Cries the stallreader, bless us! what a word on / A title page is this!" Perhaps it was Milton himself, rather than his publisher, who feared that the title "Heroic Poem" might invite ridicule and accordingly selected a more neutral term.

Once safely past the title page, however, the poet could afford to be less evasive. Both in the text of *Paradise Lost* and subsequently in his note on "The Verse" he explicitly identified it (as both Richardson and Johnson observed) as a heroic poem. In the opening lines of Book IX he deliberately accentuated, and perhaps exaggerated, his break with the epic tradition. Man's disobedience and Heaven's anger constituted a higher argument than the wrath of Turnus and Achilles or Juno and Poseidon. Although warfare had hitherto been the "only Argument / Heroic deem'd," the battle episodes and banquet scenes conventional in heroic poetry had missed the essence of true heroism. They exhibited merely the baser "skill of Artifice or Office mean," not that "which justly gives Heroic name / To Person or to Poem."

As an experienced polemicist, Milton was fully aware of the value of an aggressive defense. In his *Apology for Smectymnuus,* his defenses of the English people, and in his *Pro Se Defensio,* he had conducted a series of raids into enemy territory and had returned with trophies that would have been the envy of any Jivaro tribesman: the scalps of Salmasius and Alexander More, the unkempt tresses of a disgraced serving girl, the crowned head of a British king, and the mitered crania of several English bishops. In defending his epic argument and his unrhymed verse he again undertook the offensive, directing his attack against the weaker spots in the tradition he was attacking. To a modern reader his arguments may appear slightly disingenuous; they are accurate only if one introduces the necessary qualifications that the poet himself cleverly avoided.

In the first place, his charge that warfare was the only argument hitherto regarded as heroic is an overstatement. Even though he may have regarded the creation epics of Tasso and Du-

Bartas as divine poems rather than as heroic poetry, he must have known that numerous poets had already extolled the patience of martyrs or had turned (like himself) to the Scriptures for nonmartial themes. He could hardly have forgotten his own eulogy of Vida's *Christiad*. If few of these works merited serious consideration, the defect resided in their quality rather than in their quantity. Milton's indictment of the epic tradition is valid only as a general statement covering the majority of heroic poems or, more narrowly, the comparatively small group of epics of truly outstanding quality. Most of the latter *were* martial epics. Horace's dictum concerning the proper subject for heroic verse ("the deeds of kings and martial leaders and grievous wars") had passed virtually unchallenged.[14] In this context, Milton's break with the epic tradition in rejecting a military subject was fully as dramatic as he claimed it to be. Moreover, it also represented a reorientation of his own earlier views on the proper subject matter for epic poetry. Although his early plans for tragedies had indicated a pronounced preference for a biblical subject, his early statements concerning his epic ambitions had shown an equally marked preference for a national theme—the exploits of Brutus or Utherpendragon, Arthur or Alfred, or some other king or knight before the Norman Conquest. He had preferred a divine tragedy, but a national epic.[15]

Second, the characteristics of the martial epic that he found repugnant are typical rather of the romance than of the classical epic.[16] Although races and games are conventional in classical poetry, they usually occupy a minor part in the narrative action; they provide a temporary diversion, and sometimes comic relief, from the tensions of combat or the vicissitudes of a voyage. Other details,

14. Horace, *Ars Poetica*, in *"Satires," "Epistles," and "Ars Poetica,"* trans. H. Rushton Fairclough (Cambridge, Mass., 1966), 456: "Res gestae regumque ducumque et tristia bella" (l. 73).

15. See Milton's remarks on his literary ambitions in his *Mansus, Epitaphium Damonis*, and *The Reason of Church-Government* (*Works*, III, 237–41) and the list of dramatic subjects in the Trinity College MS (*ibid.*, XVIII, 228–45). In the dramatic notes, biblical subjects outnumber the subjects based on British history. All of the more detailed dramatic sketches, including the four outlines for a tragedy on Adam's fall, are based on scriptural narratives.

16. See Wayne Shumaker, *"Paradise Lost* and the Italian Epic Tradition," in Amadeus P. Fiore (ed.), *Th'Upright Heart and Pure* (Pittsburgh, 1967), 87–100.

> tilting Furniture, emblazon'd Shields,
> Impreses quaint, Caparisons and Steeds;
> Bases and tinsel Trappings, gorgious Knights
> At Joust and Torneament; then marshal'd Feast
> Serv'd up in Hall with Sewers, and Seneshals
>
> *(Paradise Lost,* IX, 34–38)

belong primarily to chivalric romance. Fabulous knights and fictitious battles are also more characteristic of romance than of classical epic, but even in the romances they are not always fabulous. Behind the romanticized Rolands and Olivers and Charlemagnes, there generally remained a shadow of historical truth. The charge that the martial epic neglected the better fortitude of patience and martyrdom for an inferior mode of heroism is, on the whole, just; and it effectively diagnoses one of the principal ethical defects of the conventional epic subject. This accusation, however, serves rather to deflate the traditional epic argument than to support Milton's own choice of subject. Despite the emphasis it receives in various episodes of Milton's poem, the martyr's patience is not the central theme of *Paradise Lost*. The crucial temptation scene, on which the plot turns, centers upon the trial of obedience (or, more broadly, constancy, loyalty, and love). Although the heroism of the martyr is depicted in other heroes—in the Son's *kenosis* as Suffering Servant, in Abdiel's solitary defense of truth against the scorn of multitudes, and in the constancy of the "one just man" against the contumely of the world—this is not the principal virtue subjected to trial in the temptation of Adam and Eve.[17]

As a heroic poem, *Paradise Lost* would inevitably be judged by the rules of its genre, measured against contemporary ideals of the epic and against classical and modern examples. It belonged to a well-established (though sometimes ambiguously defined) tradition and would be read in the light of this tradition. During a century or more of sustained debate over the norms of heroic poetry and the relative merits of Homer and Virgil, Ariosto and Tasso, and other ancients and moderns, critical readers had developed a sharp eye for apparent violations of the rules and for variations within the tradition itself. Milton could expect his

17. See Michael Lieb, "Milton and the Kenotic Christology: Its Literary Bearing," *ELH*, XXXVII (1970), 342–60.

readers to approach his poem both as a sacred epic in the tradition of divine poetry and as a heroic poem in the tradition of Homer and Virgil and Tasso. Insofar as his poem broke with the epic tradition in choice of subject, it behooved him to define its relationship to the tradition and to justify his innovation. This he did, with no little rhetorical ingenuity, in the passage we have just examined. His apologia, however, did not explore the full extent of his innovations on the epic tradition. These apparently went far beyond his rejection of a martial argument and his substitution of the wrath of the biblical God for the rage of fabulous divinities and legendary heroes. They involved a reconception of the pattern hero and the role of the epic person. In comparison with Godfrey and Prince Arthur, with Odysseus and Aeneas—and indeed even with Achilles—Adam seems a significantly different kind of epic protagonist.

Theoretically, the Renaissance epic attempted to form an image of heroic virtue, exhibiting this ideal in the person and actions of the epic protagonist. It was within this frame of reference that critics approached the epics of Homer and Virgil and the heroic poetry of their own contemporaries. Poems were judged not only on qualities of style and structure but also on the comparative merits of their heroes. If Odysseus was a more perfect hero than Achilles, then the *Odyssey* came closer than the *Iliad* to achieving a principal end of heroic poetry: the creation of a heroic exemplar. By the same line of reasoning the *Aeneid* could seem more heroic than Homer's epics, and the *Gerusalemme Liberata* superior as heroic poetry to all three.

The moral quality of its protagonist was, of course, merely one of several criteria by which an epic poem might be judged. Renaissance theorists were quite aware that Aristotle had regarded plot as even more important than character, and that pleasure and profit—literary and ethical values—were not precisely the same thing.[18] Nevertheless, they were also conscious of the interrelationships between moral and aesthetic criteria and between

18. See *Aristotle on the Art of Poetry,* trans. Ingram Bywater (Oxford, 1909), 21: "We maintain . . . that the first essential, the life and soul, so to speak, of Tragedy is the Plot; and that the Characters come second—compare the parallel in painting, where the most beautiful colours laid on without order will not give one the same pleasure as a simple black-and-white sketch of a portrait. We maintain that Tragedy is primarily an imitation of action, and that it is mainly for the sake of the action that it imitates the personal agents."

character and action. Just as the quality of the epic action partly conditioned the reader's response to the poem, so the quality of the hero's virtue partly determined the quality of his deeds. Heroic action sprang from heroic character; heroic virtue could best be tested and illustrated in and through a heroic enterprise. The epic poem thus provided a dynamic portrait of heroic virtue in action. The heroic image was kinetic energy rather than static power.

The same critic who regarded the plot as the soul of the poem (and the chief source of aesthetic pleasure) might simultaneously regard the heroic image as the *raison d'être* of the epic narrative, and the principal source of its ethical value. Although few theorists would have maintained that the literary merits of a heroic poem depended altogether on the moral qualities of its hero, the majority would have regarded these factors as closely interlinked. Other things being equal (some of them would have argued), the nobler the epic hero, the nobler the epic poem.

Milton himself had formerly sought an epic protagonist in whom he might "lay the pattern of a Christian *Heroe*," and he could expect his readers to look for a pattern hero in *Paradise Lost*.[19] They did look—and they disagreed sharply as to what they had found. To some, such as John Dryden and John Dennis, it appeared that Milton had, consciously or unconsciously, taken the devil for his hero: "And Milton, if the Devil had not been his hero, instead of Adam, if the giant had not foiled the knight, and driven him out of his stronghold, to wander through the world with his lady errant; and if there had not been more machining persons than human in his poem"; and, "He was resolved . . . that his Principals should be the Devil on one side and Man on the other: and the Devil is properly his Hero, because he gets the better."[20]

For others the hero was the Son of God. For Addison, Adam and Eve were the principal actors in Milton's epic, but neither was the actual hero of the poem. In answering the objection "that the hero in the *Paradise Lost* is unsuccessful, and by no means a match

19. *Works*, III, 237.
20. John Dryden, "Dedication of the *Aeneis*," in W. P. Ker (ed.), *Essays of John Dryden* (2 vols.; Oxford, 1900), II, 165; John Dennis, "The Grounds of Criticism in Poetry," in Edward Niles Hooker (ed.), *The Critical Works of John Dennis* (2 vols.; Baltimore, 1939, 1943), I, 334.

for his enemies," Addison maintained that the poem was an "epic, or a narrative poem, and he that looks for a hero in it, searches for that which Milton never intended; but if he will needs fix the name of an hero upon any person in it, it is certainly the Messiah who is the hero, both in the principal action, and in the chief episodes." [21]

For a third group the hero was Adam. Jonathan Richardson insisted that it was not Milton's

> fault if there have been those who have not found a hero, or who he is. 'Tis Adam, Adam the first, the representative of human race. He is the hero in this poem, though as in other heroic poems, superior beings are introduced. . . . He is not such a hero as Achilles, Ulysses, Aeneas, Orlando, Godfrey, &c., all romantic worthies and incredible performers of fortunate, savage cruelties; he is one of a nobler kind. . . . He is not such a conqueror as subdued armies or nations, or enemies in single combat, but his conquest was what justly gave heroic name to person and to poem. His hero was more than a conqueror through Him that loved us (as Rom. viii. 37).

Although Samuel Johnson regarded the question of the hero of *Paradise Lost* as pedantic, he censured Dryden for "petulantly and indecently" denying "the heroism of Adam, because he was overcome; but there is no reason why the hero should not be unfortunate, except established practice, since success and virtue do not go necessarily together." Cato, for instance, was Lucan's hero. Nevertheless, "if success be necessary, Adam's deceiver was at last crushed; Adam was restored to his Maker's favour, and therefore may securely resume his human rank." [22]

This variety of critical responses is interesting for the light it casts on the actual flexibility of neoclassical criticism in spite of the external rigidity of its methods and the derivative character of its terminology. The point at issue was not as trifling or irrelevant as several of them declared it to be. For many Renaissance theorists it would have seemed a question of primary importance; and for Milton himself (who had formerly written confidently of "that sublime art which . . . teaches what the laws are of a true epic poem," who had once endeavored to find a British king or knight capable of embodying the pattern of a "Christian *Heroe*," who could still condemn the subject matter of martial epic and chivalric romance as wanting "that which justly gives Heroic name /

21. Thorpe (ed.), *Milton Criticism*, 49, cf. 31.
22. *Ibid.*, 57, 76.

To Person or to Poem," and who would commend "*Sion*'s songs" for praising God and "godlike men" aright, "The Holiest of Holies and his Saints") it would have been no insignificant quibble. Their disagreement on the hero of *Paradise Lost* may be partly due to the ambiguity of their critical terminology; the word *hero* was itself equivocal, and Milton's critics themselves sometimes employed it in different senses. Moreover, some of them were reluctant to face squarely the tragic implications of Milton's fable and the coincidence of the epic hero with the tragic hero; they were still hampered by the critical commonplace that the action of an epic hero must end fortunately. (Milton's does, ultimately, through the paradox of the fortunate fall; but Adam's restoration lies beyond the scope of the fable itself and it is achieved through the merits of a different hero, "one greater Man.") Primarily, however, their division points to something new and unusual in Milton's poem. He had somehow failed to meet the expectations that his readers customarily brought to the epic, and this failure could not be explained simply by his rejection of the customary martial argument. As the point at issue was the identity of the epic hero, the principal cause of the critic's uncertainty would seem to lie in Milton's variations on the conventional heroic image—in his unusual treatment of the heroic exemplar and the traditional pattern hero.

The basic problem underlying this controversy over the hero of Milton's poem was the difficulty of reconciling Adam's apparent defeat with contemporary beliefs that a heroic poem should end fortunately. Could an epic hero follow the same pattern as a tragic hero, meeting defeat in the crucial encounter and finally disappearing from the stage (like Oedipus the King) as an exile? For Aristotle, epic and tragedy had differed primarily in their length and in their modes of imitation; both imitated the "better" sort of persons (*spoudaioi*)—sometimes even the same heroes and actions—and the same varieties of plot were common to both genres. On the other hand, Tasso had drawn a sharp distinction between the epic and tragic illustrious; in the opinion of many Renaissance critics (but by no means all), the action of an epic hero ought to conclude successfully. Although Johnson challenged this critical dogma, he did not attempt to refute it, and proceeded to argue that Milton's hero had, in fact, been successful in the end, inasmuch as he had been restored to divine favor.

Richardson similarly emphasized Adam's regeneration; in the end Milton's hero achieved "a secure recumbency upon and interest in the Supreme Good by the mediation of His Son."[23]

Dryden had based his identification of Milton's hero on Satan's success and Adam's defeat. In countering this argument, Addison could not deny that Adam, the chief actor in the poem, had failed, but he could deny that Adam was the hero of Milton's epic. Rebutting the charge that Milton's hero was unsuccessful by identifying the Messiah as hero, he parried the objection that the event of Milton's fable was unhappy by arguing that it belonged to a second kind of fable, in which "the chief actor in the poem falls from some eminent pitch of honour and prosperity, into misery and disgrace. Thus we see Adam and Eve sinking from a state of innocence and happiness into the most abject condition of sin and sorrow."[24]

The problem was further complicated by the ambiguity of the word *hero*. Since an epic frequently portrayed several persons of heroic character, Renaissance critics sometimes distinguished the protagonist as the "principal hero" or "epic person." Although they might regard his character as imperfect or even vicious, as some regarded Achilles and Odysseus, they nevertheless recognized his position as the principal hero of the poem; he was simply a hero who, insofar as he lacked the essence of true heroic virtue, did not merit his title as such. When Johnson refers to Cato as Lucan's hero, he is alluding not to the principal actor in the poem but to a model of Stoic virtue; he is using the term primarily in its ethical sense. When Dryden applies this title to Satan, and Addison to the Messiah, both are associating it with victorious action. Addison's distinction between the "hero" of *Paradise Lost* and its "chief actor" would probably have seemed arbitrary to many Renaissance critics, and on one occasion he himself uses these terms virtually synonymously, passing directly from the "principal actors of the *Iliad* and *Aeneid*," whom the authors had "chosen for their heroes," to the "principal actors" (who are not the heroes) of *Paradise Lost*.[25]

23. *Ibid.*, 57.
24. *Ibid.*, 48.
25. See *ibid.*, 47. I am grateful to another participant in the Fifth Renaissance Conference, held at the State University of New York at Binghamton in 1971, for pointing out that similar critical controversies have centered on the problem of the

Part of the difficulty may have resulted from Milton's choice of theme, which permitted him only two human beings; he was compelled, therefore, to amplify his cast of characters with "machining persons"—divine and infernal spirits and personified abstractions. Nevertheless, the principal *locus* of his narrative action remains Paradise itself, the "Silvan Scene" in which the plot unfolds. And for all the elaborate offstage machinery, the focal point of the plot is a voluntary human decision, an act of disobedience springing from an act of *proairesis* or moral choice.[26] The central action is man's own action, and the epic person or principal hero is man himself—Adam as progenitor and type of the human race. Satan and the Son, on the other hand, are essentially machining persons, and in the strictest sense neither of them can be regarded as a hero. Metaphysically they belong to spiritual orders higher than mankind; to mistake them for heroes (or godlike men) is to miss the essential characteristic of the hero: that he is a man raised above the common lot of men by his supernatural parentage, his superlative virtue, or an immortality of glory and fame.

Adam is the epic person and "principal hero" of *Paradise Lost* but is he actually a *pattern* hero? On one hand, he has been uniquely fashioned by God himself, created perfect and possessing the divine image in its pristine excellence. He is therefore a unique kind of hero—heroic or godlike man in a sense that could not be applied to his posterity, conceived and born in guilt and bearing the hereditary deformity of sin instead of divine resemblance. On the other hand, the action that the poet has chosen to imitate is the hero's transgression. The epic person of *Paradise Lost* is a godlike man who forfeits the divine image, a perfect man who falls from his perfection, a hero stripped of his heroic virtue.

To be sure, Adam repents; and in the last books of the poem we may follow the stages of his inner regeneration. The pattern of the peccant hero who errs and subsequently repents of his error is not uncommon in heroic poetry; and Milton's readers would have been familiar with this pattern in classical as well as in modern

hero of Lucan's *Pharsalia* and Statius' *Thebaid*—both of them epics of the Silver Age of Latin literature and both of them taking the fratricidal conflicts of civil war as their epic argument.

26. See John F. Huntley, "*Proairesis, Synteresis,* and the Ethical Orientation of Milton's *Of Education,*" *Philological Quarterly,* XLIII (1964), 40–46.

epic. Achilles' abstention from combat both on the island of
Scyros and after his quarrel with Agamemnon had been interpreted in this light. Like Ulysses' sojourns with Circe and Ca-
lypso and Aeneas' affair with Dido, these episodes represented
the obscuration of heroic virtue by unheroic leisure and "ignoble
ease." The same pattern could be detected in Rinaldo's infatua-
tion with Armida, Redcrosse's bondage to Duessa, or Samson's
seduction by Dalila. Adam's voluntary transgression through his
passion for Eve could be read as another variant on the same
pattern.

At this point, however, the resemblances cease. In the majority
of cases the peccant hero recovers from his temporary lapse, resumes his heroic enterprise, and triumphs decisively over his adversaries. Achilles forsakes Scyros to join the Greek hosts at Troy;
on a later occasion he renounces his anger against Agamemnon
and returns to the battlefield to wreak havoc on the Trojan forces
and to defeat their foremost champion. Odysseus resumes his
journey to Ithaca, and Aeneas his voyage to Italy. Rinaldo returns
to the crusade and wins the battle for Jerusalem. Lancelot rejoins
Arthur to slay the enemy champion and conquer Avaricum.[27]
Redcrosse resumes his enterprise, slays the dragon, and delivers
a kingdom. Samson regains his heroic virtue and wins his greatest victory over the Philistines. Adam, on the other hand (as
Dryden later complained), is driven from his castle "to wander
through the world with his lady errant."

It is hardly surprising that Milton's early critics found his variations on the conventional pattern hero disturbing—or that they
should have set out, separately, like knights-errant on solitary
quests, to locate the missing hero of the poem. Two of the machining persons, Christ and Satan, had themselves become heroic exemplars, antithetical images of true and false heroism, and their
operations had been invested with the imagery and structure of
heroic enterprises. On the human level the epic action had been
changed into a psychomachy, a moral struggle within the human
soul; on the supernatural level the epic machinery had been converted into a *daemonomachia* or a theomachy, a war of gods and
angels.[28] Although other epic poets before him—Homer and Vir-

27. See Chapter 2.
28. See Priscilla P. St. George, "Psychomachia in Books V and VI of *Paradise
Lost*," *Modern Language Quarterly*, XXVII (1966), 185–96.

gil, Tasso and Camoëns—had relied heavily on supernatural forces in organizing and constructing their plots, Milton went far beyond his predecessors in his exploitation of epic machinery. In his hands it became a duel between superhuman combatants, divine and infernal antagonists in a spiritual and cosmic war.

Moreover, unlike the majority of epic poets, Milton had transferred the heroic enterprise from the epic protagonist to the machining persons. Instead of an enterprise planned and executed by the nominal hero of the poem, he gives us an exploit conceived and brought to fruition by his "infernal machine." It is Satan who plans and achieves the conquest that gives unity to the fable, and it is he who, of all the principal characters in the poem, bears the strongest resemblance to the conventional military hero. Although he is inevitably outwitted by Providence (for who can contend against omnipotence joined with omniscience?), Milton's devil is actually the first world conqueror. One can sympathize (even though one cannot concur) with critics like Dryden who mistook him for the hero of the poem. The Son, on the other hand, is the perfect image of godlikeness, the archetype of that divine virtue of which heroic virtue is only a shadow. Three of the crucial episodes of the poem, the history of the war of the angels, the creation of the world, and the prophecy of the Incarnation and Passion, are devoted to his *aristeia*. Here again one may readily understand why critics should have mistaken him for the hero of *Paradise Lost*.

As pattern heroes Milton's Christ and Satan exhibit moral extremes beyond the conventional opposition of virtue and vice or heroic virtue and brutishness. With their extension to the divine and diabolical planes, *virtus heroica* and *feritas* approach absolute zero; they tend to become perfect good and pure evil. On the human level they are more likely to be mixed: "human kind Cannot bear very much reality." [29]

Milton's epic person was nothing less than archetypal Man himself, the original Adam whose likeness all men had inherited by nature and could "put off" only by grace. For the conventional heroic image—an ideal pattern proposed for the reader's emulation—Milton had substituted the image of the old man (the "earthy" man) that the regenerate must reject in order to "put on"

29. T. S. Eliot, "Burnt Norton," *Collected Poems, 1909–1935* (New York, 1936), 214.

the image of the new and "heavenly" man. In the portrait of Adam before his fall, readers would recognize an original perfection no longer accessible to his posterity, an image of what they might have been but never could be. In fallen Adam they would perceive an image of themselves—not a pattern of what they should be (as with the conventional epic hero), but a pattern of what they are. In Adam's gradual regeneration, culminating in recognition of his own frailty and of an ideal of perfection embodied in the woman's seed, they might behold an external image of the regenerative process operative in themselves and also an example of faith. Taken together, the various facets of Milton's epic hero form a vivid exemplar of man's original dignity and his present misery, of his weakness and his dependency on divine grace, and of his future beatitude.

For the poet and his "fit audience," awareness of the Fall and its spiritual and psychological consequences inevitably narrowed the possibility of heroic virtue and the scope of heroic action. To the natural man there remained little more than the shadow of true heroism. Perfection in action or in character, heroic virtues and meritorious deeds, the excellencies of the divine image— truth, wisdom, sanctity, and filial freedom—these lay inevitably beyond his grasp. His heroic exploits could not be true "acts of benefit," for they lacked solid virtue and essential goodness. His heroic virtues were splendid vices. Heroic activity itself became a pretentious charade: the shadow of heroic virtue pursuing the phantasm of false glory. In the context of the Fall, the heroic image could be little more than an empty mask, a shadow enclosed in armor or a "Headpiece filled with straw."[30]

The heroism of the natural man was specious. The true, substantial heroism was possible only for the regenerate, and in its fundamental principles this differed radically from the conventional epic heroism. Not only did it emphasize different virtues, but it rested on a different conception of man. If classical epic had overstressed the prowess of the martial hero, classical ethics had exaggerated the wisdom of the philosophical hero. "Ignorant of themselves" and of man's fall ("Degraded by himself, on grace depending"), the Greek philosophers had sought virtue in themselves, and "to themselves / All glory arrogate[d]." The ideals of the secular heroic tradition were not only vain and empty shad-

30. Eliot, "The Hollow Men," *Collected Poems*, 101.

ows; they were also a major obstacle to the realization of true heroism. Hardening man's pride in his own powers and achievements, they encouraged him to trust in himself rather than in Providence, to rely on his own merits rather than on divine grace, to regard his heroic exploits as his own personal achievements, and to seek his own glory and fame.

For the "new man," on the other hand, heroism was conceivable only as a gift from a higher power; the regenerate man was heroic only by grace. He could become a hero, so to speak, by act of God, as an officer becomes a gentleman by act of Congress. The power and wisdom behind his noblest exploits were those of the Spirit; whatever glory his actions merited belonged properly to the deity who had inspired them. To act heroically he must act as the instrument and agent of the divine, renouncing the merits of his own actions, trusting no longer in his own strength and wisdom, but relying instead on the imputed obedience of "one greater Man." The precondition of the spiritual heroism of the regenerate is a self-emptying, a humiliation comparable to the *kenosis* of the divine exemplar, the filial Logos.

For Milton the true hero was the saint. The truest office of a poet was to praise God aright and "Godlike men, / The Holiest of Holies and his Saints." The core of heroic virtue was actually sanctity; and this was contingent theologically upon the process of regeneration (or sanctification).[31] This is the process we see at work in fallen Adam and fallen Samson, manifested through its customary effects—repentance and faith.

If the Fall had narrowed the scope for heroic activity, it had also created the possibility for a special kind of heroism: the patient fortitude of the martyr to truth. Just as Satan's rebellion had provided the occasion for Abdiel's heroic constancy, so Adam's revolt would establish the scene for the martyr's agony and triumph, the stage of a "perverted World." The corruption of man's nature would provide the occasions for martyrdom; the regeneration of man's nature would produce the martyr himself, and the victories of the one just man.

In the eyes of its author, *Paradise Lost* was a heroic poem, but against the background of the epic tradition it presents a singularly altered image of heroic virtue: its epic protagonist is the archetypal sinner. Its infernal machinery carries the burden of

---

31. *Cf.* Milton's *De Doctrina Christiana*, Bk. I, Chap. 18.

the epic enterprise and (like the pillars of some Philistine temple) the weight of the epic plot. Its divine machinery contains the perfect images of virtues "Above Heroic" and the promise of ultimate victories that lie far beyond the scope of the narrative action. Milton's epic not only undercuts the tradition of secular epic but reduces heroic virtue itself to a contingency. If the hero's highest virtues and noblest actions really belong to the spirit, if he can acquire no valid merits by his own deeds, then the actual praise for his exploits belongs primarily to the divinity who had inspired and directed them. Heroic virtue becomes essentially a manifestation of divine virtue, heroic action the instrument of a divine action.

Rejecting the argument of wars and altering the roles of epic hero and epic machines, Milton recentered the heroic fable on the temptation crisis.[32] Heroic obedience—heroic righteousness and heroic charity—would be tested and illustrated in moral combat. Nevertheless, the poet was still under the obligation of relating an action and constructing a fable in accordance with the principles of legitimate epic imitation. He must still present his temptation crisis within the framework of a narrative plot. The easiest formula was to organize the incidents through the conventional epic machinery: divine or infernal councils, supernatural messengers, or allegorical abstractions.[33] Milton had already exploited this method in expanding the material of the conventional Gunpowder Plot epigram into a heroic (or mock-heroic) epyllion and in constructing his masque at Ludlow around a central temptation with demonic machinery.[34] He would utilize the same device in both of his epics, but with greater subtlety and ingenuity.

32. See James Holly Hanford, "The Temptation Motive in Milton," *Studies in Philology*, XV (1918), 176–94.

33. The conventions of epic machinery would subsequently be satirized, along with other traditional features of this genre, in Pope's "A Receit to make an Epick Poem"; see Norman Ault (ed.), *The Prose Works of Alexander Pope* (Oxford, 1936), 115–20. For the machines, "Scriblerus" advises the poet to "*Take of Deities, Male and Female, as many as you can use,* separating them in "*two equal parts*" and keeping Jupiter in the middle, to be excited by Juno and mollified by Venus. On all occasions the poet should remember "*to make use of Volatile* Mercury." Since "*no Epick Poem can possibly subsist*" without these machines, the "*wisest thing is to serve them for your greatest Necessities.*" For the manners of the hero, "Scriblerus" recommends "*all the best Qualities you can find in all the best celebrated Heroes of Antiquity.* . . . *But be sure they are Qualities which your* Patron *would be thought to have.*"

34. See Macon Cheek, "Milton's *In Quintum Novembris:* An Epic Foreshadowing," *Studies in Philology*, LIV (1957), 172–84.

In a "brief epic" like *Paradise Regained* it was easier to construct a well-made plot around a temptation ordeal than in a "diffuse epic" like *Paradise Lost*. Nevertheless, even the shorter poem confronted Milton with problems of structure. His biblical sources contained three different (and more or less equally stressed) temptations. A lesser poet might have given them equal emphasis, portraying them in three equally balanced episodes and possibly compromising the integrity of the plot. Milton, on the other hand, managed to avoid an episodic organization and to achieve a unified and integrated narrative by subordinating the first and third temptations to the second, by expanding the second temptation to heighten the antithesis between secular and divine kingship, and by linking them together so that each successive incident appeared to develop logically, with verisimilitude and probability, out of the preceding scene.[35] In the first temptation Satan takes his point of departure from the baptism and proclamation scene—the Father's public declaration of his Son and heir—on the banks of the Jordan. The second temptation is linked through the banquet episode with the first and with the final scene of angelic ministrations. The third temptation crisis, motivated by Satan's frustrated rage, follows immediately upon the elemental violence of the storm scene.[36] The first temptation brings the contestants together in an initial encounter, accentuating and counterpointing the disguise-and-detection motif with a subtlety worthy of Homer's Odysseus. The third temptation not only heightens the narrative tensions already developed in the preceding episodes, bringing them to the point of highest suspense (the *summa epitasis*), but also contains a reversal contrary to expectation, and, perhaps, a recognition—a *peripeteia* combined with an *anagnorisis*. Out of the three discrete temptations that his sources afforded him, Milton has molded a well-made plot—a unified action progressing, with increasing suspense, from preliminary skirmish through extended moral victory to divine miracle.

Paradise Lost presented more formidable problems in narrative construction. Like other epic writers before him, Milton overcame some of these difficulties through the conventional techniques of epic construction: divine and infernal councils and emissaries, and prophetic or retrospective episodes in direct dis-

35. Howard Schultz, *Milton and Forbidden Knowledge* (New York, 1955).
36. See Dick Taylor, Jr., "The Storm Scene in *Paradise Regained*: A Reinterpretation," *University of Toronto Quarterly*, XXIV (1955), 359–76.

course. His principal solution, however, constituted a marked innovation on epic tradition. This was nothing less than to develop
the role of his infernal adversary according to a narrative pattern
normally characteristic of human heroes, a pattern common to
protagonists as well as to antagonists. In conceiving and executing a martial enterprise—a war of conquest against a walled citadel—Satan has numerous parallels among epic protagonists:
the Greeks at Troy, the Crusaders at Jerusalem, the Britons at
Avaricum. As a military hero who penetrates an enemy stronghold in disguise and triumphs through ingenious stratagems and
plausible deceptions, he recalls Odysseus and Milton's proposed
epic on King Alfred. As an epic antagonist who provokes an unjust war against a hero favored by Providence, he resembles
Turnus and the Gothic champions at Rome. Even though Milton
has renounced a martial subject and centered his epic instead on
moral combat and spiritual trial, he nevertheless constructs his
narrative action in terms of a martial enterprise, conceived by a
council of war and executed by tactical guile. Paradise is lost—
and mankind ruined—by divine permission, human weakness,
and infernal fortitude and cunning. This is the first, and archetypal, world conquest; whatever its eventual outcome, it is initially Satan's victory.

Having briefly considered the role of Milton's infernal machinery,
let us turn to his divine machines. The loss of Eden is a temporary
defeat for man and a Pyrrhic victory for Satan. Through the merits
of "one greater Man" Satan will one day be decisively vanquished
and man restored to a fairer Paradise. Satan indeed conquers the
world, and will inhabit the air, but he cannot possess the happy
garden. From the standpoint of Heaven the loss of Eden is a cal-
culated loss. This temporary surrender of forested and moun-
tainous terrain on the frontier has been foreseen; it is part of the
celestial strategy for a total victory in the remote future. Before
the Fall, Milton deploys his divine machines to hinder Satan's enterprise. Uriel warns Gabriel, who in turn dispatches his watch to
apprehend the intruder; and the Eternal Father himself drives the
devil from Paradise by displaying a "celestial Sign." (Satan is apparently the archetypal astrologer.) Thereupon Raphael is sent to
"admonish" Adam "of his obedience" in order "to render Man
inexcusable." After the Fall, however, the celestial strategy becomes operative primarily in man's redemption—in the veiled
prophecy of ultimate restoration through the woman's seed in the

regeneration of Adam and Eve (manifested successively in their repentance and faith), and in Michael's survey of world history culminating in the *aristeia* of the future deliverer.

Although Milton has constructed his plot in terms of a holy war, representing his angels as armed warriors and (on occasion) God himself as a man of war, he nevertheless preserves the essential distinction between military valor and the higher heroism. Satan is a conqueror; the Son and his elect are "more than conquerors." Satan seeks his own honor and glory; like the majority of Homeric heroes, he stands in fear of shame. The Son and his saints, on the other hand, voluntarily shun honor and embrace ignominy, renouncing their own glory for the glory of God. Satanic wrath is counterbalanced not only by divine wrath, but more significantly by divine charity. Because Milton's war is essentially a spiritual war, psychomachy and theomachy rather than a physical conflict, he can present it, paradoxically, as a war between war and peace, as a conflict between the forces of disorder and destruction and the powers of creation and order.

On the human level and on the infernal plane, their conflict appears as warfare. On the celestial level they are reconciled in the unity of the divine intelligence; they are structural elements in a providential design.[37]

Just as Milton's holy war comprehends the struggle between war and peace, his divine machinery comprehends both divine and infernal machines. Through the doctrine of permissive evil, the infernal strategy itself serves divine ends; and Satan's enterprise is an integral part of the providential design, a design reflected in the design and structure of the poem. The Father himself is firmly in control, governing action and counteraction, supervising divine and infernal agents, inclining their wills to ends that he himself has preordained, and occasionally intervening directly to alter the course of battle by a divine miracle. In this context the only recourse for any hero who hopes for eventual victory is to ally himself with Providence, trusting unconditionally in divine wisdom and strength. The cardinal heroic virtues, accordingly, would appear to be obedience and faith, constancy and charity.

What happens to the heroic image in this context? In his archangelic rebel Milton constructs an ironically demonic image of

37. See Geoffrey Hartman, "Milton's Counterplot," *ELH*, XXV (1958), 1–12; J. R. Watson, "Divine Providence and the Structure of *Paradise Lost*," *Essays in Criticism*, XIV (1964), 148–55.

the heroic warlord, the traditional conqueror-destroyer intent on glory and glorying in his strength. This pattern is consistently maintained even in the pseudohero's bestial disguises, and it is finally completed in his victorious return to Hell. Nevertheless, with equal consistency, Milton undercuts this image at crucial points in the narrative. At the outset of his enterprise Satan encounters his deformed progeny, Sin and Death. His daughter bears the serpentine image that he must subsequently assume (though he does not yet foresee this future humiliation); and his own doom is inevitably linked with that of his monstrous son. The soliloquy on Mount Niphates, in turn, occurs immediately after Satan has completed a space journey that dwarfs the heroic voyages of classical legend and Renaissance epic—the exploits of Odysseus, Aeneas, and the Argonauts, and the navigations of Columbus and Vasco da Gama. In this scene the classical heroic values—the pursuit of honor and glory and dominion—are exposed as false and hollow; Satan faces, and recognizes, the reality of sin and guilt. His brush with the angelic guard brings further knowledge of the disfiguring effects of sin; he now learns that his glory has been visibly impaired. The sign of the scales, in turn, reveals the limitations of his strength. After aspiring to equal his Creator, he discovers the finite, and conditional, powers of the creature. Finally, after completing the image of a triumphant world conqueror, Milton abruptly shatters the heroic portrait (or heroic caricature). On previous occasions a divine miracle had put the devil to flight; on this occasion another miracle transforms the heroic image into an image of brutishness, the contrary of heroic virtue. Punished in "the shape" in which he had sinned, Satan experiences public shame instead of expected triumph and applause. In this shrewdly timed *peripeteia* Milton has reversed the normal heroic expectations. Instead of the honor his exploits had apparently merited, the pseudohero is again brought face to face with the reality of sin; this time the knowledge of sin is brought home by its punishment.

In Adam and Eve the divine image, the essence of heroic virtue, is paradoxically destroyed through acts that themselves possessed heroic associations. Eve's aspirations for divine wisdom and fellowship with the gods resemble the ambitions of the Stoic and Neoplatonic hero, and the flight scene in her dream possesses heroic as well as demonic prototypes. Although it recalls the delusions of witchcraft, it is equally reminiscent of the contemplative ascents of the classical sage and the apotheosized hero. Her readiness to test her virtue in moral combat against the Adversary links her, to a degree, with the woman warriors of classical and Renaissance epic.[38] The Vulgate had described her as a *virago* (Genesis 2:23)—a "heroine" or "female warrior"—and her tragedy stemmed in part from her desire to exercise her *virtù donnesca* rather than *virtù feminile*.[39] Adam's decision, in turn, to risk death rather than separation from his lady would be heroic in the context of chivalric romance. In both instances Milton creates a heroic image that results, paradoxically, in the obliteration of the divine image. In both cases the true image of heroic virtue is obscured and defaced by images of a conventional but spurious heroism.

38. On the female worthy and the woman warrior in Renaissance literature, see Eugene M. Waith, "Heywood's Women Worthies," in Norman T. Burns and Christopher Reagan (eds.), *Concepts of the Hero in the Middle Ages and the Renaissance* (Albany, N.Y., 1975), 222–38; Graham Hough, *A Preface to the "Faerie Queene"* (New York, 1963); R. A. Sayce, *The French Biblical Epic in the Seventeenth Century* (Oxford, 1955).

39. See Tasso, *Prose diverse*, II, 203–14, for Tasso's "Discorso della virtù feminile e donnesca," addressed to the duchess of Mantua. After discussing the divergent opinions of Plato and Aristotle on the question of whether "la virtù dell'uomo e della femina" were the same, Tasso argued that the virtues that temper ire are most appropriate for a man, whereas those that temper concupiscence are most fitting for a woman; whereas a man is dishonored by cowardice (*viltà*), a woman is shamed by *impudicizia*. Although a woman may possess fortitude (*fortezza*), this is not absolute courage, but a courage that obeys ("non l'assoluta fortezza; ma la fortezza ch' ubidisce"). The virtue that is most appropriate for a woman, Tasso continued, is temperance; this is a larger and more comprehensive virtue than modesty, inasmuch as *pudicizia* is a part of *temperanza*. From this *feminile virtù*, appropriate for a *cittadina* or a *gentildonna privata*, Tasso turns to the *donnesca virtù* befitting a noblewoman born of imperial and heroic lineage, whose own virtues equal the virile virtues of her glorious ancestors. For this virtue one no longer uses the term *femina*, but rather *donnesco*, which means ruling (*signorile*). Tasso conceives this kind of virtue consistently in heroic or quasi-heroic terms. In heroic ladies this *virtù donnesca* is a heroic virtue which rivals the heroic virtue of men. There is no distinction of works and offices between heroic women and heroic men, except for purely biological functions. Among recent or contemporary heroines eminent for thier *virtù donnesca*, Tasso praises Queen Mary, sister of Charles V; Margherita of Austria, duchess of Parma; Queen Elizabeth of England, in spite of her Protestantism; and Caterina de' Medici. The heroines of contemplation (for the contemplative as well as the active virtues are found among "donne eroiche") include Renata di Ferrara, Margherita di Savoia, and Vittoria Colonna. Finally, the duchess of Mantua herself, along with her sister, possesses all virtues of mind and of heroic intellect (*intelletto eroico*) and embodies *la virtù cristiana* in its perfection.

In the final books of the epic, the divine image is partly restored in hero and heroine alike, but neither embodies the image
in its perfection. The true pattern of heroic (or divine) virtue lies
in a pattern hero who rarely intervenes in the action on the
human plane. (In the fable he descends once—to judge and to
regenerate man—and in the angelic narratives twice—to create
and instruct man, and afterwards to redeem him.) Otherwise, the
pattern hero remains a "pattern laid up" in Heaven—to be revealed obscurely by types or more clearly through retrospective
or prospective episodes. *Paradise Lost*, like *The Argonauts*, is "an
epic in search of a hero."

The relationship between heroic idea and heroic image is only one
of the problems that confronted the Renaissance poet in attempting to embody an ideal conception of heroic virtue in the protagonist of an epic action. In concentrating on three particular
aspects of this problem, we have barely scratched the surface. We
have had to neglect the variety of heroic ideals current in the Renaissance, and the range and diversity of Renaissance epic. Our
findings have not been altogether encouraging. The purely martial epic could not, on the whole, cope successfully with the
higher virtues, since it could not effectively portray the matter in
which they could best be illustrated and tried. The allegorical epic
possessed a technique for reconciling a martial subject with the
actual matter of the virtues, but critical opinion was sometimes
hostile both to allegory and to romance, the narrative genre
probably best adapted to allegorical techniques. The epic centered primarily on moral combat encountered inevitable difficulties in the construction of the plot.

The difficulties in forming the image of a pattern hero were
equally great. The martial hero could rarely provide a perfect exemplar of the higher heroism. The allegorical hero tended at times
to become either a frivolous adventurer or a frigid abstraction.
The Christian hero could meet the preconditions of the higher
heroism only by renouncing his own virtues, his own glory, and
his own heroic deeds. To achieve a balance between heroic image
and heroic idea lay beyond the capacity of the majority of poets.
In the martial hero, the image could all too easily obscure the idea;
heroic virtue might be eclipsed rather than illustrated by the epic
protagonist. In the allegorical hero there was an equal risk that the
idea might overshadow the image. In the Christian hero, finally,

the heroic image itself tended to vanish in an ideal of impossible perfection transcending the powers of the hero and the imitative craft of the poet. Fading away like some ancient soldier, the pattern hero became reabsorbed into the archetype. The heroic image became lost in the divine image; the heroic example was overshadowed by its divine exemplar. In Milton's hands (as one of his earliest critics surmised) the heroic poem had vanished imperceptibly into the divine poem.

CHAPTER 2

Achilles in Renaissance Tradition

HOWEVER PEACEFUL the "realms of gold" may have seemed to John Keats, for the Renaissance they were the principal battlefield of a civil war. The fiefs that bards held "in fealty to Apollo" were no longer secure; both title and tenure were disputed. Nor did the "wide expanse" that Homer "ruled as his demesne" go unchallenged; there were rival claimants and pretenders.

Nevertheless, there was little direct challenge to the principle of literary suzerainty. It was the application of this idea, rather than the idea itself, that divided poets and critics. In an age when men were questioning the principles of political and religious authority, they remained surprisingly subservient to literary authority. The feudal order could decay; the order of church or state could alter; but poetic feudalism was stronger than ever. However heatedly one might argue the relative claims of the god's vassals, one did not doubt the principle of "fealty to Apollo," and one usually accepted the authority of his vicegerents Aristotle and Horace.

This very veneration for antiquity, however, provoked a crisis in allegiance. Accepting the authority of the ancients also meant reckoning with their contradictions. Confronted by their rival claims, their fundamental inconsistencies, their basic discrepancies, the poet or theorist faced a dilemma. Either he must accept the fact of their diversity, and then rationalize his preference for one authority over another, or else he must attempt to reconcile

42

them, demonstrating that their divergences were merely apparent rather than real, superficial rather than essential. Either alternative made more demands on his originality than he was usually willing to admit. Like a lawyer or theologian, he preferred to argue from traditional authority rather than from his own innovations. Yet in practice he could hardly avoid introducing his own judgment, even while professing to be merely following or interpreting the ancients. Whether he attempted to reconcile conflicting authorities or to decide definitely in favor of one over the others, he had to find arguments and reasons to support his judgment. In actuality, he was setting up a new system capable of comprehending the diverse viewpoints of antiquity. Hence, while philosophers were exercising their ingenuity in attempting to reconcile Plato with Aristotle, men of letters sought to combine the poetic theories of Aristotle and Horace.[1] Critics debated the relative merits of Greek and Roman poets or historians. Epic poets weighed the comparative claims of Homer and Virgil as models and guides. Clearly the summit of Parnassus was disputed territory, and poets and theorists alike were deadlocked in a confused struggle for its possession. At issue were both the laurel crown and the right to the succession, for the relative merit of the moderns depended in large part on that of the ancients they had accepted as their models and authorities.

Acknowledging the jurisdiction of the ancients, then, meant engaging in a battle of books over their rank. Granted their authority in formulating or exemplifying the rules of the poetic art, the question remained which of them had come closest to realizing these principles in their perfection, which of them had achieved the clearest statement of the laws of the various genres, and which of them had set the best example for future poets to follow.

One of the major problems for Renaissance poetics was the apparent discrepancy between classical theory and practice. The chief literary masterpieces of antiquity seemed at times to fall short of the standards set by its poetics. Scaliger's critical principles led him to condemn much of Homer's achievement in spite of his respect for Virgil, Homer's imitator. Beni's theory of heroic

---

1. *Cf.* Jacopo Mazzoni, *De triplici hominum vita . . . In quibus omnes Platonis et Aristotelis, multae vero aliorum . . . discordiae componuntur* (Cesena, 1576); see Marvin T. Herrick, *The Fusion of Horatian and Aristotelian Literary Criticism, 1531–1555* (Urbana, 1946).

poetry led him to censure Virgil as well as Homer and to rank both of them well below Tasso.[2] For many a Renaissance theorist, the literary imperative to imitate classical models conflicted with the Horatian and Aristotelian emphasis on the moral function of poetry. Paradoxically, even in antiquity the theoretical insistence on the ethical function of literature had led to reappraisal—and in some instances condemnation—of the established poetic tradition. A notable example had been Plato's criticism of Homer and his defense by the Stoics on allegorical grounds.[3] Transferred to a Christian context, the conflict between ethical and literary norms seemed even more intense, the gulf between moral values and the imitation of classical models still more unbridgeable. The classics might still give delight, but their ability to instruct, their value as examples for conduct, varied as the ethical standards of their critics varied. Changes in social mores or in ethical and political theory produced comparable changes in literary criticism. The Renaissance reassessment of the ancients varied, in part at least, with its own moral criteria.

The tension between ethical and literary norms was nowhere more evident than in criticism of Homer's warriors. Were they heroes or brutes? Paragons of virtue or types of vice? Had Homer depicted them as examples to be emulated—or shunned? Should they arouse admiration (the characteristic effect of the heroic poem) or abhorrence? On such points as these, Renaissance critics never reached unanimity. For some, Achilles and Odysseus and Agamemnon were exemplars of heroic virtues—fortitude, wisdom, and the qualities of the perfect leader. For others, they were negative examples, embodiments of vice. Achilles was brutish and violent, Odysseus guileful and skilled in fraud, Agamemnon arbitrary and tyrannical. For a third group of commentators, they represented a distinct failure on Homer's part. He had intended to portray valor and prudence and effective leadership, but had fallen short of his aim.[4] For most critics, however,

2. *Select Translations from Scaliger's Poetics*, trans. Frederick Morgan Padelford (New York, 1905), 36, 73–81; J. E. Spingarn, *A History of Literary Criticism in the Renaissance* (New York, 1899), 133–34, 123; Paolo Beni, *Comparazione di Omero, Virgilio, e Torquato*, in *Opere di Torquato Tasso* (6 vols.; Florence, 1724), VI.

3. *The Works of Plato*, trans. Benjamin Jowett (4 vols.; New York, 1936?), I, 52–53, 192–97; II, 75–77, 82–87, 378–96.

4. Cf. Beni, *Comparazione*; Torquato Tasso, *Le Prose diverse di Torquato Tasso*, ed. Cesare Guasti (2 vols.; Florence, 1875), I, 115; G. Gregory Smith (ed.), *Elizabethan Critical Essays* (2 vols.; Oxford, 1904), I, 165. John Dryden, *Critical and Miscellaneous Prose Works*, ed. E. Malone (3 vols.; London, 1800), III, 433–34, praises Achilles'

Homer's characters embodied neither complete virtue nor absolute vice. They were, on the whole, heroic figures, but not perfect heroes. Tarnished by vice, their virtues fell demonstrably short not only of Christian heroism but also of the examples set by the best classical worthies.

For the poets who took the *Iliad* as their model, Achilles in particular proved a stumbling block. Although they might retain the basic outline of his role as essential to the plot, they could hardly transfer his character whole cloth from Homer without incurring blame for celebrating a vicious hero. They must, accordingly, alter the motives for his conduct. They must find better reasons for his breach with his commander and his abstention from combat. They must eliminate the outrages inflicted on the body of his dead enemy. They must adapt him to the moral and military code of the Cinquecento. In short, the archaic Greek warrior must be refined, polished, civilized, brought up to date. He must be transformed into a Renaissance gentleman.

Although interesting in their own right, these Renaissance refinements on the Homeric hero are primarily significant for their bearing on literary history. They reflect the impact of changing moral criteria on poetic tradition.[5] Superficially the actions of Achilles' successors conform to the pattern set by their classical forebear, and their roles have comparable importance for the development of the fable. But this resemblance is sometimes deceptive. Ethically, these Renaissance heroes are often very unlike Achilles, and as a result the real significance of their actions can be strikingly different. They act from loftier motives and with stricter decorum.

---

courage, but censures his "pride and disobedience to his General," his "brutal cruelty to his dead enemy," and "the selling of [Hector's] body to his father." Plato (*Works*, II, 87–92) condemns Homer's picture of Achilles' lamentations and the hero's cupidity and brutality: "Neither will we believe or acknowledge Achilles himself to have been such a lover of money that he took Agamemnon's gifts, or that when he had received payment he restored the dead body of Hector, but that without payment he was unwilling to do so. . . . As little can I believe . . . that he dragged Hector round the tomb of Patroclus, and slaughtered the captives at the pyre."

5. Tasso's *Discorsi del poema eroico* takes Achilles' vices as a point of departure for arguing Aeneas' greater conformity to the chivalric ideal. The charges of "avarice and cruelty" that Plato had raised against Homer's hero cannot be gainsaid. Virgil, on the other hand, better observed "general decorum," investing Aeneas with every "chivalric virtue" (*virtù di cavaliero*). See Tasso, *Prose*, ed. Francesco Flora (Milan, 1935), 430–32.

In the following pages I shall reexamine four heroes of this type—Ruggiero in Ariosto's *Orlando Furioso*, Corsamonte in Trissino's *Italia Liberata*, Lancilotto in Alamanni's *Avarchide*, and Rinaldo in Tasso's *Gerusalemme Liberata*.[6] Three of these works closely resemble the *Iliad* in plot and character, while the fourth reveals significant affinities with Statius' *Achilleid*. In varying degrees all four poems attempt to bridge a gulf of over a thousand years and adapt classical motifs to the indigenous chivalric tradition. Finally, all four are linked by their common relation to Tasso. It is significant that the latter's *Discorsi del poema eroico* devotes considerable space to criticizing the epics of Ariosto, Alamanni, and Trissino.[7] Reexamination of the Achilles pattern in these three works should throw additional light on Tasso's presentation of Rinaldo in the *Gerusalemme*.

The salient characteristic of the Achilles pattern is the dual motif of the hero's withdrawal and return. All four of these Cinquecento poets recognized its significance for the structure of the plot and accordingly gave it a prominent—in some cases a central—position in the fable. Yet, as they were well aware, it was by no means peculiar to the Achilles of the *Iliad*. Statius had based his *Achilleid* on an earlier episode in the hero's career that illustrated the same motif. Furthermore, there was a third, and extremely popular, literary tradition that offered numerous analogues. From Homer's *Odyssey* to Boiardo's *Orlando Innamorato*, epic and romance had portrayed heroes alienated from their enterprises by love or magic, yet ultimately liberated and restored to the path of honor. From all three of these sources Tasso and his predecessors derived their versions of the Achilles pattern and its significance for the development of the plot.

But plot was not all. By investing the obvious contrasts inherent in this pattern with moral import, they transformed it into a schema of ethical contraries. They reinterpreted the hero's withdrawal and return as a moral dichotomy, the opposition of vicious indolence and strenuous virtue. Hence Tasso's account of Rinaldo's alienation from Godfrey and subjection to Armida shows no little complexity. Indebted to Statius as well as to Homer, it com-

6. For summaries of the plots of these epics, see Antonio Belloni, *Il poema epico e mitologico* (Milan, n.d.).

7. *Cf.* Tasso, *Prose diverse*, I, 71ff.

bines aspects of two different episodes in Achilles' career: his temporary withdrawal from the Trojan War after his quarrel with Agamemnon and his earlier attempt to evade military duty by disguising himself as a maiden at Lycomedes' court. Yet the ethical contrasts Tasso emphasizes in his version of the Achilles pattern are those conventionally associated with the Circe legend and its Renaissance analogues.

In the *Achilleid*, Statius proposes to celebrate the hero's emergence from retirement—"to summon him forth from his hiding-place in Scyros with Dulichian trumpet" ("heroa velis Scyroque latentem Dulichia proferre tuba"). Knowing that her son is fated to die young, Thetis disguises him as a damsel and leaves him at Lycomedes' court on Scyros, where he secretly espouses the king's daughter Deidameia. Here he remains, occupied in womanly pastimes, until Odysseus exposes his disguise. When the wily Ithacan includes arms among his gifts to the maidens of the court, Achilles rises to the bait. Yet his own reactions are paradoxical. The sight of the weapons inspires him with enthusiasm for the war, but the reflection of his own image in the shield fills him with shame at his unseemly metamorphosis. "But the bold son of Aeacus no sooner saw before him the gleaming shield enchased with battle-scenes . . . and leaning against the spear, than he shouted loud . . . , and Troy fills all his breast . . . But when he came nearer, and the emulous brightness gave back his features and he saw himself mirrored in the reflecting gold, he thrilled and blushed together."[8] The essential features of this scene find a place in Cinquecento epic. Both Ruggiero and Rinaldo exhibit the same antithesis of effeminate idleness and martial valor, the same duality of moral lapse and recovery, the same inner progression from self-forgetfulness to self-recognition.

The *Orlando Furioso* develops the parallel between Ruggiero's enforced idleness and that of Achilles. Both warriors are destined to die young, yet achieve immortal fame in battle. Just as Thetis had attempted to forestall Achilles' fate by hiding him at Lycomedes' court, so Ruggiero's teacher Atlante tries to circumvent his destiny by holding him captive in an enchanted castle, where he leads a life of luxurious ease. When this device fails, the enchanter attempts a further ruse to keep him from the battle-

---

8. *Statius*, trans. J. H. Mozley (2 vols.; Loeb Classical Library; London, 1928), II, 508–509, 573.

field. Brought to Alcina's island by Atlante's hippogriff, Ruggiero falls victim to her charms, physical as well as magical. Like Achilles, he neglects his military obligations and remains in unseemly bondage to his mistress until reason restores him to self-knowledge and the path of duty. In thus diverting Ruggiero from the pursuit of honor to inglorious ease, Atlante is motivated by the same considerations that had prompted Thetis to conceal Achilles.

> So did Atlante, not with evil mind,
> Give to Rogero this so bad direction,
> But of a purpose thereby to withdraw
> His fatal end that he before foresaw
>
> . . . .
>
> Esteeming less his honor than his ease,
> A few years' life than everlasting fame.

Ruggiero's apparel, like Achilles' garments on Scyros, has moral significance as an index of his idle and sensuous life. These ornaments, so unbefitting the hero or warrior, signalize his alienation from himself.

> About his neck a carc'net rich he ware
> Of precious stones, all set in gold-well-tried;
> His arms, that erst all warlike weapons bare,
> In golden bracelets wantonly were tied;
> Into his ears two rings conveyèd are
>
> . . . .
>
> His locks, bedewed with waters of sweet savor,
> Stood curlèd round in order on his head;
> He had such wanton womanish behavior
> As though in Valence he had long been bred;
> So changed in speech, in manners, and in favor,
> So from himself beyond all reason led
> By these enchantments of this am'rous dame
> He was himself in nothing but in name.[9]

In this state of sensual ease, the hero forgets his overlord, his lady, and his own honor. Only the exhortations of the "good witch" Melissa and the magic ring of reason reclaim him from his "lunga inerzia" and restore him to self-knowledge. This transition from sensual ignorance to knowledge and from carnal vice to rational

---

9. Ludovico Ariosto, *Orlando Furioso*, ed. Rudolf Gottfried, trans. Sir John Harington (Bloomington, 1963), 161–63.

virtue receives further emphasis through Ruggiero's flight from Alcina to Logistilla.

Tasso's Rinaldo likewise reenacts the role of Statius' Achilles. Sunk in ignoble ease in Armida's bower, he is roused by the sight of his friends' armor, much as Achilles had been stirred by his first glimpse of the weapons Odysseus had brought.

> So far'd Rinaldo when the glorious light
> Of their bright harness glister'd in his eyes,
> His noble sprite awaked at that sight,
> His blood began to warm, his heart to rise;
> Though drunk with ease, devoid of wonted might,
> On sleep till then his weaken'd virtue lies.

As in the case of Achilles and Ruggiero, his condition of sensual bondage finds expression in vestiary symbolism, and his recovery is analogous to that of both heroes. Like Ruggiero, he comes to a true knowledge of himself through reason; like Achilles, he is humiliated by his reflection in the shield.

> Upon the targe his locks amaz'd he bent,
> And therein all his wanton habit spied,
> His civet, balm, and perfumes redolent,
> How from his locks they smok'd and mantle wide;
> His sword, that many a Pagan stout had shent,
> Bewrapt with flow'rs hung idly by his side,
> So nicely decked that it seem'd the knight
> Wore it for fashion sake, but not for fight.[10]

In the *Gerusalemme*, as in the *Achilleid*, the process of self-recognition hinges on the shield as a symbol of reason; in the *Orlando*, upon the magic ring.

Thus Tasso fuses two motifs derived from the *Iliad* and the *Achilleid*—Achilles' withdrawal to his tents after his quarrel with Agamemnon and Statius' account of the hero's disguise and discovery on Scyros. Ariosto, on the other hand, draws largely on the episode described in the *Achilleid* rather than on the *Iliad*. But both poets also exploit the Circe myth. Alcina and Armida are modeled, to a considerable degree, on the classical sorceress. The scenes depicting the inglorious idleness of Ruggiero and Rinaldo combine the motif of sensual enchantment by a beautiful witch with the motif of Achilles on Scyros.

10. Torquato Tasso, *Jerusalem Delivered*, ed. Roberto Weiss, trans. Edward Fairfax ([London], 1962), 400–401.

Similarly, Trissino invests the motif of Achilles' withdrawal with details suggestive of the Circe legend. When Corsamonte forsakes Belisarius' camp, he departs to the peninsula of Circe in search of the fay Plutina (*i.e.*, wealth). Here he resides in a "sontuoso, e bel pelagio" with "abbondanza d'ottime vivande" while the unhappy Romans remain in "periglio estremo" from the Goths.[11] Thus the motif of Achilles' withdrawal inherited from both Homer and Statius undergoes moral development. Through the addition of elements derived from the Circe myth, it becomes an exemplum of sensual vice and a stage in the inner development of the hero in his progress toward ethical perfection.[12] In the hands of Ariosto, Trissino, and Tasso, it is transformed into an allegorical statement of the antithesis between pleasure and duty, vice and heroic virtue.

Thus the Cinquecento converted the hero's withdrawal from military action into a moral crisis. As a phase in his education in the nature of virtue and vice, it culminated in an act of *proairesis*, a positive moral choice based on right reason and self-knowledge. Yet in thus moralizing this motif, Renaissance poets found it necessary to alter numerous details in their classical sources and models. In particular, the quarrel between the warrior and his commander must be placed on a higher level. By Cinquecento standards the abusive epithets Achilles and Agamemnon had heaped on each other appeared unseemly, and the grounds of their dissension trivial or base. Such a slanging match befitted neither a hero nor a king. Epic decorum demanded a weightier cause of dispute than a concubine, and the dispute itself should be conducted in the loftier terms appropriate to their character and rank. Accordingly, even though Trissino, Alamanni, and Tasso deliberately imitate the quarrel scene of the *Iliad*, they alter the motives and circumstances that lead to the breach in order to meet Renaissance standards of the heroic *ethos* and the heroic poem.

Most of these Cinquecento successors of the *Iliad* heighten and develop Homer's emphasis on honor (*timē*) to produce a more consistent and characteristic image of magnanimity. Like the *Iliad*

---

11. G. G. Trissino, *Italia Liberata*, in *Opere* (2 vols.; Verona, 1729), I, 141–42.

12. See Merritt Y. Hughes, "Spenser's Acrasia and the Circe of the Renaissance," *Journal of the History of Ideas*, IV (1943), 381–99.

itself, they abound in such epithets as "great-souled" and "great-minded." As in the *Iliad*, a sense of wounded honor is a primary cause of the hero's alienation from his commander. In these Renaissance epics, however, the motif of honor is "moralized" through the influence of Aristotle's discussion of magnanimity, the Platonic definition of the warrior's *thymos*, and the contemporary emphasis (in theory and practice alike) on the moral function of the epic.[13] Ethical commonplaces concerning the magnanimous man—his pursuit of honor and great actions and his contempt for riches and pleasure—place Achilles' conduct in a different perspective. To delineate the hero's "magnitude of mind," the Renaissance poet sharpens the ethical contrasts in his behavior—between high exploits and inglorious ease, between concern for honor and the temptations of sensual pleasure and wealth. He heightens the antithesis between true magnanimity and its contrary—vanity or pride—and between rational valor and ungoverned wrath, true fortitude and rashness.[14] Such antitheses are especially marked in Tasso's Rinaldo and several of his Renaissance predecessors.

Trissino's *Italia Liberata* bases the quarrel of Corsamonte and Belisarius on that of Achilles and Agamemnon. As in the *Iliad*, a woman is the cause of their dispute, but (again as in the *Iliad*) the real issues are merit and honor. Trissino not only refines the character and motivation of his antagonists but also elevates the station of the woman over whom they contend. Elpidia, the daughter of the prince of Taranto, petitions Belisarius to bestow her in marriage on Corsamonte, whose great merits have made him worthy of her hand. Yet another warrior, the "fiero Acquilino," objects. Arguing that his own merits equal Corsamonte's, he urges Belisarius to refuse Elpidia's request and instead reserve her as a reward for valor after the impending battle with the Goths at

13. Aristotle, *Nicomachean Ethics*, Bk. IV, Chap. 3, in *The Student's Oxford Aristotle*, trans. W. D. Ross (6 vols.; London, 1942), V. See Torquato Tasso, *Discorso della virtù eroica e della carità*, in *Prose diverse*, II, 187–202, for a comparison between heroic virtue and magnanimity. For Plato's view on *nous* and *thymos* in the individual and in the state and on timocracy ("the government of honor"), see *Works*, I, 80–89, 166–69, II, 146–49, 156–57, 166–68, 307–12, 363.

14. One should not be misled by Ross's translation, which ambiguously renders Aristotle's *megalopsychos* as the "proud man" rather than as the "magnanimous man." In Ross's translation, the excess of this virtue is "vanity." In Milton's *De Doctrina Christiana* (Bk. I, Chap. 9) "pride" and an "ambitious spirit" are opposites of magnanimity.

Rome. Most of the other warriors approve this suggestion, but Corsamonte greets it with "little patience and great disdain," preferring to settle the issue by duel. Although Belisarius intends to bestow Elpidia ultimately on Corsamonte, he conceals his intent and postpones his verdict until after the battle. Outraged by this development, Corsamonte casts patience to the winds as "food of base minds" and attacks Acquilino with drawn sword. Thereupon Belisarius, likewise kindled with "disdain" and "ire," bars Corsamonte altogether from candidacy for the princess' hand. The hero then quits the camp in disgust, complaining that it affords neither scope for the pursuit of honor nor reward for virtue. "Alas, do not remain, Corsamonte, in this camp, where no reward is given to virtue. Seek another fortune, for the nobleman who seeks honor should never remain under the governance of a changeable and unjust commander." [15] Just as Achilles had withdrawn with Patroclus to his own tents, Corsamonte departs with his "fedele Achille," and only the abduction of Elpidia by the Goths brings him back into the war.

Like Trissino, Alamanni ennobles the Achilles pattern by attributing to his hero Lancilotto a higher and more chivalric motivation than that of Homer's protagonist. Lancelot's breach with Arturo stems from the envy displayed by the king's nephew, Gaveno, and from Lancelot's own gallantry in releasing Claudiana, the captive daughter of the king of Avaricum (Bourges). When Arthur sides with Gaveno and accuses Lancelot of aiding the enemy by his unauthorized action, the hero withdraws from the field with his faithful comrade Galealto. Only after the latter has been slain, like Patroclus, does the hero return to combat. Alamanni's epic bears a much closer resemblance to the *Iliad* than does Trissino's. As the author's son declares, "egli ha voluto imitare . . . l'Iliade del grande Homero: perciò che dove in quella l'assedio di Troia si descrive, in questa l'assedio di BORGES si dimostra. . . . Et in somma vedrà, che egli con ogni studio, e diligenza si è ingegnato di volere quasi una TOSCANA ILIADE formare." [16]

Like its Greek prototype, the "Tuscan Iliad" takes as its argu-

---

15. Trissino, *Italia Liberata*, I, 113–15.

16. Luigi Alamanni, *La Avarchide* (Florence, 1570), Dedicatory epistle by Batista Alamanni. Luigi Alamanni had desired to imitate Homer's *Iliad*, composing a "Tuscan *Iliad*." Whereas Homer had described the siege of Troy, Alamanni would describe the siege of Bourges.

ment the hero's anger against his king and the tragic results of their quarrel for their companions. "Sing, o Muse, the wrath and ardent ire of Lancelot son of King Ban against King Arthur, which caused the British and French troops to lament so bitterly, and caused so many illustrious souls, afflicted and extinguished, to leave their limbs in bloody grief, the unworthy prey of cruel fowls and dogs, as pleased Him who leads and reigns." In the *Iliad*, however, Apollo's revenge for Agamemnon's insult to his priest precipitates the train of events that leads to the quarrel. In the *Avarchide*, on the other hand, the cause is Gawain's envy of Lancelot's heroic virtues. "What was the cause of so great a quarrel? Gawain, Lord of Orkney, who envied the agreeable virtues of Lancelot." Aggrieved because he cannot espouse Claudiana himself and jealous of the hero's merits, Gawain accuses his rival of insubordination to his king. By restoring the princess and her brothers to their father, Lancelot has, he charges, impeded the progress of the war. In reply, Lancelot indignantly accuses his adversary of envy and complains of the insult to his own honor. Arthur, in turn, pays tribute to the hero's "true prowess" and "rare valor," but rebukes his imprudence and pride and commands him to render the same obedience as his peers. Interrupting angrily, Lancelot rebuffs the charge of ingratitude, refuses the lands Arthur offers him, and insists that he prizes nothing except honor. "I value not at all riches, possessions, kingdom or tribute. All seems trifling to me except that true honor which is merited by the virtue which springs from us and feeds the mind with immortal food." In reply Arthur urges the superior merit of a monarch. Reproaching Lancelot for attempting to exercise his valor in council rather than in war and against his friends and his sovereign instead of against his enemies, the king accuses him of outrages and scorn. "He always despises and opposes my opinion. He is unwilling to accept me as greater than he. He values no one else and disdains every man, this soul full of pride and wrath." Attempts to reconcile the two men prove vain. Lancelot, angered more than ever ("sdegnato più che mai") by Arthur's charges, refuses to serve him any longer. Like Achilles, he departs in wrath predicting that "one day you will long in vain for my return" ("un giorno Bramerete anco indarno il mio ritorno").[17]

Alamanni invests his hero with an *ethos* notably higher than

17. *Ibid.*, 1, 3–4, 5, 8.

that of Achilles. Lancelot's anger is directed primarily against Gawain rather than Arthur, and at the beginning of the quarrel scene he professes "obbedienza" and "integro amore" to his sovereign. In remaining apart from the conflict, he does not, he declares, desire Arthur's ruin, but intends only to punish ingratitude: "The noble breast cannot delight in another's misfortune." [18] Gawain's envy of Lancelot's merits actually enhances his heroic stature; that heroic virtue must suffer from envy, and honor from detraction, was a commonplace familiar even to Sir John Falstaff. As in the *Iliad*, the quarrel arises over a woman, but here again Alamanni consciously elevates the motifs he derives from Homer. Claudiana is a king's daughter, not a mere concubine like Briseis; and Lancelot's chivalrous conduct toward her signalizes his ethical superiority to Achilles. Finally, Alamanni intensifies the emphasis on honor, already explicit in the *Iliad*, in order to heighten his portrait of magnanimity.

In Tasso's epic, as in Alamanni's, the hero's breach with his commander springs from a rival's envy. Jealous because Rinaldo has been nominated to lead the expedition on Armida's behalf, the Norwegian prince Gernando publicly slanders him, but is slain by the hero in single combat. Informed that he must stand trial for manslaughter, Rinaldo is indignant, feeling that his commander, Godfrey of Bouillon, has requited his faithful service with insult and injury. On the advice of friends he forsakes the camp, confident that without him the crusaders must suffer reverses and Godfrey ultimately recognize his indispensability. By attributing this argument to advisers rather than to Rinaldo himself, Tasso attempts to exonerate his hero of the possible charge of desertion. [19] As in other Cinquecento epics based on the *Iliad*, a woman is indirectly involved in the quarrel, but in this case her connection is even more tangential. The issue at stake between Rinaldo and Gernando is not Armida herself, but the question as to who is the worthiest to conduct the enterprise on her behalf. The central issue is merit and honor; and, as in the *Avarchide*, the author exploits the conventional antithesis between envy and heroic virtue.

In all three epics the alienation scene serves a structural function comparable to that in the *Iliad*. It complicates the plot by es-

18. *Ibid.*, 12.
19. Tasso, *Jerusalem Delivered*, V.

tranging the most valiant of the warriors and thus temporarily paralyzing the epic enterprise. It also serves, as in the *Iliad*, to highlight the concept of honor. Nevertheless, in their actual development of the quarrel, these Renaissance epics differ markedly from their classical prototype. They tend to ennoble both the hero and his commander. In the *Iliad* the chief responsibility for the quarrel lies with Agamemnon. In these Cinquecento poems, however, the commander does not precipitate the quarrel, and the blame rests with an inferior—Acquilino, Gawain, Gernando. Whereas Agamemnon had outraged his best warrior by seizing his concubine, none of the commanders in these later epics is guilty of this offense. Belisarius does not seek Elpidia for himself, Arthur does not desire Claudiana, Godfrey is indifferent to the charms of Armida. In two cases—those of Corsamonte and Rinaldo—the breach results from the hero's violent assault on his rival or accuser. Indeed, in Rinaldo's case, Tasso avoids an open quarrel with Godfrey; there is a quarrel scene that results in the hero's forsaking his camp, but Rinaldo's quarrel is actually with Gernando rather than Godfrey. Tasso carefully avoids the indecorum both of exposing his hero to the charge of insubordination and of degrading his commander by imitating the taunts and jibes of Achilles and Agamemnon.[20]

In these Renaissance quarrel scenes both contestants are idealized. The commanders are wiser and less culpable than Agamemnon, and the aggrieved warriors more temperate than Achilles. Except for their impatience and anger, they approach Renaissance ideals of valor and magnanimity.

A tendency to moralize the quarrel scene appears in all three epics. In the *Avarchide* the various warriors and councillors who attempt to compose the quarrel pass ethical judgments on the contestants.[21] In the *Gerusalemme*, Godfrey and Achilles become

20. Plato, *Works*, II, 89–90: "Are not the chief elements of temperance . . . obedience to commanders and self-control in sensual pleasures? . . . What of this line,

> O heavy with wine, who hast the eyes of a dog and the heart of a stag,

and of the words which follow? Would you say that these, or any similar impertinences which private individuals are supposed to address to their rulers, whether in verse or prose, are well or ill spoken?"

21. In the quarrel scene in Alamanni's *La Avarchide*, Galealto and Lago offer advice to both contestants (pp. 5–8) in an attempt to resolve their conflict. Subsequently Arthur's ambassadors to Lancelot point out the path of duty (pp. 166–71).

allegorical types of two different faculties of the human soul—the
rational and the irascible—and thus correspond to the *nous* of
Plato's philosopher-kings and the *thymos* of his warrior-class.[22]
Hence the alienation and reconciliation of the two men acquires
moral and psychological significance. The former symbolizes the
divorce of reason and passion in the human soul, the refusal of
the lower power to obey the higher, the separation of the irascible
and rational faculties in man. The latter represents the return to
the state of natural justice and natural obedience, in which the
lower faculties obey the higher. Tasso lifts the Homeric quarrel
scene to the level of moral philosophy.

Besides mitigating and extenuating Achilles' quarrel with his
commander, Renaissance poets also attempted to alter other aspects of his behavior that violated contemporary conceptions of
decorum. The most flagrant breach of the chivalric ideal—the indignities inflicted on Hector's corpse—had incurred severe censure from contemporary critics; such a scene could find no place
in any Cinquecento epic that seriously claimed to celebrate heroic
virtue. Hence, despite their superficial fidelity to the *Iliad*'s account of Achilles' duel with Hector, both Trissino and Alamanni
scrupulously avoid tarnishing their heroes by imitating the victor's outrage to his foe. Although Corsamonte avenges his lady's
abduction by slaying the Gothic Hector, Turrismondo, he does
not press his vengeance beyond death. Although he rejects his
adversary's offer of friendship and threatens to leave his body to
dogs and vultures, he never carries out his threat: "When I have
you dead, and your soft flesh will be the food of vultures and
dogs." Instead, he respects Turrismondo's dying request and con-
signs the body to the latter's friends for decent burial. "But I do
not want to feed on dead bodies. Die assured that I shall not allow
any insult to your limbs, but shall return them to your people
when it pleases them." The motif of desecration of the dead
is transferred from Corsamonte to his friend Achille. After
Corsamonte has been treacherously slain, Achille avenges his

Maligante urges Lancelot to cast aside "ira" and "sdegno," for excessive obduracy
is characteristic rather of the proud man than the magnanimous. Lancelot himself
confesses that anger has driven him from the "dritto cammin" (p. 171), and
Galealto later observes that revenge can be carried beyond the limits of true magnanimity (p. 211).
    22. Cf. Tasso, *Prose diverse*, I, 303–307.

murder by tying the traitors, heads downward, to fierce horses and dragging their bodies seven times around Corsamonte's burial mound.[23] Trissino has altered the details of Achilles' vengeance as he found them in Homer in order to invest his own hero with greater nobility.

Although Alamanni usually imitates the *Iliad* much more closely than does Trissino, his hero provides an even more striking contrast to Achilles in his treatment of his enemy's corpse. When Lancelot rejoins Arthur's forces after Galealto's death and slays the Celtic Hector, Segurano, he conducts himself with consistent generosity toward his antagonist. Unlike Achilles, he offers Segurano his life, and slays him only after the "crudo Hiberno" has indignantly rejected his offer of peace. Thereupon, filled with "dolcissima pietate," he orders that his antagonist's body be cleansed of blood and dust and wrapped in silk. In contrast to Achilles, who had accepted Priam's ransom for Hector's body, Lancelot magnanimously refuses the treasures Clodasso (king of Avaricum) offers him. He restores the bodies of Segurano and the king's son Clodino without ransom, for he desires honor rather than wealth. "The scepter and crown and golden garment which you have brought are Clodasso's. Know that I thirst for true honor, not for gain."[24] By these significant variations on the *Iliad*, Alamanni avoids the accusations of cruelty and cupidity so frequently leveled against Homer's hero. Since the magnanimous man traditionally aimed at honor rather than wealth, both Trissino and Alamanni take pains to demonstrate their heroes' indifference to riches and to exonerate them from the charges of avarice that critics had raised against Achilles. In emphasizing this facet of magnanimity, both poets drew on the ambassador scene in the *Iliad*, Book IX. Just as Achilles had rejected the gifts and offers Agamemnon had sent him, Corsamonte and Lancelot refuse the gifts and promises of their commanders. Although Belisarius offers the angry hero honors, treasures, and Elpidia's hand, Corsamonte spurns these gifts. "I do not want to accept them, even if you should give me all the treasure that Rome ever possessed and that the Ruler of the world now possesses. The enemy's gift is no true gift."[25]

23. Trissino, *Italia Liberata*, I, 220–21, 240. Cf. Plato's criticism of the analogous scene in the *Iliad* (*Works*, II, 92).

24. Alamanni, *La Avarchide*, 320.

25. Trissino, *Italia Liberata*, I, 142–43.

Similarly, though Arthur's ambassadors offer costly gifts—
cities, ships, treasures, the king's own sister-in-law as wife—Lancelot indignantly rejects them as base bribes. "The ingrate thinks
that at the vilest price he can restore land and gold. He does not
recall that I am accustomed to give kingdoms and treasure, not to
take them." He bids them inform their king that he disdains such
gifts. "I do not value his promised gifts. I have enough kingdoms
and honors, without his, from the infinite and immortal goodness. . . . Thanks to this goodness the spirit aspires so high that it
does not admire the base treasure here below." [26]

Lancelot exhibits a similar indifference to riches after the battle
and his reconciliation with Arthur. Although the king offers him
a reward "nostro Scettro, e tutto il Regno," the hero refuses and
asks only to be invested with the "segno" of "Cavalleria"—sword,
girdle, and spurs. "The crowns, the lands, the gems and the gold
and the other greater things dear to the world, save these for those
who are greedy. For me it is enough that my martial labor makes
virtue shine with illustrious deeds and that I employ my strength
and life in bringing aid to the oppressed." [27] An analogous indifference to "wealth or sovereign power" in his pursuit of honor
and heroic deeds characterizes Tasso's Rinaldo.

Behind these Cinquecento epics lay a complex heritage—the example set by classical epic; the values and tastes formulated by the
medieval tradition of chivalric romance; contemporary critical
opinion which tended to extol Greek and Roman epics as literary
models, but to censure aspects of their morality. It is hardly surprising, therefore, that the heroic poet felt impelled to imitate the
ancients and yet radically alter them. Indebted as they are to classical epic for their versions of the Achilles legend, all four poems
convert the latter into an exemplum of the characteristic vices and
virtues of the magnanimous man; they essay, in varying degrees,
to adapt Achilles' behavior to the chivalric ideal. Ariosto borrows
elements of the hero's concealment on Scyros. Trissino and Alamanni imitate the Homeric quarrel scene. Tasso draws on Homer
and Statius alike, combining both withdrawal motifs in his account of Rinaldo's estrangement from Godfrey.

All four poems tend to moralize this motif by sharpening ethi-

---

26. Alamanni, *La Avarchide*, 168–71.
27. *Ibid.*, 294.

cal contrasts, by eliminating the more objectionable aspects of Achilles' conduct, and by increasing the amount of moral commentary on the part of the author, the protagonists, and the minor characters. Emphasizing the distinctive attributes of magnanimity—concern for honor and great actions, preoccupation with merits and deserts, contempt of pleasure and riches—they transform the Homeric into the chivalric *ethos*. They convert the *ferus* and *saevus* Pelides into a Renaissance nobleman.

CHAPTER 3

Bacon and the Scientist as Hero

WHAT HAS Bacon to do with Hercules, or Verulam with Gibraltar? Alcuin and Tertullian once raised similar questions apropos of Christ and Ingeld, Athens and Jerusalem, and perhaps literary history itself has answered them. Anglo-Saxon scops eulogized the saints in the idioms of Teutonic heroic poetry, portraying Christ with his disciples as an evangelical warrior-prince surrounded by a comitatus of apostolic athelings. Greek and Latin churchmen, mindful perhaps of Saint Basil's exhortation to plunder the Egyptians, diverted the classical heroic tradition into the channels of sacred eloquence, celebrating biblical themes in verse and oratory: a precedent that Renaissance apologists for "divine poetry" would cite with approval and that Reformation and Counter-Reformation writers would follow with zeal and occasional skill.

Nevertheless, heroic *topoi* might serve to extol the scientist as well as the soldier and the saint, the man of learning as well as the man of war and the man of God. Like the celebrants of Christian heroism, the apologists for secular erudition—philologists, moralists, and natural philosophers, who were usually far more at home in the academic cloister than in the military camp—exploited the vocabulary of heroic myth to magnify their own vocations and the achievements of fellow scholars. Just as Stoic apologists had eulogized the sage's victory over his passions in the idiom of the field, just as Christian orators had exhorted their

congregations to be "more than conquerors" in the warfare between flesh and spirit, so the scientist and humanist in their turn
evoked the imagery of bloodlust and "infinite manslaughter" in
their literary combat against ignorance. The Battle of the Books
was still a theme for encomium rather than burlesque; it had not
yet become identified with the mock-heroic.

Like many of his contemporaries, Bacon employs heroic *topoi*
to extol the honor or *honestas* of learning. Of particular significance are his emphasis on the practical as well as the theoretical
value of knowledge; his stress on the physical conquest of nature
through intellectual enterprise; his eulogy of the scholar not
merely as "well-thinker" but as "well-doer," as *euergetes* and
benefactor; and his insistence, paradoxically, on the intrinsic
nobility of the "base" mechanical arts. In thus utilizing heroic
commonplaces as topics of honor or nobility, he observes the conventional ends of deliberative and demonstrative rhetoric as
Ciceronian tradition had defined them: "In the deliberative
type," Cicero had declared in the *De Inventione*. "Aristotle accepts
advantage [*utilitas*] as the end, but I prefer both honour [*honestas*]
and advantage. In the epideictic speech it is honour alone." In the
Rhetorica ad Herennium, on the other hand, honor or *honestas* is
classified as a subdivision of utility.[1]

For many of Bacon's contemporaries and successors, few images could have been more challenging than his adaptation of the
motif of Hercules' Columns and his transformation of the motto
Ne plus ultra into *Plus ultra*. This metaphor brought the scientist
into conscious rivalry not only with the greatest of classical heroes (for Hercules had long since become the paradigm and archetype of heroic virtue) but with the greatest and most extensive of
world empires (for the phrase *Plus ultra* had served as motto and
emblem for Charles V).[2] Pindar himself, moreover, had exploited

1. Cicero, *De inventione*, trans. H. M. Hubbell (London, 1949), 324–25; Cicero,
Ad C. Herennium libri IV de ratione dicendi, trans. Henry Caplan (Cambridge, Mass.,
1954), 160–61. For Bacon's views on rhetoric, see Karl R. Wallace, *Francis Bacon on
Communication and Rhetoric* (Chapel Hill, 1943); Wilbur Samuel Howell, *Logic and
Rhetoric in England, 1500–1700* (Princeton, 1956); Robert Hannah, *Francis Bacon:
The Political Orator, with a Short Study of His Rhetorical Theory and Practice* (New York,
1926); Paolo Rossi, *Francis Bacon: From Magic to Science*, trans. Sacha Rabinovitch
(Chicago, 1968), 135–223.

2. For examples of this motif in Renaissance emblem literature, see Arthur
Henkel and Albrecht Schöne (eds.), *Emblemata, Handbuch zur Sinnbildkunst des XVI
and XVII Jahrhunderts* (Stuttgart, 1967), cols. 1197–99. Jacobus Typotius, in *Symbola
divina & humana pontificum imperatorum regum* (Frankfurt, 1652), 45, depicts two

this motif in the Isthmian Odes, in praising the ancestors of Melissus of Thebes. "And by far-reaching deeds of native valour, did they touch the pillars of Heracles; and let none pursue prowess that passeth beyond that bound!"[3] This was an image that already possessed emphatically heroic associations, in classical myth and panegyric and in recent history, and to readers who encountered it in the text of *The Advancement of Learning*, on the illustrated title page of the *Magna Instauratio*, or in the writings of Bacon's early disciples, the comparisons it evoked must have seemed startling in their ambition and audacious in their confidence. Bacon's image did not merely imply the superiority of moderns to ancients; it also promised an empire over nature—achieved by and through the lowly mechanical arts—which might rival the dominions of the Holy Roman Emperor Charles V and of Philip II of Spain.

Behind Bacon's encomium of the scientist as hero lies a rich and complex tradition, incorporating the conventions of epic and rhetoric, history and myth. Before analyzing his use of heroic *topoi* in his own writings, let us briefly reconsider three aspects of this intellectual and literary background: first, the ideal of the military hero, and Renaissance reactions against this norm; second, the argument from nobility in Renaissance defenses of arts and sciences; third, the ideal of the contemplative hero, the worthy who excels less in fortitude than in wisdom, who achieves his victories on the page or in the laboratory rather than in the field, and who triumphs through the labors of the mind. It is against this background—the tensions and conflicts within the European heroic tradition; the diversity of Renaissance heroic ideals; and, in particular, the glorification of "contemplative heroes" in imagery borrowed from martial epic and myth—that we must examine Bacon's eulogy of the experimental scientist as heroic benefactor: founder, discoverer, conqueror; an exemplar not only of heroic wisdom but of heroic charity.

"Res gestae regumque ducumque et tristia bella," Horace's statement of the proper subject for epic verse, "the deeds of kings and

---

emblems belonging to Charles V and including both the Columns of Hercules and the motto *Plus Ultra*.

3. *The Odes of Pindar*, trans. Sir John Sandys (London, 1915), 460–61. See also Erasmus, *Adages* (1599), col. 571, "Ultra Herculis columnas."

martial leaders and grievous wars," epitomizes the central tradition in European heroic literature. Besides expressing the dominant themes of Greek and Latin epic, it foreshadowed, and in part
conditioned, the views of later poets and critics. The heroic
poem, declared Tasso, should portray "the ideal of a perfect
knight," deriving its subject from "the noble and magnanimous
actions of heroes." Wars have been "hitherto the only Argument
Heroic deem'd," Milton would complain, less than a century afterwards; fallen man has mistaken "Might" for "Valour and Heroic
Virtue" and martial exploits for "the highest pitch of human
Glory." As Dryden would declare in the preface to *Annus Mirabi-
lis*, "I have chosen the most heroic Subject which any Poet could
desire. I have taken upon me to describe the motives, the beginning, progress and successes of a most just and necessary
War. . . . All other greatness in subjects is only counterfeit, it
will not endure the test of danger; the greatness of Arms is only
real; other greatness burdens a Nation with its weight, this supports it with its strength."[4]

Such views, however, represented merely one important facet
of the heroic tradition; they did not adequately summarize the
tradition as a whole. Although epic fable and poetic myth decisively shaped this tradition, they did not absolutely determine
it. Moralists and theologians, physicians and metaphysicians,
and indeed seventeenth-century scientists, all contributed their
share to its development. The martial heroism, conventional in
epic verse, possessed a formidable rival in the heroism of the
mind; poets and philosophers alike debated the relative merits of
the active and the contemplative hero. Conceptions of heroic
character, passion, or action, though strongly molded by epic
theory and practice, were neither uniform nor standard. There
was no single or universal paradigm of the hero; he was, in fact, a
composite ideal, combining varied and sometimes inconsistent
stereotypes. Moreover, the very word *hero* was an equivoque, a
term notorious for multiple and sometimes contradictory senses.
Poets and rhetoricians were not alone in recognizing and exploiting its ambiguities.

The result of these ambiguities was a heroic tradition as no-

4. Torquato Tasso, *Prose*, ed. Francesco Flora (Milan, 1935), 362, 401; John
Milton, *Paradise Lost*, Bk. IX, ll. 28–29, Bk. XI, ll. 689–94; James Kinsley (ed.), *The
Poems and Fables of John Dryden* (London, 1962), 44–46.

table for its complexity and variety as for its continuity. Mythographers, for instance, usually depicted the heroes as demigods, the offspring of mixed marriages between gods and mortals, men immortalized or even deified for their labors. Pythagoreans and Neoplatonists described them as separated essences or purified souls; the heroes constituted an aerial order ranking slightly below daemons and gods. Aristotelian tradition stressed the hero's moral eminence and "excess of virtue," defining him as a "godlike man" and identifying heroic virtue as a "superhuman virtue, a heroic and divine kind of virtue."[5] Saint Augustine transferred the term to Christian martyrs ("our heroes"), and medieval schoolmen applied Aristotle's definition to the saints, men eminent for heroic sanctity and for charity *in gradu heroico*.

Such concepts as these, sometimes complementary, sometimes contradictory, to poetic ideals of martial heroism, not only modified epic representations of the hero but in several instances induced a reappraisal of the epic tradition itself. Renaissance poets might consciously model their epics on the *Iliad* and their heroes on Achilles; yet as a rule they scrupulously avoided the latter's excesses in action and passion. Even though Tasso preferred a military argument, he insisted that the epic hero be eminent in Christian piety. Although Dryden would likewise favor a martial subject, he would nevertheless draw a sharp contrast between the true "Man of Honour" and "those Athletick Brutes whom undeservedly we call Heroes." Milton would explicitly reject the martial argument, censuring it as not justly heroic.[6] Preferring spiritual to physical combat, he would extol more humane and less feral virtues—wisdom and faith, obedience and charity—above brute strength.

In Renaissance prose treatises—defenses and eulogies of particular arts and sciences, histories and biographies, and panegyrics of particular nations or cities or men—heroic conventions performed a rhetorical function. Insofar as they aided the writer to magnify or extol, they served the ends of demonstrative oratory, the rhetoric of praise. (Significantly, Renaissance rhetoricians often placed both epic and encomium in this category.) Insofar as they enabled him to persuade his readers to a certain course

5. *The Basic Works of Aristotle*, ed. Richard McKeon (New York, 1941), 1036–37.
6. Kinsley (ed.), *Poems and Fables of John Dryden*, 518; *Paradise Lost*, Bk. IX, ll. 30–41.

of action, toward ends and means that seemed expedient and honorable, heroic conventions also pertained to deliberative oratory, the rhetoric of exhortation. Like the epic poet, the orator employed "notable examples" for the sake of exhortation and praise. Such a theme as the heroic virtues of Socrates, for instance, might serve the ends of both demonstrative and deliberative rhetoric, praising the philosopher himself but also exhorting his posterity to emulate him. An encomium on the nobility of painting might similarly perform a dual office, praising the art itself (and indirectly complimenting its practitioners), but also exhorting the audience to seek the delights of connoisseurship and the responsibilities of patronage.

Lavish in superlatives, the heroic tradition served as a conventional language for encomium. It provided the strongest, though also the most extravagant, idiom of praise. Inevitably the seventeenth-century apologists for the natural sciences made much the same use of it as spokesmen for other sciences and arts in the preceding century. For these too, the topics and imagery of the heroic tradition buttressed their appeals to the argument from nobility. Just as Alberti had insisted that painting ought to rank among the liberal rather than the mechanical arts, and Leonardo had extolled the superiority of painting to poetry and sculpture, apologists for the natural sciences refuted charges of baseness by insisting on the nobility of their subject matter and the honorable ends they served.[7] In Bacon's hands, the same rhetorical techniques, the same arguments from *honestas* and *utilitas*, could serve as instruments to exalt the lowly mechanical arts, to demonstrate their dignity and nobility as well as their usefulness.

Thus the first book of *The Advancement of Learning* (and of the expanded Latin version, *De Augmentis Scientiarum*) exploits the topics of nobility and utility for an extended demonstration of the "Dignity" and "Proficience" of learning. Its rhetorical strategy and its genre are closely analogous to those of the apologies that other men of eloquence and erudition—Leonardo, Alberti, Sidney, Daniel—had composed on behalf of their own favorite arts or sciences. Like other apologists for learning, Bacon appeals

7. Leon Battista Alberti, *On Painting*, trans. John R. Spencer (Rev. ed.; New Haven, 1966); Jean Paul Richter (ed.), *The Literary Works of Leonardo da Vinci* (2nd ed., rev. and enl.; London, 1939); Sir Anthony Blunt, *Artistic Theory in Italy, 1450–1600* (London, 1968).

not only to *honestas* but to *utilitas;* he stresses the profitableness as well as the nobility of learning. For both kinds of *topoi*, moreover, he heightens his argument and his style through elements derived from the heroic tradition. Science has already begun to conquer (he suggests), and may continue to conquer, new realms beyond the Pillars of Hercules, farther than the greatest of mythical heroes had penetrated. Since knowledge is power, the natural philosopher, the student of nature, may subject greater natural forces to his command than the strongest of classical worthies, accomplish nobler acts of benefit for the public good than the ancient benefactors, and achieve more admirable wonders than the heroes of epic and romance. The scientist, or the fortunate monarch who employs him, is potentially a discoverer of new worlds and a conqueror of wider empires. He is a benefactor and a hero.

A commonplace of Renaissance poetic theory, the ideal of the contemplative hero was also a recurrent theme in demonstrative rhetoric. As such, it profoundly affected the language of encomium, the arguments and images employed in eulogizing men eminent in the arts and sciences: poets and painters, philologists and philosophers.

In its later forms, the distinction between active and contemplative heroes was a complex blend of Aristotelian and Neoplatonic concepts. Although Aristotle's definition of *virtus heroica* had applied primarily to the moral rather than the intellectual virtues, he had nevertheless exalted the life of the philosopher (the *vita contemplativa*) over the active life, inasmuch as "perfect happiness is a contemplative activity."[8] In this distinction, later writers found justification for positing a "contemplative hero," eminent in the intellectual virtues and in the characteristic pursuits of the contemplative life; such a hero would, *a fortiori*, excel the active hero as far as the contemplative life surpassed the active and philosophical wisdom (theory) surpassed practical wisdom (prudence). Plato had similarly exalted the philosopher over the warrior, inasmuch as *nous* excels *thymos* and the rational faculty the irascible. Neoplatonists in turn developed the Platonic notion of poetry and love as divine furor and the conception of philosophy as an intellectual love of the Good into an ideal of the philos-

8. Aristotle, *Basic Works*, 1106.

opher as inspired mystic. This ideal found expression in late-classical lives of the philosophers, where both Pythagoras and Apollonius of Thyana appear as heroic figures, and in Bruno's influential treatise on the "Heroic Frenzies." In the Renaissance, terms such as *hero* and *divinus vir* (or indeed *deus*) became common idioms of praise for scholars and artists. Antonio Francini would subsequently hail John Milton as "Fabro quasi divino," whose country produced "superhuman heroes" and whose "celestial virtue" merited "celestial rewards" greater than those of Apollo. To expound his "merto alto, e preclaro" was impossible, and he could be praised only "con lo stupore." Marvel is the characteristic effect of heroic virtue, and heroic poetry, and Francini's praise would be echoed by Carlo Dati; Milton's gifts of mind and body moved the senses to wonder, *ad admirationem*.[9]

The distinction between active and contemplative heroes was not, however, always firmly drawn. Certain of the intellectual virtues were clearly necessary for the active hero; it was axiomatic that practical wisdom (prudence) must underlie all the moral virtues. Homer had praised his heroes for skill in council as in combat, and even Achilles, thanks to divine intervention, had managed to curb his anger and refrain from slaying a king. The active hero must, moreover, possess no small skill in the arts of combat. As Dryden recognized, "the Knowledge of Warfare" is commendable "in a Man of Courage and of Resolution; in him it will direct his Martial Spirit; and teach him the way to the best Victories, which are those that are least bloody, and which tho' atchiev'd by the Hand, are manag'd by the Head."[10]

Of all the Homeric heroes, Odysseus seemed best to exemplify the intellectual virtues in a heroic degree; by the Renaissance he had become a type of heroic prudence or heroic wisdom, and the contrast between the two Homeric epics as images of contrasting ideals of heroism had become proverbial. Tasso regarded the *Odyssey* and Dante's *Commedia* as "figures of the life of the contemplative man," and the *Iliad* as an image of the active hero. Aeneas, in his opinion, represented a mixed heroism, active throughout the greater part of the fable, but contemplative in the underworld scenes of Book VI. Tasso's own hero, Godfrey of

9. John Milton, *Paradise Regained, the Minor Poems and Samson Agonistes*, ed. Merritt Y. Hughes (Garden City, N.Y., 1937), 6–12.

10. Kinsley (ed.), *Poems and Fables of John Dryden*, 518.

Bouillon, likewise conjoined the two modes of heroism, active as leader of the First Crusade, contemplative in his vision of the celestial Jerusalem. Thomas Wilson approved Saint Basil's view that whereas the *Iliad* described "strength and valiauntnesse of the body," the *Odyssey* set forth "a lively paterne of the minde."[11] Chapman similarly declared that whereas the *Iliad* described "Predominant Perturbation," the *Odyssey* portrayed "overruling Wisedome. . . . in one, the Bodie's fervour and fashion of outward Fortitude to all possible height of Heroical Action; in the other, the Mind's inward, constant and unconquered Empire, unbroken, unaltered with any most insolent and tyrannous infliction."[12] Most Renaissance critics were, moreover, thoroughly familiar with Horace's view that Ulysses provided a "useful exemplar" of virtue and sapience.

The contemplative hero, renowned for heroic wisdom, was thus fully established in Renaissance epic theory, though poets might experience no little difficulty in endeavoring to portray such a hero in a genre that by definition sought to imitate an action. Some resorted to allegory; some, like Tasso, portrayed a mixed hero. Others, like Milton, would portray a spiritual monomachy: a "great duel, not of arms, / But to vanquish by wisdom hellish wiles."[13]

Before turning to Bacon's text, let us briefly consider some of the conventional types of the contemplative hero: the philosopher, the orator, the poet, the painter, and (finally) the scientist.

11. See John M. Steadman, *Milton and the Renaissance Hero* (Oxford, 1967), 9–10.

12. O. B. Hardison, Jr. (ed.), *English Literary Criticism: The Renaissance* (New York, 1963), 205.

13. Milton, *Paradise Regained*, Bk. I, ll. 174–75. For the complexity of the Renaissance heroic tradition and the variety of forms it assumed in the literature and thought of the period, see *inter alia* Merritt Y. Hughes, "Milton and the Sense of Glory" and "The Christ of *Paradise Regained* and the Renaissance Heroic Tradition," both in *Ten Perspectives on Milton* (New Haven, 1965); Hughes, "Merit in *Paradise Lost*," *Huntington Library Quarterly*, XXXI (1967), 3–18; Frank Kermode, "Milton's Hero," *Review of English Studies*, n.s., IV (1953), 317–30; Burton O. Kurth, *Milton and Christian Heroism* (Berkeley, 1959); E. M. W. Tillyard, *The Miltonic Setting, Past and Present* (Cambridge, 1938); Eugene M. Waith, *The Herculean Hero in Marlowe, Chapman, Shakespeare, and Dryden* (New York, 1962). The function of heroic imagery in the encomiastic verse of the period has been examined by Ruth Nevo in *The Dial of Virtue: A Study of Poems on Affairs of State in the Seventeenth Century* (Princeton, 1963).

Not surprisingly, few of the spokesmen for these types were altogether free from professional bias. Most of them employed heroic terminology primarily to extol their own vocation and its masters. Philosophers heroized philosophers, rhetoricians their own kind. The apotheosis of scholars and artists, then as now, was partial, relative, and prejudiced. Few rhetoricians entered the philosopher's Elysium, and the orator left few offerings at the metaphysician's *heroon*. The heroes, it would appear, preserved their loyalties and antagonisms after death as in life.

First we should note the euhemerist element in both classical and Renaissance mythography. By explaining the myths of gods and heroes as fabulous distortions of the deeds of actual men, the mythographers fostered a decidedly comprehensive conception of the hero. Not all of the men and women thus heroized had been warriors; some of them had been inventors, who had benefited their people by discovering, introducing, and teaching new arts or sciences. Others, though not inventors, had exhibited superhuman excellence in the arts and brought them to new perfection. Such persons were in a sense contemplative heroes, and a grateful posterity had accorded them divine or semidivine honors. Within this frame of reference, with this precedent behind them, Renaissance writers could, without breach of decorum, apotheosize the virtuosi and inventors of their own age.

If Plato had exalted the philosopher as one conversant with a higher mode of existence than that of ordinary men, the realm of ideas, his followers literally deified the contemplative. "There is," declared Plotinus, "a third kind of men, that of divine men, . . . whose penetrating eye contemplates the splendor of the intelligible world, and who finally take their flight . . . beyond the clouds and darkness of this world." Such men have "*become* divine," or rather are "part of the eternal Being of the divine that is beyond becoming. . . . Such is the life of gods and of divine and blessed men, detachment from all things here below, scorn of all earthly pleasures, and flight of the alone to the alone." The superiority of contemplative virtue to active virtue, he continues, is implicit in Homer's "double assertion that Heracles is in Hades and that he is among the gods. . . . He seems to say that Heracles, because he possessed practical virtue and because of his great qualities, was judged worthy of being a god, but that, as he possessed only practical virtue, but not the contemplative virtue . . .

he could not be admitted into the world above entirely and something of him remained below." [14]

The Stoics, in turn, idealized the philosopher as a heroic figure:
a godlike man who, realizing the divine element within him, recognized that he was a "son of Zeus," conformed his own will to
the divine, and remained unmoved by the vicissitudes of time.
Subduing his own passions, he was a conqueror over himself;
retaining his inner freedom in adversity as in prosperity and unaffected by external circumstances, he illustrated the triumph of
virtue over fortune. Whether he engaged in the active or contemplative life, his wisdom and magnanimity made him indifferent to fame and superior to traditional heroes.

For all his indifference to fame, the Stoic sage nevertheless received the hero's conventional reward of praise. Zeno surpassed
all men, declared Diogenes Laertius, in the virtues of abstinence
and endurance, "in dignity of demeanor," and in happiness. He
"climbed the summits of Olympus," asserted Antipater of Sidon,
but did not seek to "emulate the immortal toils of Hercules." Instead he "found a new way for himself to the highest heaven, by
virtue, temperance, and modesty." Zenodotus hailed him as
"God-like Zeno," the founder of "a great novel school" and parent
of liberty, and compared him to an older culture hero, Cadmus,
"who gave to Greece her written books of wisdom." Epictetus
observed, "The great heroic style . . . belongs . . . to Socrates and
men like him," for Socrates was "a kinsman of the gods in very
truth." The heroes, according to Diogenes Laertius, were "the
souls of virtuous men which have left their bodies." Wise men,
he adds, are "godlike, for they have something divine in them."
Seneca similarly describes tranquillity of mind as "most exalted
and godlike."

The Stoic sage was likewise notable for magnanimity, a virtue
closely associated with *virtus heroica*. Diogenes Laertius defined
this as "a knowledge of engendering a lofty habit, superior to all
such accidents as happen to all men indifferently"; for "magnanimity of itself can raise us above everything." Marcus Aurelius,
in turn, described this virtue as "the elevation of the intelligent
part above the pleasurable or painful sensations of the flesh,

14. Joseph Katz (ed.), *The Philosophy of Plotinus: Representative Books from the
Enneads* (New York, 1950), 29, 126, 155, 158.

and above that poor thing called fame, and death, and all such things."[15]

The Epicureans were scarcely more restrained in eulogizing their own founders and philosopher-heroes. Lucretius exalted Epicurus above all other authors of "excellent and godlike discoveries." It is impossible, he declared, to "frame a poem worthy of the grandeur of . . . these discoveries" or to "devise praises equal to the deserts of him who left us such prizes won and earned by his own genius." For Epicurus was verily "a god . . . , who first found out . . . wisdom, and who by trained skill rescued life from such great billows and such thick darkness." Epicurus had surpassed all other inventors now worshipped as culture heroes or as gods. The poet continues.

> Compare the godlike discoveries of others in old times: Ceres is famed to have pointed out to mortals corn, and Liber the vine-born juice of the grape. . . . But a happy life was not possible without a clean breast; wherefore with more reason this man is deemed by us a god. . . . I[f] you shall suppose that the deeds of Hercules surpass his, you will be carried still farther away from true reason. For what would yon great gaping maw of Nemean lion now harm us and the bristled Arcadian boar? . . . None methinks: the earth even now . . . abounds to repletion in wild beasts. . . . But unless the breast is cleaned, what battles and dangers must then find their way into us in our own despite!

The man who has subdued the passions and "banished them from the mind by words, not arms, shall he not have a just title to be ranked among the gods?"

Lucretius' heroes are "the inventors of all sciences and graceful arts": Homer, Democritus, and (above all) Epicurus, "who surpassed in intellect the race of man." Epicurus was the "glory of the Greek race," the "discoverer" of the nature of things, a "godlike intellect"; and in praising him, Lucretius very nearly converts his didactic treatise into a heroic poem.

> When human life to view lay foully prostrated . . . crushed down under the weight of religion, . . . a man of Greece ventured first to lift up his mortal eyes to her face and first to withstand her to her face. Him neither story of gods nor thunderbolts nor heaven with threatening roar could quell; they only chafed the more the eager courage of his soul, filling him with desire to be the first to burst the fast bars of nature's portals. Therefore the living force of his soul gained the day: on he passed far beyond the flaming walls of the world and

15. Moses Hadas (ed.), *Essential Works of Stoicism* (New York, 1961), 11–12, 27, 34, 44, 58; Whitney J. Oates (ed.), *The Stoic and Epicurean Philosophers* (New York, 1940), 228, 241, 564.

PACIFIC UNIVERSITY LIBRARY
FOREST GROVE, OREGON

traversed throughout in mind and spirit the immeasurable universe; whence
he returns a conqueror to tell us what can, what cannot come into being; in
short on what principle each thing has its powers defined, its deepest bound-
ary mark.

Epictetus was content merely to compare the Stoic philosopher
with Heracles; the monsters were analogous to the trials the Stoic
must undergo in order to train and display his virtue. Plotinus
regarded Heracles as inferior to the true contemplative. Lucretius
exalted his Epicurean hero immeasurably above and beyond
Alcides.[16]

For Renaissance humanists, the ideal of the contemplative hero
was not only personally flattering but rhetorically useful; it lent
itself readily to the praise of letters and learned men. Erasmus
(as a modern iconographer observes) consciously invited comparison between Alcides' labors and his own contemplative struggle against ignorance.[17] In his writings he applied conventional
heroic terminology to the labors of scholars and to the spiritual
warfare of the Christian. In the *Querela Pacis*, for instance, Peace
turns from the "courts of princes" inasmuch as they are "not the
home of peace but rather the real source of war" and seeks refuge
instead among scholars. "Good letters," she argues, "produce
men; philosophy, more than men; theology, gods." The terminology of this passage is heroic, but the tone soon shifts to mock-
heroic, for Peace encounters among scholars "a new kind of warfare, not as bloody but just as foolish," waged with "venomous
pens," not with daggers. "In the same university logicians war
with rhetoricians, theologians dispute with lawyers. In the same
profession the Scotist fights with the Thomist, the Nominalist
with the Realist, the Platonist with the Peripatetic."[18] Erasmus'
Enchiridion Militis Christiani not only evoked the heroic concept in
its very title but amplified the biblical convention of spiritual warfare through comparisons with pagan worthies. Erasmus' treatment of the crossroads motif derived not only from Scripture but
from the classical tradition of Hercules' Choice; and he defined

16. Oates (ed.), *Stoic and Epicurean Philosophers*, 70, 82, 115, 135, 163–64, 235; *cf.*
192.

17. See William S. Heckscher, "Reflections on Seeing Holbein's Portrait of
Erasmus at Longford Castle," in Douglas Fraser, Howard Hibbard, and Milton J.
Lewine (eds.), *Essays in the History of Art Presented to Rudolf Wittkower* (London,
1967), 128–48.

18. John P. Dolan (ed.), *The Essential Erasmus* (New York, 1964), 180–81.

the opposition of spirit and flesh in terms reminiscent of *virtus heroica* and its contrary (brutishness or *feritas*): "To sum up, . . . the spirit makes us godlike; the flesh, brutish."[19]

Like the philosopher, his major rivals, the poet and rhetorician, claimed heroic status, urging the superiority of eloquence to theory as an instrument of moral persuasion. If philosophy could teach, poetry and rhetoric could not merely teach but also delight and move. The poet and orator could, therefore, be greater benefactors than the philosopher. To buttress their claims to heroic eminence, both might point to culture heroes and divinities famous for their eloquence—Orpheus and Musaeus, Hermes and Hercules Gallicus. Both, moreover, could appeal to Plato: the *Ion* had described the poet as a man directly inspired by a god, possessed by divine fury or enthusiasm; the *Cratylus* in turn had tentatively (and perhaps ironically) associated the word *heros* with rhetoricians and sophists. Later writers emphasized the exceptional endowments requisite for excellency in these arts. Cicero and Quintilian demanded of the orator the highest moral and intellectual attainments in addition to verbal skill; literary theorists required similar, if not greater, abilities of the poet. The latter must not only be eminent in intellectual virtues and conversant with the whole encyclopedia of arts and sciences, a *poeta doctus*; he must also possess the highest moral virtues in order to become a fitting vehicle for divine inspiration. Renaissance critics seriously debated whether or not Dante himself was the hero of his poem and whether or not a poet could be rightly called a hero.

Especially significant for the ideal of the poet as hero was Longinus' treatise *On the Sublime (Peri Hypsous)*. Even though its influence was not fully apparent until the late seventeenth and eighteenth centuries, this book had been published both in Italy and Switzerland during the Cinquecento. In emphasizing many of the qualities that literary theory associated primarily with heroic poetry and the heroic *ethos*, such as "wonder" and "greatness of soul," it reinforced the conception of the poet as hero. Through its stress on "great genius" it gave additional support to the concept, already a literary commonplace, of the poet as a divinely inspired *vates*. For "nothing is so grand as noble passion . . . which, as in the stress of madness and inspiration, breathes forth

19. Raymond Himelick (ed.), *The Enchiridion of Erasmus* (Bloomington, 1963), 80, 88–94.

its language as one possessed by a god, and, as it were, utters it with all the divine afflatus of a prophet." Longinus believed that "Aeschylus ventures on images of a most heroic character." The creations of "transcendent genius" produced in the hearers not persuasion but ecstasy. True sublimity is the "ring of greatness in the soul," and "expressions of transcendent genius fall to the province of men of the highest spirit." When "we come to greatness of genius in literature . . . we must conclude . . . that men so great . . . are superior to what is merely mortal; that other things reveal their users men, while sublimity raises them near to the greatness of soul of God." [20]

From the magnanimity of orator and poet to the heroism of other artists was an easy and probable transition. It was, moreover, a challenge that Renaissance apologists for the arts of design sometimes found difficult to resist. The epithet "divine," commonly applied to poets of the stature of Homer and Virgil and Dante, was soon extended to painters and sculptors. Vasari's *Lives of the Painters* bordered at times on hero worship, and later critics lauded Michelangelo's "divine energy" and "sublimity" in terms reminiscent of Longinus. Michelangelo had painted heroically, they argued, because he had possessed a heroic soul.

For Bacon and his seventeenth-century successors, the advancement of learning and the nobility and utility of the physical sciences were heroic themes; and in celebrating them, they turned to the commonplaces of the heroic tradition. The natural scientist and the inventor were godlike men, exercising the gift of godlike reason in the interests of the public good. The founders of new sciences, the discoverers of new methodologies and new arts, were intellectual heroes, more eminent in deeds of peace than conventional heroes in acts of war. They were greater benefactors than the martial hero, for they served man instead of destroying him. They were greater conquerors, for they extended their empire not merely over a fraction of the globe but over nature herself. The physical scientist possessed the dignities of active and contemplative heroes alike; the results of his labors were not only noble but useful.

Such encomia were often reminiscent of Lucretius' eulogy of

20. Longinus, *On the Sublime*, trans. Benedict Einarson (Chicago, 1945), 4, 15–16, 33, 63, cf. also 59.

Epicurus (likewise an explorer of nature's secrets) and of other founders of schools or inventors of the arts and sciences. Nevertheless, there was one significant difference. Lucretius had eulogized his hero primarily for the moral and psychological effects of his doctrine; by revealing the causes of natural phenomena, Epicurus had freed man from the terrors of religious superstition. The seventeenth-century writers, on the other hand, generally praised the scientist not only for his courageous discovery of new truths but also for the utility and practical value of his discoveries. Although Lucretius' poem was widely read and admired in the later years of the sixteenth century and throughout the seventeenth, even his admirers usually shrank from the religious implications of his system. Although Bacon might quote the powerful indictment "Tantum Religio potuit suadere malorum" to condemn the violence and fanaticism of the wars of religion, he never explicitly challenged the role of Providence in the government of the world.

These seventeenth-century eulogies of the scientist must be viewed not merely against the Lucretian background but also against the entire heroic tradition: the reaction against the purely martial hero, the use of heroic *topoi* in encomia, the relative claims of active and contemplative and "mixed" heroes, and the rivalry between different modes of contemplative heroism. The exaltation of the scientist often, though not invariably, entailed the corresponding depreciation of his rivals: the metaphysician, the rhetorician, and the poet.

On the whole, Bacon's conceptions of heroism are traditional. In the *Essays* (1597–1625) he covered a wide variety of heroic ideals, ranging from martial vainglory to Christian charity.[21] Extolling magnanimity, a comprehensive virtue often regarded as nearly synonymous with *virtus heroica*, he observed that atheism not only "destroys man's nobility" (if he "be not kin to God by his spirit, he is a base and ignoble creature") but also "destroys . . . magnanimity and the raising of human nature." For when a man

21. Except where otherwise specified, all references to Bacon's writings are based on James Spedding, Robert Leslie Ellis, and Douglas Denon Heath (eds.), *The Works of Francis Bacon* (14 vols.; London, 1858–74), hereafter cited parenthetically in text as *WFB*. The complete text of the *Advancement* and selections from other writings have been conveniently collected in the one-volume edition published by the Modern Library and based on the Spedding-Ellis-Heath edition; see Hugh G. Dick (ed.), *Selected Writings of Francis Bacon* (New York, 1955).

"resteth and assureth himself upon divine protection and favour," he "gathereth a force and faith which human nature in
itself could not obtain" (*WFB*, VI, 414–19).

Although Bacon believed arms to be essential for "true greatness of kingdoms and estate," he was nevertheless highly critical
of the ideal of the "fortunate conqueror." He condemned revenge
as a "kind of wild justice" that ought to be eradicated by law. In
fortitude he recognized the characteristic "virtue of Adversity," a
"more heroical virtue" than temperance, the proper "virtue of
Prosperity." In Hercules' liberation of Prometheus he beheld the
"mystery" of "Christian resolution, that saileth in the frail bark of
the flesh through the waves of the world." Adversity best discovers virtue, Bacon maintained; "the pencil of the Holy Ghost
hath laboured more in describing the afflictions of Job than the
felicities of Salomon." The "mould of a man's fortunes is in his
own hands"; Cato's fortitude of mind and body, *robur corporis et
animi*, could have made his fortune anywhere (*WFB*, VI, 444–49,
384–86, 472).

In urging the plantation of colonies, Bacon argued that these
had traditionally ranked "amongst ancient, primitive, and heroical works." Like Saint Augustine, he emphasized the higher heroism of the saint and martyr. Martyrdoms were to be reckoned
"amongst miracles"; they "seem to exceed the strength of human
nature," as does "superlative and admirable holiness of life"
(*WFB*, VI, 457, 514).[22]

Philanthropy and the pursuit of truth are also described in heroic terms. Man was created "for the contemplation of heaven and
all noble objects." Stressing the "difficulty and labour" of dis-

22. The essay "Of Honour and Reputation" (*WFB*, VI, 505–506) exploits commonplaces of the heroic tradition in distinguishing five degrees of "sovereign honour" and five degrees of "honour in subjects." The former include (1) "founders of
states and commonwealths," such as Cyrus and Caesar, Ishmael and "Ottoman";
(2) lawgivers like Lycurgus and Solon and Justinian, or Eadgar and Alfonso el
Sabio; (3) liberators and saviors, such as Augustus, Henry VII of England, and
Henry IV of France; (4) defenders or extenders of empires; and (5) just and benefi-
cent monarchs known as the fathers of their countries. Among subjects, the greatest honors belong to those heroes who "sacrifice themselves to death or danger for
the good of their country," such as Regulus and the Decii. The ordinary degrees of
honor pertain to *participes curarum* (the king's "right hands"), *duces belli* ("great
leaders" in his wars), favorites and *negotiis pares*. Perhaps the most striking feature
of this essay is its omission of inventors and discoverers. In other contexts Bacon
frequently extols them as deserving the highest honors.

covering theological and philosophical truth, Bacon nevertheless
regarded it as "the sovereign good of human nature." In civil business, he continued, truth is "the honour of man's nature." *Philanthropia* or "Goodness" is the greatest of "all virtues and dignities of the mind," for it is the very "character of the Deity" and
corresponds to the theological virtue Charity, which "admits no
excess, but error." Whereas the angels fell through excessive desire of power and man through excessive desire of knowledge,
"in charity there is no excess; neither can angel or man come in
danger by it" (*WFB*, VI, 377–79, 397, 403).

In their range and variety, and perhaps in their inconsistency,
the opinions expressed in the *Essays* are faithful to the compre-
hensiveness and complexity of the heroic tradition. To a degree
they underlie ideas of heroism that Bacon expresses elsewhere, in
greater detail and with greater coherence. Nevertheless, they are
not fully representative of his views on the nobility of science and
on the scientist as hero. (The *Essays* are, after all, counsels "Civill
and Morall" rather than treatises on natural history.) For a clear
statement and just index of these opinions we must turn to *The
Advancement of Learning* (1605) and similar writings. It is there,
rather than in the *Essays*, that he combines the ideal of philanthropy with that of the heroism of truth to eulogize the scientist as benefactor. It is there that he elevates the method of experiment and the lowly mechanical arts into objects of the highest
praise. In his essay "Of Honour and Reputation," he omits the
inventor and the discoverer altogether; in *The Advancement of
Learning*, on the other hand, he deifies them.

Like other masters of rhetorical technique, Bacon fully appre-
ciated the value of heroic *topoi* and heroic imagery as instruments
of praise and exhortation. Moreover, in applying them to the
praise of learning and learned men, he had a rich and varied tradition, classical as well as Renaissance, behind him. On this tradition he could draw at will, in praise of art or contemplation, martial exploits or scientific experiments, the empire of arms or that
of the arts. Since the primary function of such imagery was rhetorical, one should not be surprised to find him varying his heroic
topoi with his subject or altering his emphasis according to the
occasion of his discourse, the end he hoped to achieve by it, and
the audience to which it was directed. In his letter to Burghley
and his proem to the *De Interpretatione Naturae*, he applied heroic
commonplaces to himself. In *The Advancement of Learning* he ex-

ploited similar heroic arguments to praise King James. In both instances his use of heroic commonplaces was rhetorically conditioned. In the letter to Burghley they served as ethical proof. In the opening paragraphs of the *Advancement* they performed a function conventional in most exordia; they helped the speaker to ingratiate himself with his audience through flattery.

"I confess," Bacon wrote to Burghley in 1592, "that I have as vast contemplative ends, as I have moderate civil ends: for I have taken all knowledge to be my province." Disavowing any desire for honor or activity, he observed nevertheless that his "ordinary course of study and meditation" was "more painful than most parts of action are"; and he proceeded to describe his scholarly ambitions through the metaphor of just government and heroic benefaction. Motivated, he implied, by *philanthropia*, he proposed to free his province of roving brigands and pillagers and to introduce "profitable inventions and discoveries" instead (*WFB*, VIII, 109). In this passage he borrowed the heroic imagery of the civil life to extol the pursuits of the *vita contemplativa*, representing the latter paradoxically not only as a form of activity but also as an enterprise attended with more formidable labors than the *vita activa*. Liberal and scientific studies were not (as often asserted) a mere leisure pastime, but a labor fully as arduous as active political life.

In the "Proemium" to the *De Interpretatione Naturae*, Bacon returned to the conception of the inventor as philanthropist. Conscious of his own merits, but indifferent to fortune and fame, he aimed at the service of mankind ("ad utilitates humanas") through the contemplation of truth. The dignity of knowledge could best be "fortified" by "utility and operation" ("utilitatibus et operibus munitur"); and the inventor was a potential benefactor worthy of the loftiest honors.

> I discovered that nothing is of such estimation towards the human race, as the invention and earnest of new things and arts, by which man's life is adorned. For I perceive that, even in old times among rude men, the inventors and teachers of things rude were consecrated and chosen into the number of the gods; and I noted that the deeds of heroes who built cities, or were legislators, or exercised just authority, or subdued unjust dominations, were circumscribed by the narrowness of places and times. But the invention of things, though it be a matter of less pomp, I esteemed more adapted for universality and eternity. Yet above all, if any bring forth no particular invention, though of much utility, but kindleth a light in nature, which from the very beginning illuminates the regions of things, which lie contiguous to things already invented, afterwards being elevated lays open and brings to view all the abstrusest

things; he seems to me a propagator of the empire of man over the universe, a defender of liberty, a conqueror of necessities.[23]

In Lucretius we have encountered a similar deification of inventors and, in particular, the heroization of the natural philosopher as conqueror and benefactor. Like Lucretius, Bacon is sketching the ideal of a contemplative hero in terms usually associated with martial and civic heroism. These *topoi* were conventional, and much later in the century Milton could still treat them as commonplaces. Denying that "Might only" constitutes heroic virtue or martial conquest heroic enterprise, he would condemn the conquerors as destroyers and dismiss their resounding titles as pompous vanities.

> and for Glory done,
> Of triumph, to be styl'd great Conquerors.
> Patrons of Mankind, Gods, and Sons of Gods,
> Destroyers rightlier call'd and Plagues of men.[24]

> Then swell with pride, and must be titl'd Gods,
> Great Benefactors of mankind, Deliverers,
> Worship't with Temple, Priest and Sacrifice?
> One is the Son of *Jove*, of *Mars* the other,
> Till Conqueror Death discover them scarce men,
> Rolling in brutish vices, and deform'd.[25]

In these passages Bacon and Milton employ similar heroic *topoi*, but for different ends—Milton in order to discredit the secular conception of heroic virtue, Bacon in order to extol the contemplative hero, the man of science.

From the *De Interpretatione Naturae* let us return to *The Twoo Bookes of Francis Bacon of the Proficience and Advancement of Learning Divine*

23. For the Latin text, see *WFB*, III, 518–20. The English translation quoted above has been taken from Basil Montagu (ed.), *The Works of Francis Bacon* (16 vols.; London, 1825–34), XV, 103. In this passage Bacon contrasts the "knowledge, whose dignity is fortified by utility and operation" with "that unwarlike learning, which is nourished by ease, and flourishes by praise and reward, which sustains not the vehemency of opinion, and is the sport of artifices and impostures," and which is ultimately "overcome by the impediments" it encounters. "Atque ista quidem imbellis doctrina, quae otio alitur . . . iis quae dixi impedimentis obruitur. Longe alia ratio est scientiae, cujus dignitas utilitatibus et operibus munitur." As Virgil Whitaker has remarked to me, the military connotation of the verb *munitur* ("is fortified") is of central importance for the imagery of this passage.

24. Milton, *Paradise Lost*, Bk. XI, ll. 694–97, in *Complete Poems and Major Prose*, ed. Merritt Y. Hughes (New York, 1957).

25. Milton, *Paradise Regained*, Bk. III, ll. 81–86.

and Humane. Although, strictly speaking, this work belongs to deliberative rhetoric, inasmuch as it exhorts the king to patronize Bacon's program for the reformation and advancement of learning, it also exploits the methods of demonstrative and judicial oratory. Early in Book I, for instance, Bacon, an accomplished forensic orator himself, takes the brief for the defense, endeavoring to "deliver" learning "from the discredits and disgraces which it hath received," and thus crosses into the proper domain of judicial rhetoric (*WFB*, III, 264). Conversely, in blaming the current defects of learning on the scholastic and "magistral" methods common in the universities, on the humanists' preoccupation with manner rather than matter and words rather than things, on excessive reverence for antiquity, and on the frailty of the human understanding with its propensities for fashioning and revering *eidola*, he resorts to an alternative function of forensic oratory—accusation.

On the ends and methods of demonstrative rhetoric, praise or blame, he draws even more heavily. The first part of his discourse concerns "the excellency of learning and knowledge, and the excellency of the merit and true glory in the augmentation and propagation thereof." The second book, in turn, treats "the particular acts and works . . . which have been embraced and undertaken for the advancement of learning, and again what defects and undervalues I find in such particular acts" (*WFB*, III, 263–64). In asserting the dignity of learning, Bacon fully exploits the topics of nobility as well as those of profit; and it is in this respect that his use of heroic imagery is most significant. The heroic tradition could serve both demonstrative and deliberative ends; and we should avoid drawing too sharp a distinction between demonstrative and deliberative topics in Bacon's book. His use of the rhetoric of praise for the purpose of exhortation is, after all, consistent with the principles of Cicero (who had included *honestas* as well as *utilitas* among the topics of deliberative oratory) as well as those of Aristotle (who had recognized that certain topics were common to all three branches of oratory and that all three might advantageously borrow arguments from one another). In Bacon's discourse, judicial and demonstrative arguments serve deliberative ends; just as his defense of learning argues the latter's dignity, his praise of its dignity supports his central argument: that the advancement of learning is a worthy object for royal patronage.[26]

26. The same rhetorical pattern underlies Bacon's expanded Latin translation

In this exordium to the *Advancement*, Bacon sagaciously appeals to the *topos* of heroic wisdom, a theme equally appropriate
to the subject of his book and to its royal audience. (The English
Solomon must indeed have been "the wisest fool in Christen-
dom" if he did not recognize the extravagant flattery for what it
was, a conventional rhetorical technique for winning favorable
attention from the speaker's audience, in spite of the author's assurance "that this which I shall say is no amplification at all.")
Bacon is "possessed with an extreme wonder" at James's excellence in the "virtues and faculties which the philosophers call
intellectual," his princelike eloquence, his admirable understanding capable of comprehending "the greatest matters" as well
as the least, and the "universality and perfection" of his learning.
Such erudition is "almost a miracle," for not since Christ's time
has there been a monarch "so learned in all literature and erudition, divine and human." James I surpasses the kings of France,
Spain, England, and Scotland, and the emperors of Rome and
Greece and the West. Like Hermes Trismegistus he combines "the
power and fortune of a King" with "the knowledge and illumination of a Priest, and the learning and universality of a Philosopher" (*WFB*, III, 261–63).

After thus evoking the image of the king himself as a contemplative hero, Bacon draws the inference essential for the central argument of his book; such heroic wisdom can best merit
renown, the conventional reward of *virtus heroica*, by founding an
establishment for the advancement of learning. "This propriety
inherent and individual attribute in your Majesty deserveth to be
expressed not only in the fame and admiration of the present
time, nor in the history or tradition of the ages succeeding; but
also in some solid work, fixed memorial, and immortal monu-

---

of the *Advancement*. This first book of the *De Augmentis Scientiarum* performs the
same rhetorical function as the first book of the English treatise; it stresses the
excellence of learning and the merit of those who labor for its advancement: "de
Scientiae et Literarum per omnia excellentia agendum est; et simul de merito
eorum, qui in iisdem provehendis operam strenue et cum judicio impendunt."
The eight remaining books of the Latin treatise correspond to the second book of
the English version, pointing out which areas of knowledge had already been
explored and which required further exploration ("quid in hoc genere huc usque
actum sit et perfectum; insuper et ea perstringet quae videntur desiderari") and
reviewing "what has hitherto been done by kings and others for the increase and
advancement of learning and what has been left undone" ("quid principes viri
aliique huc usque ad literarum amplificationem attulerint, quid praetermiserint").
See *WFB*, I, 433, 485, IV, 284.

ment, bearing a character or signature both of the power of a king and the difference and perfection of such a king" (*WFB*, III, 263).

His exordium completed, Bacon now turns, appropriately, to the proposition of his treatise: the dignity of learning and the "merit and true glory" of advancing it. Ironically, it was not the learned Scot but his grandson, the "Merry Monarch," who became the titular founder and patron of the type of establishment Bacon envisaged.

Although Bacon utilizes heroic *topoi* primarily for extolling King James, he nevertheless employs them freely throughout the first book of his treatise. After his death Socrates "was made a person heroical, and his memory accumulate with honours divine and human." Antiquity conferred higher honors on inventors than on other worthies. Among the heathen the highest honor was "to obtain to a veneration and adoration as a God"; apotheosis or *relatio inter divos* was "the supreme honour which man could attribute unto man . . . ; for there were reckoned above human honours, heroical and divine." In the "attribution and distribution" of these honors, moreover, "antiquity made this difference: that whereas founders and uniters of states and cities, lawgivers, extirpers of tyrants, fathers of the people, and other eminent persons in civil merit, were honoured but with the titles of worthies or demi-gods; such as were Hercules, Theseus, Minos, Romulus, and the like; on the other side, such as were inventors and authors of new arts, endowments, and commodities towards man's life, were ever consecrated amongst the gods themselves; as was Ceres, Bacchus, Mercurius, Apollo, and others." Whereas the merit of the former was confined merely to an age or a nation, that of the latter was permanent and universal. "The former again is mixed with strife and perturbation; but the later [*sic*] hath the true character of divine presence, coming in *aura leni*, without noise or agitation" (*WFB*, III, 301–302).

Heroic wisdom does not preclude other heroic virtues, for intellectual eminence is often associated with martial eminence; they appear not only in the same eras but often in the same persons. Experience demonstrates "that both in persons and in times there hath been a meeting and concurrence in learning and arms, flourishing and excellent in the same men and the same ages." Thus Alexander the Great was "Aristotle's scholar in philosophy," and Julius Caesar was "Cicero's rival in eloquence." In Egypt and Assyria and in Persia, Greece, and Rome, "the same times that are most renowned for arms are likewise most admired for learning; so that the greatest authors and philosophers and the greatest captains and governors have lived in the same ages" (*WFB*, III, 269).

In support of this argument Bacon invokes the commonplace of the dual fortitude—of body and mind—in terms that imply the superiority of the latter: "for as in man the ripeness of strength of the body and mind cometh much about an age . . . ; so in states, arms and learning, whereof the one correspondeth to the body, the other to the soul of man, have a concurrence or near sequence in times" (*WFB*, III, 269–70).

Far from disposing men to sloth and idleness, learning accustoms the mind to "perpetual motion and agitation." Whereas other men seek activity for profit or honor, only learned men truly love activity ("business") for itself. Although scorned as private or obscure, the "life of contemplative men" is often ranked above the "civil life" in liberty and dignity. Learned men are magnanimous; "the largeness of their mind can hardly confine itself to dwell in the exquisite observation or examination of the nature and customs of one person." They are also patriotic, esteeming the "preservation, good, and honour of their countries or masters before their own fortunes or safeties" (*WFB*, III, 272, 276–79).

Citing both divine and human testimony for the "true dignity and value of learning," Bacon briefly surveys both sacred and profane history. Seeking the "dignity of knowledge in the archtype or first platform," which is "the attributes and acts of God," he finds a "lively image of a contemplative life" in Abel, and observes that the Scriptures themselves "have vouchsafed to mention and honour the name of the inventors and authors of music and works in metal." Moses possessed the learning of the Egyptians, and the Book of Job abounds in natural philosophy. Solomon compiled a "natural history of all verdure," and the ancient bishops and fathers of the church were "excellently read and studied in all the learning of the heathen." From secular history Bacon selects "the most eminent and selected examples" to illustrate the "felicity of times under learned princes," ranging from the Caesars to Queen Elizabeth. There "was not a greater admirer of learning or benefactor of learning" than Trajan: "a founder of famous libraries, a perpetual advancer of learned men to office, and a familiar converser with learned professors and preceptors." Alexander "esteemed it more to excel other men in learning and knowledge than in power and empire," and Julius Caesar aspired "as well to victory of wit as victory of war: undertaking . . . a conflict against the greatest champion with the pen that then lived, Cicero the orator" (WFB, III, 295–99, 303–308, 311).

Learning enhances "imperial and military virtue" as well as "moral and private virtue." It is "hard to say whether arms or learning have advanced greater numbers." Finally, the "monuments of wit and learning" are far "more durable than the monuments of power or of the hands" (WFB, III, 314, 317–18).

While arguing the concurrence and indeed the interdependence of learning with arms, Bacon consistently emphasizes the superiority and higher dignity of the former. Many of his arguments derive from the commonplaces of nobility. Although such pseudosciences as alchemy, astrology, and natural magic have more affinities with man's imagination than with his reason, nevertheless their "ends or pretences are noble." In their emphasis on words rather than matter, the humanists have ranked the less noble before the nobler object of study; but the scholastic philosophers have done worse: "for as substance of matter is better than beauty of words, so contrariwise vain matter is worse than vain words." Again, the dignity of commandment is "according to the dignity of the commanded." Command over galley slaves is "a disparagement rather than an honour"; similarly, there is but "small honour" in a schoolmaster's command over children. The "commandment of knowledge" is therefore "higher than the commandment over the will: for it is a commandment over the reason, belief, and understanding of man, which is the highest part of the mind, and giveth law to the will itself" (WFB, III, 285, 289, 316).

Bacon is as keenly aware of the vanities and distempers of learning as of its dignity. If learning has its heroes, it also possesses its pseudoheroes and impostors; and it is the task of the rhetorician (as of the scientist) to differentiate between them. As Bacon himself emphasizes, the hero worship directed toward the ancients has been one of the most formidable obstacles to the further advancement of learning. In attacking the excessive reverence paid to authority and the "idols of the Theatre" (as he later called them), he found himself compelled, paradoxically, to dethrone many of the conventional monarchs of learning and to strip them of the heroic honors traditionally accorded them.

To a certain degree the apparent inconsistencies in Bacon's attitude varied with rhetorical context. In one passage he could find it expedient to cite the ancients for "human testimony," in another, to expose their feet of clay. Thus, protesting against "too great a reverence, and a kind of adoration of the mind and understanding of man," he condemns the intellectualists. Although they have been "commonly taken for the most sublime and divine philosophers," they have actually "withdrawn themselves too much from the contemplation of nature and the observations of experience," and accordingly "tumbled up and down in their own reasons and conceits" (WFB, III, 292). In this context, Bacon discredits one type of conventional and contemplative hero as no more than an anti-hero, the exemplar of a vain and false heroic wisdom.

In another passage he distinguishes between two modes of sapience, the one impatient of doubt, the other characterized by "due and mature suspension of judgment," in imagery reminiscent of the Choice of Hercules. In the classical fable the alternatives were virtue and vice (or pleasure); in Bacon's treatise, the choice lies between solid and empty wisdom. "For the two ways of contemplation are not unlike the two ways of action commonly spoken of by the ancients; the one plain and smooth in the beginning, and in the end impassable; the other rough and troublesome in the entrance, but after a while fair and even. So it is in contemplation; if a man will begin with certainties, he shall end in doubts; but if he will be content to begin with doubts, he shall end in certainties" (WFB, III, 293).

Nevertheless the goal of learning, "the last or furthest end of knowledge," is not wisdom for wisdom's sake, but "the glory of the Creator and the relief of man's estate." As the end of active and contemplative philosophy alike should be "the use and benefit of man," the true dignity and exaltation of knowledge is to be found in a conjunction of action and contemplation. The type of heroism that Bacon extols most highly, therefore, belongs to the mixed variety: a blend of action and contemplation comparable to the conjunction of Saturn and Jupiter, "the planet of rest and contemplation" and "the planet of civil society and action" (WFB, III, 294).

This, too, was a conventional heroic ideal. In place of the Aristotelian *triplex vita* (the voluptuous, active, and contemplative lives) Varro, and Saint Augustine after him, had proposed an alternative triad (action, contemplation, and the mixed life consisting of both). In the Middle Ages both classifications were current. Although many of the schoolmen followed Aristotle's division, other theologians preferred the Augustinian; and in Walter Hilton and Richard Rolle, and in *Piers Plowman* it is the mixed life that is the noblest of the three, for it provides the perfect exemplar of *caritas*. In medieval theology, moreover, instruction ranks among the spiritual acts of mercy or *misericordia*. Similarly for Bacon, the "corrective spice, the mixture whereof maketh knowledge so sovereign, is Charity." Quoting the *locus classicus* in I Corinthians 13, he adds his own comment: "not but that it is an excellent thing to speak with the tongues of men and angels, but because if it be severed from charity, and not referred to the good of men and mankind, it hath rather a sounding and unworthy glory than a meriting and substantial virtue." Perhaps it is significant that the father of Salomon's House "had an aspect as if he pitied men" (*WFB*, III, 154, 266). On the surface, Bacon's contemplative hero displays a remarkable resemblance to the inventors and natural philosophers extolled by Lucretius; upon closer examination, however, he reveals a more fundamental likeness to the mixed hero of Christian tradition. In the final analysis, he, too, is an exemplar of heroic charity.

Although heroic *topoi* are most apparent in the first book of *The Advancement of Learning*, they also recur throughout the second book. Quoting Aristotle's definition of heroic virtue ("heroicam sive divinam virtutem"), Bacon turns to the "celsitude of honour" that Pliny attributed to Trajan and to the heroic excellence of charity; "only love doth exalt the mind," and "only charity admitteth no excess." He commends the poet for feigning "acts and events greater and more heroical" than true history and for conducing to magnanimity and morality as well as delight. Virgil had won as much glory for his "observations of husbandry as of the heroical acts of Aeneas"; similarly, the principles of moral philosophy, the "Georgics of the mind," are "no less worthy than the heroical descriptions of Virtue, Duty, and Felicity" (*WFB*, III, 343, 419, 442–43).

Bacon extols the heroic virtue of magnanimity, observing that just as "*there are minds which are proportioned to great matters, and others to small*," so likewise "*there are minds proportioned to intend many matters, and others to few*." In another passage he elaborates the parallel between martial and intellectual prowess. "It hath pleased God to ordain and illustrate two exemplar states of the

world for arms, learning, moral virtue, policy, and laws; the state
of Graecia, and the state of Rome." In Aristotle he finds an intellectual conqueror comparable to Alexander. "For this excellent
person Aristotle, I will think of him that he learned that humour
of his scholar, with whom it seemeth he did emulate, the one to
conquer all opinions, as the other to conquer all nations." He alludes to the Neoplatonic conception of illumination by "divine
influxions" or divine *fury*. He compares the "credulous and superstitious conceits" of natural magic to the "fables of romantic
heroes" (*WFB*, III, 335, 352, 361–62, 380, 434).

Returning to the "Art of Inquiry or Invention," he deplores the
utter "deficience" of any art for the "invention and discovery of
arts and sciences." The "inventions and originals of things" are
usually referred "rather to chance than to art, and rather to
beasts, birds, fishes, serpents, than to men. . . . So that it was no
marvel (the manner of antiquity being to consecrate inventors)
that the Aegyptians had so few human idols in their temples, but
almost all brute" (*WFB*, III, 384–85).

Finally, in an extensive discussion of the relative merits of the
active and contemplative lives, Bacon decides in favor of the former, inasmuch as the public good exceeds private interest. Although "the contemplative life hath the pre-eminence" in regard
to "the pleasure and dignity of man's self," consideration of the
public benefit "decideth against Aristotle" on the issue of "the
preferment of the contemplative or active life." For that "contemplation which should be finished in itself without casting
beams upon society, assuredly divinity knoweth it not" (*WFB*, III,
419–24).

In an age that still idolizes the painters and sculptors of the Renaissance, it is easy to overlook their struggle to assert the dignity
and nobility of their vocations and to free the arts of design from
the stigma of the base mechanical arts. In a century that rewards
its natural scientists with public honors as well as public funds
and bestows peerages and substantial royalties on its inventors, it
is equally easy to underestimate Bacon's struggle to prove the dignity of natural philosophy and the nobility of the mechanical arts
themselves. Even though the actual subject of his treatise was
learning in general, even though he surveyed the entire province
of the arts and sciences, he clearly believed that the proficience
and advancement of learning must be achieved primarily through

new methods in natural philosophy and, in particular, through the development and perfection of the despised mechanical arts. For "the use of History Mechanical is of all others the most radical and fundamental towards natural philosophy; such natural philosophy as shall be operative to the endowment and benefit of man's life." Unfortunately, he complained, the "History of Nature Wrought or Mechanical" of his own time had consisted largely of agriculture and manual arts, rejecting "experiments familiar and vulgar. For it is esteemed a kind of dishonour unto learning to descend to inquiry or meditation upon matters mechanical." But "it cometh often to pass that mean and small things discover great better than great can discover the small" (WFB, III, 332).

To stress the nobility of natural science, Bacon emphasized the nobility of its object: nature herself. The marvels of nature aroused wonder (which was itself "the seed of knowledge" and "broken knowledge"). The "contemplation of nature" could demonstrate the "power, providence, and goodness" of the Creator, a knowledge truly "divine in respect of the object, and natural in respect of the light." Just as "all works do shew forth the power and skill of the workman . . . ; so it is of the works of God" (WFB, III, 266–67, 349–50).

The analogy between the divine workman and his human counterpart could be rhetorically exploited either to the advantage or disadvantage of the mechanical arts. Bacon turned it to their advantage, partly by emphasizing the divine honors formerly paid to inventors, partly by stressing the major changes that a few chance inventions (the printing press, the mariner's compass, and gunpowder) had effected in human society, partly by presenting the discovery of an art of invention as an act of supreme benefit and charity, and finally by extolling the scientist and inventor as conquerors of nature. As Bacon was well aware, the ambiguities of the term *invention* were a rhetorical asset; by emphasizing the divine honors that antiquity had bestowed on inventors, he could eulogize not only the isolated mechanical inventions that had changed the face of the world but also the art of discovery and, in particular, the "invention of Forms," which was "of all other parts of knowledge the worthiest to be sought" (WFB, III, 355). By stressing not only the wonders of nature but also the potential marvels of the mechanical arts, he invested both the natural philosopher and the inventor with heroic dignity.

Aristotle had defined the hero as a "godlike man" (*theios anèr*), and theologians as well as moral philosophers had associated likeness to God with heroic virtue. Although Bacon argued that knowledge is power, he also insisted that knowledge must be combined with charity; and in his discussion of this point, with its reiterated stress on godlikeness—in power, wisdom, and love (a triad traditionally associated with the three persons of the Trinity)—we may perhaps detect a comparison between the merits of the active, contemplative, and mixed lives. For "aspiring to be like God in knowledge, man transgressed and fell; . . . but by aspiring to a similitude of God in goodness and love, neither man nor angel ever transgressed or shall transgress." For "unto that imitation we are called. . . . Only love doth exalt the mind," and "if a man's mind be truly inflamed with charity, it doth work him suddenly into greater perfection than all the doctrine of morality can do" (*WFB*, III, 443).

Similarly, the man who aims at the public good, through action, contemplation, or both, is superior to the man who pursues his own private good, whether active or passive. For "this Active Good" of the individual is by no means identical with "the good of society, though in some cases it hath an incidence into it: for although it do many times bring forth acts of beneficence, yet it is with a respect private to a man's own power, glory, amplification, continuance. . . . For that gigantic state of mind which possesseth the troublers of the world, such as Lucius Sylla, and infinite other in smaller model . . . pretendeth, and aspireth to active good, though it recedeth furthest from good of society" (*WFB*, III, 425).

Bacon's heroic ideal—his conception of the scientist as a benefactor laboring through power, knowledge, and charity for the greater good of man and the greater glory of God—provided him with a standard of measurement whereby he might judge and revalue the older, more conventional conceptions of heroism. Although his conception of the hero was different from Milton's, we may find in the thought of both men a critique and revaluation of the heroic tradition.

Less significant, but perhaps more sensational, as heroic *topoi* were the images of the voyager and the magician. For Bacon's contemporaries these were not merely conventional figures in classical and Renaissance epic (where the voyager was usually cast as hero, and the magician not infrequently as villain). They were also historical figures; and the age regarded them with a mixture of credulity, skepticism, and admiration. The voyages of Odysseus and the Argonauts might have been fables; but those of Drake and Raleigh were real, and both Columbus and Vasco da Gama had been celebrated as epic heroes. These Renaissance mariners had not only out-traveled Hercules and Dionysos; they had also forced revision and reappraisal of classical cosmography. From their exploits, accordingly, Bacon drew one of his favorite images for contrasting the achievements of the moderns with those of the ancients and for his eulogy of the new science.

> For it may be truly affirmed to the honour of these times, and in a virtuous emulation with antiquity, that this great building of the world had never through-lights made in it, till the age of us and our fathers. . . . But to circle the earth, as these heavenly bodies do, was not done nor enterprised till these later times: and therefore these times may justly bear in their word, not only *plus ultra*, in precedence of the ancient *non ultra*, and *imitabile fulmen* in precedence of the ancient *non imitabile fulmen*, . . . but likewise *imitabile coelum*; in respect of the many memorable voyages, after the manner of heaven, about the globe of the earth.

Again, "why should a few received authors stand up like Hercules' Columns, beyond which there should be no sailing or discovering, since we have so bright and benign a star as your Majesty to conduct and prosper us?" This is heroic rhetoric; but Bacon is more modest in applying the same image to his own endeavors. *The Advancement of Learning* is merely a coasting voyage, "*premendo littus iniquum*" (WFB, III, 322–23, 340, 361).

The magus was a more dubious figure than the voyager, alternatively revered and vilified. If the Three Magi had been canonized, Simon Magus (who had received quasi-divine honors as "some great one" and as "the great power of God") had been excoriated both for his sorcery and for his simony. If Tasso's Ismeno is thoroughly evil, Spenser's Merlin is depicted favorably. Ariosto's Melissa is a benevolent sorceress, and the motives of Atlante (who embodies the euhemerist interpretation of Atlas as an astrologer) are creditable.

The same moral ambiguity is apparent in Renaissance dramatic treatments of the magician. In *Friar Bacon and Friar Bungay* his magical attainments are a source of comedy. Essentially he is a "merry jester" like the heroes of Tudor jestbooks, a sort of academic Till Eulenspiegel. In Calderon's *Magico Prodigioso* and Marlowe's *Dr. Faustus,* on the other hand, he is a tragic figure. Calderon's magician has sold himself to Lucifer but subsequently saves his soul by repenting and perishing as a Christian martyr. Faustus combines features of the practical joker and the tragic hero—more tragic indeed than Calderon's Cipriano, as he dies without hope of grace.

Shakespeare's Prospero, on the other hand, represents an idealized type of the magician-hero (and he is also, incidentally, a voyager). He has acquired his powers through study rather than by a pact with the devil, and he employs them without malice, in the cause of political justice and domestic concord. A contemplative hero, he regains his dukedom and frees it from tyranny not by force of arms but by wisdom. Unlike most of the sorcerers in Renaissance drama, he has no contact with the powers of darkness; there is no whiff of infernal brimstone about him. Instead of a grotesque fiend, he commands the graceful Ariel as his familiar. He detests the black magic of Caliban's dam and her intercourse (conventional in witchcraft) with the devil. (If Caliban sometimes resembles the domestic devils of Renaissance comedy, he recalls, even more vividly perhaps, the grumbling servants of classical comedy. Although begotten by an incubus on a witch, he is not a supernatural being and has no supernatural powers. He is an archetypal savage, not an infernal spirit.)

Shakespeare has taken deliberate pains to divest his sorcerer of infernal associations and to emphasize his divergence from the pattern of the usual state magician. Like Francis Bacon's magus, Prospero is a benefactor. He too realizes that knowledge is power, and he uses his power well. In a sense, his fortunate island is also a New Atlantis.

Although the picture of the magician as a variant of the contemplative hero is most strongly marked in *The Tempest* (which appeared too late to be directly relevant to Bacon's view of the magus), elements of the heroic tradition are nevertheless apparent in the earlier dramas. In Greene's comedy, the contest in magic serves as a test of merit; it is a monomachy between contemplative champions not unlike the duels or jousts between warriors. If personal fame is involved in the rivalry of Friar Bacon and Friar Bungay, both national and academic honor is at stake in their contest with the German sorcerer Vandermast. The contestants engage in conventional heroic rodomontade, vaunts, taunts, and mutual disdain. Boasting that he has "given nonplus" to all his previous opponents, Vandermast summarizes his victories in an epic catalog—Padua, Siena, Florence, Bologna, Rheims, Louvain, Rotterdam, Frankfort, Lutetia, Orleans, and now Oxford—and demands to be crowned with laurel, the victor's meed of praise. The contest centers, moreover, upon a traditional emblem of *virtus heroica*, Hercules and the Garden of the Hesperides. The spectacle of three scholars exercising their skills in conjuring up, and actually commanding, the *eidolon* of the greatest of classical heroes may strike the modern reader as ironic, but one doubts that Greene intended it that way. This is a contest for eminence in the intellectual virtues, waged for royal honors between the champions of England and the Empire; and in its outcome, when Hercules obediently executes Friar Bacon's commands and transports the overconfident adversary back to Hapsburg, one may perhaps find an implicit comparison between contemplative and active heroism.[27]

The moral ambiguities that accompanied the magician of epic and drama were scarcely less pronounced in the "magicians" of history. The alchemists, the astrologers, and the exponents of natural magic might acquire lucrative practices and high honors

27. Although Greene utilizes heroic terminology frequently in this play to extol Friar Bacon and his schemes, much of this praise is conditional, and the schemes themselves prove abortive. In Act I, scene ii, Clement hails the friar as

> A man supposed the wonder of the world;
> For if thy cunning work these miracles,
> England and Europe shall admire thy fame,
> And Oxford shall in characters of brass,
> And Statues, such as were built up in Rome,
> Eternize Friar Bacon for his art.

Moreover, the friar himself foreshadows his illustrious namesake in his ideal of the scholar as benefactor. He intends to employ his skills on behalf of public good—including, of course, national defense.

> And I will strengthen England by my skill,
> That if ten Caesars lived and reigned in Rome,
> With all the legions Europe doth contain,
> They should not touch a grass of English ground.
> The work that Ninus reared at Babylon,
> The brazen walls framed by Semiramis,
> Carved out like to the portal of the sun
> Shall not be such as rings the English strand
> From Dover to the market-place of Rye.

See Gerald Eades Bentley (ed.), *The Development of English Drama, An Anthology* (New York, 1950). Milton would subsequently employ similar *topoi* in his own heroic poetry. Samson is described as "The miracle of men," and the magnificence of Pandaemonium is compared to that of Babylon.

at Renaissance courts; but they might just as frequently have to flee for their lives, accused either of charlatanism or of black magic. The extravagant claims Paracelsus advanced on his own behalf (in medicine and alchemy, theology and philosophy) were scarcely more extravagant than the partisan admiration and indignation he aroused in his disciples and enemies. If one epigrammatist, Baptista Possevinus, consigned Agrippa to hell,

> stygii Rex fuit iste lacus.
> Quare etiam custodem habuit, dum viveret, Orci,
> Cui nunc in tenebris praeda daret comitem,

a later writer, Thomas Vaughan, would apotheosize him:

> Sic Agrippa ingens, duplici quoque sufficit orbi,
> Fractaque diversas fabrica monstrat opes.
> .   .   .   .
> Sic vivens, moriensque docet, dumque altus in astra
> Tendit, habet magicas parca vel ipsa manus.

In Vaughan's opinion, Agrippa would merit the praises that Hermes Trismegistus had accorded to mankind, *theon oraton*, and that Panætius had bestowed on Plato, "*Hominem divinum, sanctissimum, sapientissimum et Homerum philosophorum.*" [28]

While dismissing the natural magic of his own day as fabulous and superstitious, Bacon deliberately retained the term itself but applied it specifically to one of the "two parts of natural philosophy,—the Inquisition of Causes, and the Production of Effects; Speculative, and Operative; Natural Science, and Natural Pru-

---

28. Arthur Edward Waite (ed.), *The Works of Thomas Vaughan* (London, 1919), 69, 71. Both Latin quotations occur in Thomas Vaughan's *Anima Magica Abscondita*. Waite translates the passages as follows. Baptista Possevinus:

> Know, here entomb'd, abysmal Styx's King,
> On earth protected by a guard from hell
> But in perdition now his warder's prey.

Thomas Vaughan:

> So great Agrippa for two worlds sufficed
> And powers diverse displayed in broken frame.
> .   .   .   .
> He taught in life and teaches yet in death,
> And whilst ascending high amidst the stars
> Some magic potence still his hands dispense.

Waite also translates *theon oraton* as "a manifested god" and the Panætius quotation on Plato as "the most divine, most holy, most wise man and the Homer of philosophers."

dence. . . . And here I will make a request, that for the latter (or at least for a part thereof) I may revive and reintegrate the misapplied and abused name of Natural Magic; which in the true sense is but Natural Wisdom, or Natural Prudence, taken according to the ancient acception, purged from vanity and superstition." Later in the same treatise he further subdivided Natural Prudence (*i.e.*, the active branch of natural philosophy) into three parts: Experimental, Philosophical, and Magical. The "true Natural Magic . . . is that great liberty and latitude of operation which dependeth upon the knowledge of Forms"; and the natural magic of his own times was "as far differing in truth of nature from such a knowledge as we require, as the story of King Arthur of Britain, or Hugh of Bourdeaux, differs from Caesar's commentaries in truth of story. For it is manifest that Caesar did greater things *de vero* than those imaginary heroes were feigned to do. But he did them not in that fabulous manner" (*WFB*, III, 351, 362–63).[29]

Bacon's ideal of the mixed hero who united action and contemplation and employed his knowledge of nature for man's benefit presupposed, then, the cooperation and harmonious development of the two principal branches of natural philosophy, active and speculative. Natural Prudence must supplement Natural Science; if the second of these could discover the truths of nature, her underlying principles and essential forms, the first could harness this truth for the production of "great effects." The role of the natural magician was thus literally "magnificent," and its fulfillment presupposed a magnanimous man. The magus, as Bacon conceived him, was as superior to the conventional magician-hero as truth to falsehood.

---

29. The *De Augmentis* (*WFB*, IV, 366–67) develops this heroic imagery and the themes of *utilitas* and *honestas* still further.

> But I must here stipulate that magic, which has long been used in a bad sense, be again restored to its ancient and honourable meaning. For among the Persians magic was taken for a sublime wisdom, and the knowledge of the universal consents of things; and so the three kings who came from the east to worship Christ were called by the name of Magi. I however understand it as the science which applies the knowledge of hidden forms to the production of wonderful operations; and by uniting (as they say) actives with passives, displays the wonderful works of nature.

In contrast to this true natural magic, the false magic is full of "credulous and superstitious traditions and observations"; its experiments are frivolous, and "wonderful rather for the skill with which the thing is concealed and masked than for the thing itself." In amplifying his remarks on this subject, Bacon has given

Between *The Advancement of Learning* (1605) and the *Novum Organum* (1620), Bacon looked frequently to classical myth for images and comparisons that might amplify and illustrate the pursuit of truth. In the *Filum Labyrinthi sive Formula Inquisitionis* he indirectly exploited the Hercules myth and the fable of Theseus and Ariadne to symbolize his search for a methodical art of invention capable of producing new discoveries. Lamenting that the present state of knowledge ("especially that of nature") did not extend to "magnitude and certainty of works," Bacon complained that extant inventions were imperfect and that new ones were "not like to be brought to light but in great length of time." Through excessive admiration of antiquity and authority, men had "cut themselves off from further invention"; "sciences are at a stay," and the "columns of no further proceeding are pitched." Believing that new inventions were impossible and expecting "no great works . . . from art, and the hand of man," natural philosophy had lost confidence in man's power and fallen victim to "artificial despair." Meanwhile the "vain promises and pretences" of the pseudosciences—alchemy, astrology, and magic—had hindered the further invention of works of benefit. The "ignominy of vanity had abated all greatness of mind" (*WFB*, III, 496–99, 503).

Such passages as these combine classical allusions with ethical commonplaces of the heroic tradition: magnanimity, confidence, and fortitude; greatness of mind and of enterprise; trial of the hero's powers, proof of his merit, admiration for his deeds. *The Wisdom of the Ancients* exploits the imagery of classical myth to weigh the relative merits of active and contemplative heroism. Orpheus, Bacon explains, is "an easy metaphor for philosophy personified," and just as "the works of wisdom surpass in dignity and power the works of strength, so the labours of Orpheus surpass the labours of Hercules" (*WFB*, VI, 720).

Always a favorite image with Bacon, the voyage metaphor became a visual (as well as verbal) emblem in the *Instauratio Magna* (1620). Bearing the motto "Multi pertransibunt & augebitur scientia," the title page portrayed a ship sailing between the Pillars of Hercules into the open seas. This image (already amply elaborated in the *Advancement*) recurs in the preface to the *Instauratio*.

---

additional emphasis to the concept of the marvelous and to the ideal of heroic wisdom.

In the propensity of his contemporaries to overrate their store (*opes*) of knowledge and underestimate their strength (*vires*), Bacon finds "scientiis columnae tanquam fatales." From "an extravagant estimate of the value of the arts which they possess, men seek no further; or else from too mean an estimate of their own powers, they spend their strength in small matters and never put it fairly to the trial in those which go to the main. These are as the pillars of fate set in the path of knowledge; for men have neither desire nor hope to encourage them to penetrate further" (*WFB*, IX, 3; I, 125).[30]

If the advancement of learning is a voyage of discovery, and the scientist (or his patron) the chief pilot, the new methodology serves as a mariner's compass. "[B]efore the ocean could be traversed and the new world discovered, the use of the mariner's needle, as a more faithful and certain guide, had to be found out; in like manner . . . before we can reach the remoter and more hidden parts of nature, it is necessary that a more perfect use and application of the human mind and intellect be introduced" (*WFB*, IV, 18).

Besides the voyage metaphor, the *Instauratio* recapitulates other heroic motifs reminiscent of Bacon's earlier treatises: the Choice of Hercules, the labyrinth image, and the ideal of the scientist as a benefactor and an exemplar of heroic charity. Bacon has undertaken a "solitary" and difficult "enterprise" for the "benefit of the human race." This is nothing less than a "total reconstruction of sciences, arts, and all human knowledge, raised upon the proper foundations." Through this program he hopes, in part, to restore the cognitive powers darkened by Adam's fall, to recover the intellectual dominion Adam had lost, to regain man's original empire over nature. Proposing to restore to its perfect and original condition that "commerce between the mind of man and the nature of things, which is more precious than anything on earth," Bacon regards "all other ambition as poor in comparison." The "matter is either nothing, or a thing so

---

30. *Cf.* also *WFB*, III, 340, for a similar combination of voyage imagery with the theme of the advancement of learning and the prophecy in Daniel: "And this proficience in navigation and discoveries may plant also an expectation of the further proficience and augmentation of all sciences. . . . For so the prophet Daniel speaking of the latter times foretelleth, *Plurimi pertransibunt, et multiplex erit scientia* [Many shall pass to and fro, and knowledge shall be multiplied]: as if the open-

great that it may well be content with its own merit, without seeking other recompense" (*WFB*, IV, 7–8).

Adapting heroic commonplaces to the ends of deliberative
rhetoric, to arguments from use as well as from honor, Bacon
combined the appeals to *utilitas* and *honestas*. From their fusion
he drew some of his strongest hortatory arguments on behalf
of the neglected philosophy of nature, the base experimental
method, and the despised mechanical arts. In this way, heroic
commonplaces served as topics both of dehortation and of exhortation. Admiration or wonder had been conventionally regarded
as the characteristic effect of heroic poetry, the affection properly
aroused by heroic deeds. Among Bacon's major problems as
rhetorician, as propagandist for the great instauration, was the
need to transfer admiration from the ancients to the moderns,
from the science of classical antiquity to that of the future. On one
hand, he must dehort his contemporaries from their veneration
of Greek and Roman authors and from their correlative despair
in their own powers. On the other hand, in exhorting them to
undertake the new and difficult enterprise he proposed, he must
arouse their confidence in their own strength and kindle hope of
success.

Since overestimating the existing store of knowledge has been
a major obstacle to the further progress of learning, Bacon must
dissuade his contemporaries from bestowing undue veneration
on the arts they already possess. It is "absolutely necessary, that
the excess of honour and admiration with which our existing
stock of inventions is regarded be . . . stripped off, and men be
duly warned not to exaggerate or make too much of them." Similarly, the excess of honor must be stripped from the ancients and
from the schoolmen. In contrast to the mechanical arts, which are
"continually growing and becoming more perfect," scholastic tradition has been static. It has produced no new discoveries, no
increase of learning "worthy of the human race." Instead, "barren
of works" and "full of questions," philosophy and the intellectual
sciences "stand like statues, worshipped and celebrated, but not
moved or advanced." The schoolmen have been merely a "succession of masters and scholars, not of inventors" (*WFB*, IV, 13–16).

---

ness and through passage of the world and the increase of knowledge were appointed to be in the same ages."

The admiration of authority, in turn, discourages the progress of learning, for it is "hardly possible at once to admire an author, and to go beyond him." Even if a few individuals may have endeavored to "make trial for themselves, and put their own strength to the work of advancing the boundaries of the sciences," they have not "ventured to cast themselves completely loose from received opinions" (*WFB*, IV, 16).

In the *Novum Organum*, as in the *Advancement*, Bacon attempts to counter the excessive honors and admiration bestowed on the ancients themselves or on the present stock of inventions. It is not "only the admiration of antiquity, authority, and consent," he declares, that has retarded knowledge, "but also an admiration for the works themselves of which the human race has long been in possession." Yet if one will reflect how long it has taken to perfect such things, how little they owe to "observations and axioms of nature," and "how easily and obviously" and casually they may have been discovered, one will "easily cease from wondering, and on the contrary will pity the condition of mankind, seeing that in a course of so many ages there has been so great a dearth and barrenness of arts and inventions." Similarly, whatever wonder one feels at our "immense variety of books" will be dissipated on examining their contents; "after observing their endless repetitions, . . . he will pass from admiration of the variety to astonishment at the poverty and scantiness of the subjects which till now have occupied and possessed the minds of men." The wonder accorded natural magic similarly lacks foundation; whatever works it has produced aimed merely at "admiration and novelty" rather than at "utility and fruit" (*WFB*, IV, 82–84).[31]

Proposing to leave the "honour and reverence due to the ancients . . . untouched and undiminished," Bacon refuses to follow their road and endeavors instead to "open a new way for the understanding, a way by them untried and unknown." Acting

31. Distinguishing his own science of invention from the "invention" pertaining to the rhetorician and the logician, Bacon declares that "the end which this science of mine proposes is the invention not of arguments but of arts; not of things in accordance with principles, but of principles themselves; not of probable reasons, but of designations and directions for works." Their effects are likewise different: "the effect of the one being to overcome an opponent in argument, of the other to command nature in action." Bacon's scientist surpasses the rhetorician just as his art of invention is both nobler and more beneficial in its ends and effects. See *WFB*, IV, 24.

"merely as a guide to point out the road," he is nevertheless "a pioneer, following in no man's track, in his search for the 'New Continent.'" In publishing his conjectures, "which make hope in this matter reasonable," he follows the example set by an early heroic voyager—Christopher Columbus. "[B]efore that wonderful voyage of his across the Atlantic, . . . he gave the reasons for his conviction that new lands and continents might be discovered besides those which were known before; which reasons, though rejected at first, were afterwards made good by experience, and were the causes and beginnings of great events" (WFB, IV, 41, 91, 102).[32]

In attempting to remove despair of the further advancement of learning and to awaken hope, Bacon dwells at length on "the errors of past time," and exhorts his contemporaries to make "trial" of their own strength: "by not trying we throw away the chance of an immense good; by not succeeding we only incur the loss of a little human labour." We cannot call in "any of the ancients to our aid and support," but must rely instead "on our own strength." Although it may seem "a strange and a harsh thing that we should at once and with one blow set aside all sciences and all authors," nevertheless "new discoveries must be sought from the light of nature, not fetched back out of the darkness of antiquity" (WFB, IV, 98, 102, 108–109).

As in his previous works, Bacon makes extensive use of the topoi of honestas and utilitas in order to demonstrate both the nobility and the benefit of natural philosophy, the experimental method, and the mechanical arts. "Of all signs there is none more certain or more noble than that taken from fruits." From all the philosophical systems of the Greeks one can scarcely adduce a single experiment tending to the benefit of man. The "experimental part of medicine was first discovered," and men "philosophised" about it later. The "true and lawful goal of the sciences" is to endow human life with "new discoveries and powers," but this end can be achieved only through a new kind of natural philosophy leading to "new assurance of works and new light of axioms." Natural philosophy, that "great mother of the sciences," has "with strange indignity been degraded to the

32. Cf. Bacon's further use of the metaphor of the "coasting voyage" (WFB, IV, 23): "Having thus coasted past the ancient arts, the next point is to equip the intellect for passing beyond."

offices of a servant; having to attend on the business of medicine or mathematics." But in fact no real progress can be achieved in the sciences "unless natural philosophy be carried on and applied to particular sciences, and particular sciences be carried back again to natural philosophy" (WFB, IV, 73–74, 79–80).

The task of advancing the boundaries of knowledge and thereby extending the human empire over nature thus belongs essentially and primarily to natural philosophy. The goal of the natural philosopher (and a fortiori of his royal patron) is the noblest of all ambitions, inasmuch as it aims at nothing less than universal dominion, seeking power and sovereignty not so much for an individual or a country as for humanity. Distinguishing three kinds or "grades of ambition in mankind," Bacon brands as "vulgar and degenerate" those who merely "desire to extend their own power in their native country." The second class, who "labour to extend the power of their country and its dominion among men," display more dignity but "not less covetousness." The ideal of the third group, those who "endeavour to establish and extend the power and dominion of the human race itself over the universe," is "without doubt both a more wholesome thing and a more noble than the other two" (WFB, IV, 114).

This ambition is nothing less than the restoration of man's original birthright, dominion over all creatures forfeited by the Fall. "Only let the human race recover that right over nature which belongs to it by divine bequest, and let power be given it; the exercise thereof will be governed by sound reason and true religion." The labor and the honor of reestablishing Adam in his original dignity must inevitably fall to the natural scientist, with his knowledge of the laws of nature and the principles or forms of things. For the "empire of man over things depends wholly on the arts and sciences" and man cannot "command nature except by obeying her" (WFB, IV, 114–15).

Ambition may, however, be a heroic vice as well as a spur to noble achievements, and Bacon takes pains to emphasize its dangers. There is "in man an ambition of the understanding, no less than of the will, especially in high and lofty spirits." This has led to the "apotheosis of error," to the corruption of philosophy by superstition or the "admixture of theology," and to the creation of systems "fanciful and tumid and half poetical" (WFB, IV, 66).

As in the Advancement, Bacon recalls the divine honors traditionally accorded inventors, emphasizing both the utility and the nobility of their discoveries. The "introduction of famous discoveries appears to hold by far the first place among human actions." Whereas antiquity bestowed honors "no higher than heroic" on the men who "did good service in the state," it "awarded divine honours" to the "authors of inventions." Whereas "civil benefits" are limited to particular places and times and are generally attended with violence and confusion, "the benefits of discoveries" are peaceful and may extend to "the whole race of man" and throughout all time. The scientific inventor is, accordingly, a greater hero, a more eminent benefactor, than the national worthies commonly hailed as heroes: the "founders of cities and empires, legislators, saviours of their country, and quellers of tyrannies" (*WFB*, IV, 113).

Like apologists for painting and poetry, Bacon advances a further argument for the nobility of the inventor, the analogy with the divine workman. "Discoveries are . . . new creations, and imitations of God's works," and by means of his inventions man may imitate "the *magnalia* or marvels of nature" (*WFB*, IV, 99, 113).

In recent discoveries, "unknown to the ancients"—printing, gunpowder, and the magnet—Bacon finds not only an "argument of hope" for further "noble inventions" in the future but additional evidence that knowledge is power. "For these three have changed the whole face and state of things throughout the world; the first in literature, the second in warfare, the third in navigation; . . . insomuch that no empire, no sect, no star seems to have exerted greater power and influence in human affairs than these three mechanical discoveries" (*WFB*, IV, 99–100, 114).

Discoveries, however, are less noble than the art of discovery; and the inventor must yield the preeminence to the inventor of the science of invention. If men accord divine honors to the inventor of "one particular discovery" (regarding as "more than man" the person who has been able "by some benefit to make the whole human race his debtor"), the discoverer of the science of invention is a still greater benefactor: "how much higher a thing to discover that by means of which all things else shall be discerned with ease!" Just as beholding the light is more excellent than "all the uses of it," so "the very contemplation of things, as they are" is "more worthy than all the fruit of inventions." The invention of causes (in the idiom of the *Advancement*) is more

noble than the production of effects; and natural science is superior to natural prudence (*WFB*, IV, 115; III, 351–52).

Bacon's heroes of science—the naturalist, the inventor, the experi-
menter, and the founder of scientific institutions—lacked only
one adornment to render them the peers (or perhaps the superi-
ors) of classical heroes: celebration in heroic poetry. The *New Atlantis* attempted, in its own way, to remedy this deficiency. In the
broadest sense of the term, it is a heroic poem, combining several
of Bacon's favorite themes within a narrative framework equally
heroic, the motif of the voyage. Although it lacks "measure of
words," it is nevertheless poetry of a sort; for, as Bacon himself
observes, a "Feigned History . . . may be styled as well in prose as
in verse." Although it is ironical to find Bacon giving rein to the
imagination in the service of reason and experiment, glorifying
the discovery and utilization of the "laws of matter" in a medium
that "may at pleasure join that which nature hath severed, and
sever that which nature hath joined," it is hardly surprising, inasmuch as "the duty and office of Rhetoric is *to apply Reason to
Imagination* for the better moving of the Will." In utilizing the
"Feigned History" of poetry as the vehicle of his scientific program, Bacon was faithful to the views on rhetoric and poetic expressed earlier in *The Advancement of Learning*.

> The use of this Feigned History hath been to give some shadow of satisfaction
> to the mind of man in those points wherein the nature of things doth deny it;
> the world being in proportion inferior to the soul; by reason whereof there is
> agreeable to the spirit of man a more ample greatness, a more exact goodness,
> and a more absolute variety, than can be found in the nature of things. There-
> fore, because the acts or events of true history have not that magnitude which
> satisfieth the mind of man, poesy feigneth acts and events greater and more
> heroical. . . . So as it appeareth that poesy serveth and conferreth to mag-
> nanimity, morality, and to delectation (*WFB*, III, 343, 409).

Poetry not only portrays heroic deeds; it also stimulates its readers to heroism, stirring their latent greatness of spirit, their magnanimity. With this view of the office and function of the heroic
poet, Bacon might legitimately celebrate the heroes of science in a
feigned history, restoring the hero to that realm of fiction and
fable where the majority of classical heroes properly belonged
and where readers nurtured on epic and romance might expect to
find him.

"This fable my Lord devised," wrote Bacon's chaplain and biog-

rapher, "to the end that he might exhibit therein a model or description of a college instituted for the interpreting of nature and
the producing of great and marvellous works for the benefit of
men." He had also intended to include "a frame of Laws, or of the
best state or mould of a commonwealth," but had been prevented
by his work on "the Natural History" (*WFB*, III, 127). If completed, the fable would have reflected two principal occupations
of Bacon's public and private career, his labors for the advancement of natural philosophy and his endeavors as legalist and
statesman.

In celebrating the ideal of the scientist as benefactor, Bacon
accords heroic honors to the royal founder of Salomon's House
and to the chief inventors and their discoveries. Endowed with
"noble and heroical intentions," Solamona is adored after death
as "a divine instrument, though a mortal man." Among his many
"excellent acts . . . one above all hath the pre-eminence," the
"erection and institution of . . . the noblest foundation . . . that
ever was upon the earth; and the lanthorn of this kingdom."
Dedicated to "the finding out of the true nature of all things," and
to "the study of the Works and Creatures of God," the College of
the Six Days' Works seeks God's glory "in the workmanship of
them" and man's benefit "in the use of them." One of the galleries
in Salomon's House contains the statues of "all principal inventors": Columbus, "who discovered the West Indies"; the inventors of ships, ordnance and gunpowder, printing, music, and
letters; the inventors of glass, silk, wine, sugars, corn, and bread;
the inventors of "observations of astronomy" and "works in
metal"; and the inventors of "excellent works . . . you have not
seen" (*WFB*, III, 144–46, 165–66).

Although the primary function of the *New Atlantis* is to eulogize the *magnalia* of natural science and natural magic—the
speculative and operative branches of natural philosophy—the
narrative framework Bacon selected for his fable was already
firmly established in the heroic tradition. Eminently adaptable to
all three types of heroism (active, contemplative, or mixed), the
voyage motif was equally capable of manifesting the hero's prudence and fortitude in action, his patience in adversity, or his
wisdom in contemplation. Moreover, the journey had long been a
conventional vehicle for presenting scientific or speculative material within the framework of a more or less unified fable. The
journeys described in the *Odyssey*, the *Divina Commedia*, and the

sixth book of the *Aeneid* had been allegorized as images of speculation. Similarly, the astral voyages portrayed in the literature of
dream visions (such as the *Somnium Scipionis*) could be, and often
were, regarded as allegories of contemplation. For his blueprint
of an ideal commonwealth under the leadership of an idealized
college of scientists, Bacon chose a vehicle conventionally associated not only with the heroic tradition but also with the literature
of speculation. Perhaps the most significant difference between
his work and the latter is that the journey finds its end not so
much in a vision of the afterlife as in a portrait of an ideal state of
society in this life. Concerned less with contemplation of the
heavens than with the examination of things on earth, preoccupied rather with earthly creatures than with angels and other
"separated substances," it is oriented, on the whole, toward the
physical rather than the metaphysical. Its end is technology
rather than eschatology.

Nevertheless, Bacon's fable also serves a practical end. Like
other Utopias—those of Plato and Cicero, More and Campanella—it functions as a rhetorical exemplum; it is an instrument of persuasion. Despite its remote and exotic setting, this
imaginary island serves as a hortatory argument for the author's
own island. Its royal foundation for "the knowledge of Causes
and secret motions of things; and the enlarging of the bounds of
Human Empire" is, in effect, a plea for Bacon's own program for
scientific reform. The parallel extends to the very name of the
royal benefactor. Solamona, the founder of Salomon's House,
some nineteen hundred years before, bore a name prophetic (or
rather reminiscent) of King James, the "English Solomon"; and in
the *New Atlantis* as in *The Advancement of Learning*, Bacon exploits
the rhetorical possibilities inherent in this epithet in the interests
of natural philosophy. In both it is not merely the breadth of the
Hebrew king's learning that makes him an effective example for
rhetorical exhortation; it is specifically his interest in natural science, in the "study of the Works and Creatures of God." Primarily
it is Solomon's lost "Natural History . . . of all plants, from the
cedar of Libanus to the *moss that groweth out of the wall*, and of all
things that have life and motion" that interests Bacon (*WFB*, III, 145,
156). It is a precedent that he may exploit rhetorically in appealing
to the British Solomon to subsidize his scheme. In both works he
resorts to this *topos*, but in the *New Atlantis* his emphasis on Solomon as an exemplar of the natural philosopher is even more pronounced than in the *Advancement*.

Both works, in fact, belong to deliberative rhetoric. Like the *Advancement*, the scientific romance is a rhetorical exhortation to the English king, in favor of the author's ambitious and still unrealized program for natural philosophy. Despite their fundamental differences in method and genre (the one, a formal oration seeking to persuade by means of logical proof; the other, a quasi-poetic fiction endeavoring to persuade through inductive methods, by example), they aim nevertheless at essentially the same end—to persuade the king to endow an institution for the advancement and utilization of natural philosophy. The *Advancement* argues the imperative need for such an establishment by surveying the current deficiencies of the arts and sciences of the present. The *New Atlantis*, on the other hand, portrays the merits of such an establishment, and the future benefits that may result therefrom, by drawing a glowing, though imaginary, picture of what Britain herself might (and could) become through the type of program Bacon has proposed. Like many other Utopias, this is in substance a vision of the future, though represented as contemporary. Substituting geographical for chronographical distance, the author has made his imaginary commonwealth (his vision of a future Britain transformed by science) remote in space rather than in time.

Like England, the New Atlantis is a Christian state, and Bacon stretches the resources of the Christian marvelous in order to make it so. Like England, it enjoys the natural protection afforded it by the sea. Like England, it has benefited by the rule of a sage-king, another Solomon in wisdom. What Solamona accomplished for his island monarchy, the British Solomon may similarly achieve for his own island domain. What the New Atlantis is now, the new Britain, the England of the future, can potentially become.

Bacon is often regarded rather as a propagandist for the experimental method than as a master of experiments, rather as the *buccinator* of the advancement of learning than as a major scientist. The trumpet was nevertheless a conventional symbol of heroic poetry, and one of the strongest and most resonant tomes in Bacon's propaganda for the Great Instauration was the heroic. The motto *Plus ultra* not only evoked the image of Hercules, a proverbial symbol of *virtus heroica*, but pointed the way toward a nobler mode of conquest. Through his knowledge of the book of nature, the scientist could not only accomplish greater endeavors for the

public good; he might also achieve a higher knowledge of the
Creator through His works. Through his inventions and discoveries, moreover, he could assist and perfect nature. It was a commonplace of Renaissance critical theory that the poet and painter,
by means of selective and "ideal" imitation, might improve on
nature. The scientist could do likewise through judicious exercise of the mechanical arts.

Bacon's followers made effective use of heroic *topoi* in arguing
the nobility and profitableness of experimental science. Like the
artists of Renaissance Italy, they faced the problem of exonerating
their vocation from the charge of baseness and the traditional
prejudice against the mechanical arts. In 1635, for instance, Alexander Read condemned chemical principles in medicine as
"meerly factive, commonly called mechanicall, and so unworthy
of a Philosopher." His "remarkable hostility to any matter requir-
ing practical and manual activity," R. F. Jones observes, "increases
in the conservatives as the century advances. Knowledge, they
held, must be a matter of the brain only." To counter this prejudice
against the experimental method, its apologists resorted to tactics
not dissimilar to those that the partisans of arts of design had
found effective. Employing the conventional techniques of demonstrative rhetoric, they argued the nobility of experiment,
drawing freely on topics generously provided by the heroic tradition. Glanvill waxed eloquent in praise of the "glorious Under-
takers," those "free-spirited Worthies" of his century who would
soon fill the world with wonders. Such "illustrious Heroes" as
Descartes, Gassendi, Galileo, Tycho Brahe, Harvey, More, and
Digby, and other "generous Vertuoso's" dwelt "in a higher Region
than other Mortals," making a "middle species" between Platonic
gods and common humanity. "This is not the first example of the
'heroizing' of scientists," as Jones points out; and this attitude
"clearly anticipates modern hero-worship of the masters of science."[33] The inventor of the mariner's compass (Glanvill subsequently declared) had accomplished more for mankind than
"a thousand Alexanders and Caesars" or "ten times the number of Aristotles."[34] Copernicus' "Heroicke Hypothesis" moved
seventeenth-century observers to admiration, an emotion conventionally associated with the heroic poem. Samuel Parker per-

33. Richard Foster Jones, *Ancients and Moderns: A Study of the Rise of the Scientific Movement in Seventeenth-Century England* (2nd ed.; Berkeley, 1961), 80, 143–45.

34. J. B. Bury, *The Idea of Progress* (New York, 1955), 93.

ceived in the scientist's curiosity "a gallant and heroical Quality," so long as it confined itself prudently to the evidence of the senses. For Henry Power the members of the Royal Society were "the enlarged and Elastical souls of the world," and their endeavors were truly "Heroick."[35]

To critics of the new science, such language must have appeared not merely hyperbolic but paradoxical. For scientific conservatives, nurtured in the belief that the manual or mechanical arts were ignoble, such a phrase as "noble Experiment" must have seemed little more than oxymoron. As the century advanced, however, it became increasingly aware of the practical as well as the theoretical benefits promised by the "new science." With Bacon's insistence that "knowledge is power" and Descartes' assertion that it could "render ourselves the lords and possessors of nature," the philosopher acquired a more valid title to heroic eminence than the warrior.[36] His conquests were greater, inasmuch as they extended not merely over a small fraction of the globe but over nature herself. The dominion he promised was, moreover, both intellectual and physical; his empire of the mind conferred positive control over nature.

As eminent in natural prudence as in natural wisdom and in works as in thought, the scientist as Bacon conceived him was both active and contemplative hero. That near-contemporaries, spokesmen for the "new philosophy" during the last three-quarters of the century, should hail Bacon himself in heroic terms was no more than poetic justice. For Rawley, he was a man of "divine understanding." For the contributors to the *Manes Verulaminani* he was "Verulamius Heros"—"noster Heros [qui] traderet scientias Aeternitati"; the Columbus who has conquered a New World with new arts:

> Calpen superbo Abylamq; vincit remige
> Phoebi Columbus, artibus novis Novum
> Daturus *Orbem.*

Comenius linked him with Campanella as a "Hercules, who has debelled monsters and purged the Augean stables" through his attacks on Aristotelian philosophy. Gassendi lauded his "heroic daring": "Ausu verè Heroico novam tentare viam est ausus, sperareque fore ut, modo illi strenuè diligenterque insistatur,

35. Jones, *Ancients and Moderns,* 189–94, 290.
36. Basil Willey, *The Seventeenth-Century Background* (New York, 1953), 96.

nova tandem eaque perfecta condi haberique Philosophia pos-
sit." To the University of Oxford he seemed "a literary Hercules,
who has further advanced the pillars of learning, deemed by
others immovable." For Cowley he resembled Moses, who had
led "our wandring Praedecessors" through the wilderness to the
border of the "blest promis'd Land." For Leibniz he was "divini
ingenii vir." [37]

The image of Bacon as contemplative hero, intellectual voyager
and conqueror, had become conventional by the end of the seventeenth century, and it retained its currency, if not its freshness,
during the following century. In David Mallet's *Life of Francis Bacon*
one reencounters the heroic *topoi* that Bacon's early admirers had
applied to him and that he himself had so frequently exploited as
themes for eulogy and exhortation. If Bacon's successors, "tread-
ing in the path he struck out for them, have gone farther and
surveyed it more exactly than he did; yet to him is the honour of
their discoveries in a manner due. It was *Columbus* alone who
imagined there might be a new World; and who had the noble
boldness to go in search of it, thro' an ocean unexplored and immense." But Bacon is not only an intellectual mariner; he is also,
in Mallet's opinion, the conqueror of an empire of the mind. The
"noble aim to which he directed all his philosophic labours" was
the "universal advancement of science. . . . What *Caesar* said, in
complement [*sic*], to *Tully* may, with strict justice, be applied to
him; that it was more glorious to have extended the limits of
human wit, than to have enlarged the bounds of the *Roman
world*." [38]

Despite their professed distrust of rhetorical ornament, Bacon's followers were not at all averse to employing it on behalf of
the Great Instauration and its prophet. Like the master himself,
they could rise (or stoop) to heroic imagery in the cause of naked
truth, in defense of the experimental philosophy and in praise of
its trumpeter, the inventor of a viable method of invention.

37. Bacon, *Novum Organum*, ed. Thomas Fowler (Oxford, 1878), Introduction,
passim; W. G. C. Gundry (ed.), *Manes Verulamiani* (London, 1950), pp. 3–4, 27 of
photofacsimiles.
   38. David Mallet, *The Life of Francis Bacon*, in *The Works of Francis Bacon* (4 vols.;
London, 1740), I, lxiii, lxv.

PART II

The Tempter as Anti-Hero

And either this is the reason why they are called heroes, or it is because they were wise and clever orators and dialecticians, able to ask questions (erotan), *for* eirein *is the same as* legein *(speak). Therefore, when their name is spoken in the Attic dialect, . . . the heroes turn out to be orators and askers of questions, so that the heroic race proves to be a race of orators and sophists.*

—Plato, Cratylus

CHAPTER 4

Satan and the Unjust Discourse

A CENTURY ago, few scholars would have welcomed the notion of Milton as a rhetorician. Rhetoric was still largely a term of reproach—indeed, a dirty word. It was a label that critics applied to literature that fell demonstrably short of true poetry; a literature in which manner prevailed over content, gesture over sincerity; a literature rich in applied ornament but poor in essential truth; a literature in which a superficial mastery of technique disguised a fundamental lack of vision and conviction; a literature decorative, methodical, specious—in a word, meretricious.

In the last decades, however, the term has rehabilitated itself. The painted meretrix (to which Milton and so many of his predecessors compared it) has become a respectable matron. To stress the rhetorical techniques underlying Renaissance poetry no longer implies veiled or explicit censure. After the studies of Donald L. Clark and many others, we can accept the full implications of Milton's rhetorical training and experience, and their significance for his prose and poetry, without batting an eyelash.[1] Po-

---

1. See *inter alia* the following works: J. B. Broadbent, "The Rhetoric of *Paradise Lost*" (Ph.D. dissertation, St. Catharine's College, Oxford, 1956); Donald L. Clark, *John Milton at St. Paul's School: A Study of Ancient Rhetoric in English Renaissance Education* (New York, 1948); W. E. Gilman, *Milton's Rhetoric: Studies in his Defense of Liberty* (Columbia, Mo., 1939); Thomas Kranidas, *The Fierce Equation: A Study of Milton's Decorum* (The Hague, 1965); Wilbur Samuel Howell, *Logic and Rhetoric in England, 1500–1700* (Princeton, 1956); Walter J. Ong, S.J., *Ramus, Method, and the Decay of Dialogue* (Cambridge, Mass., 1968); Arnold Stein, *Answerable Style: Essays*

etry and rhetoric no longer seem antithetical, but rather complementary. And we have come to realize, gradually, that one reason
why Milton was so successful a poet is that he was so accomplished a rhetorician.

Yet there is, perhaps, more truth in the first view than we may
care to acknowledge; and on this point Milton held a somewhat
broader view of the rhetorical art than either our contemporaries
or their immediate precursors. In his own writings he follows the
traditional distinction between the beneficial and the injurious
types of oratory—a difference dependent largely on the speaker's
moral purpose and comparable, roughly, to the distinction between logic and sophistic. In his prose he has much to say about
both kinds, and both find representation in his poetry.[2] Indeed he
often intensifies the contrast by stressing the opposition between
these two extremes of eloquence in the same scenes—in the dialogues between the Lady and Comus, Abdiel and Satan, or Christ
and his demonic Adversary. True and false eloquence, logic and
sophistry, just and unjust discourse—these antithetical concepts
of rhetoric appear in Milton's poetry, as in his prose; and in many
instances each is instrumental in defining and clarifying its contrary. Their traditional opposition can be traced (like so much else
in Western rhetoric) back to the ancient Greeks.

In Aristophanes' *Clouds* a wily rustic seeks, somewhat surprisingly, the consolations of philosophy. Looking for some new
scheme to evade his creditors, he enrolls his son in Socrates'
school for a tutorial in dialectic. "Teach him both methods of reasoning," the old man urges, "the strong and also the weak, which
by false argument triumphs over the strong; if not the true, at
least the false, and that in every possible way. . . . He must always, always be able to confound the true."[3]

Socrates consents to give the youth the very best of all possible
tutors, Just and Unjust Discourse themselves. The two modes of
disputation promptly make their entrance, already engaged in a

on *"Paradise Lost"* (Minneapolis, 1953); Rosemond Tuve, *Elizabethan and Metaphysical Imagery* (Chicago, 1947).

2. *Cf.* Milton, *Of Education,* in Frank Allen Patterson (ed.), *The Works of John
Milton* (18 vols.; New York, 1931–38), IV, 286, on "a graceful and ornate Rhetoric."
The Patterson edition is hereinafter cited as *Works.*

3. Whitney J. Oates and Eugene O'Neill, Jr. (eds.), *The Complete Greek Drama*
(2 vols.; New York, 1938), II, 575–83.

violent wrangle. In the course of their debate truth clearly loses, discountenanced. "I am beaten," confesses Just Discourse. "Debauchees! in the name of the gods, receive my cloak: I pass over to your ranks." Unjust Discourse, on the other hand, triumphantly conducts the pupil into the classroom, promising to make him an accomplished sophist.

Nor is truth the indisputable victor in *Paradise Lost*. Among Milton critics, Satan's "persuasive rhetoric" and "glozing lies" have won notable converts, some of them far more sapient than Eve. We may pass over Blake, Shelley, and the earlier generations of Satanists. Our own generation can afford us sufficient examples. Not a few scholars have taken Satan's competent sophistries at their face value. He really believes (*they* believe) what he is saying. The devil himself is not so much a devil that he cannot be sincere! This is a large and, in Milton's idiom, a vicious pill—yet they swallow it without gagging. For it bears that reassuring label, "fidelity to the text."

"Satan . . . does not degenerate," A. J. A. Waldock insisted; "*he is degraded.*" In the opening books of *Paradise Lost*,

> there is hardly a great speech of Satan's that Milton is not at pains to correct, to tone down and neutralize. He will put some glorious thing in Satan's mouth, then, anxious about the effect of it, will pull us gently by the sleeve, saying (for this is what it amounts to): "Do not be carried away by this fellow: he *sounds* splendid, but take my word for it. . . ." We have in fact . . . two levels: the level of demonstration or exhibition, and the level of allegation or commentary: and [between them] there is disagreement. What is conveyed on the one level is for a large part of the time not in accord with what is conveyed on the other. Milton's allegations *clash* with his demonstrations.[4]

Like most other spokesmen for "the Devil's part," Waldock confused moral purpose and rhetoric. He ignored the distinction between *ethos* and *dianoia*, character and thought.[5] This difference was of primary importance in Aristotle's *Poetics*; and so, presumably, it was for Milton himself. On occasion, moreover, it can be very significant indeed, especially when the speaker himself proves to be a disciple of Unjust Discourse. Satan and Belial alike excel in sophistical oratory. What Milton is actually demonstrat-

4. A. J. A. Waldock, *"Paradise Lost" and Its Critics* (Cambridge, 1947), 77–80, 83.

5. For fuller discussion of this point, see John M. Steadman, "Character and Rhetoric in *Paradise Lost*," in Ronald D. Emma and John Shawcross (eds.), *Language and Style in Milton* (New York, 1968). Cf. *Aristotle's Treatise on Rhetoric*, trans. Theodore Buckley (Bohn ed.; London, 1850), 197.

ing in their speeches, on the so-called level of exhibition, is precisely what he is also emphasizing on the level of commentary.
This, in a word, is the character of the archsophist, the archetypal
deceiver. The essence of such a type is, of course, that he should
deceive. He should seem to be what he is not, to be speaking truth
when he is uttering falsehood, to be persuading to good when he
is actually exhorting to evil. The last thing one expects of such a
person is a revelation of his true "moral purpose," his actual character. If one accepts this premise, then the alleged clash between
the two levels of demonstration and commentary tends to disappear. The demonstration is, in fact, an exhibition of the sort of
specious rhetoric against which Milton's commentary so appropriately warns us.

In the Neo-Aristotelian poetic theory of the Renaissance, three of
the principal elements of tragedy (and, of course, epic as well) are
mythos, ethos, and *dianoia*—that is, fable, character, and thought.
"The Fable," as Aristotle defines it, is "simply . . . the combination of the incidents . . . in the story. . . . Character is what
makes us ascribe certain moral qualities to the agents; and
Thought is shown in all they say when proving a particular point
or . . . enunciating a general truth." Thought is simply "the
power of saying whatever can be said, or what is appropriate to
the occasion." The critic must not confuse it with character. In the
speeches of tragedy (and equally in epic dialogue) the element of
thought belongs properly to politics and to rhetoric. "The older
poets," Aristotle observes, "make their personages discourse like
statesmen"; the "moderns" make them speak "like rhetoricians."
Finally, "the Thought of the [dramatic] personages is shown in
everything to be effected by their language—in every effort to
prove or disprove, to arouse emotion (pity, fear, anger, and the
like), or to maximize or minimize things."[6]

Tasso's *Discourses on the Heroic Poem* develop still further the
rhetorical function of *dianoia*.

> In Character it is chiefly the moral habits which are demonstrated. In Thought,
> it is the habits of the intellect—and particularly prudence, which is one of the
> intellectual virtues. [The functions of *dianoia* are] to demonstrate, to solve, to
> move the affections . . . , to amplify or diminish, or make known the greatness
> or smallness of things. Hence this part of poesy contains everything treated

6. *Aristotle on the Art of Poetry,* trans. Ingram Bywater (Oxford, 1951), 36,
38–39, 66.

in rhetoric, inasmuch as poetics is a more comprehensive art than rhetoric. *Dianoia* accomplishes these functions through speech, which is an index of the power of the mind, whereas the Fable accomplishes them through portraying things and events.[7]

In spite of the complexity of Milton's Satan, one can at times distinguish fairly clearly between character and rhetoric, or *ethos* and *dianoia*—between his real and his fictitious intent. Let us take one of the more "heroic" passages in his opening speech in *Paradise Lost*.[8]

> yet not for those,
> Nor what the Potent Victor in his rage
> Can else inflict, do I repent or change
> Though chang'd in outward lustre; that fixt mind
> And high disdain, from sence of injur'd merit,
> That with the mightiest rais'd me to contend.
>
> . . . .
>
> To bow and sue for grace
> With suppliant knee, and deifie his power
> Who from the terrour of this Arm so late
> Doubted his Empire, that were low indeed,
> That were an ignominy and shame beneath
> This downfall.
>
> (*PL*, I, 94–99, 111–16)

At the end of this passage Milton again "plucks us by the sleeve" (as Waldock would have put it): "So spake th' Apostate Angel, though in pain, / Vaunting aloud, but rackt with deep despare." To Waldock this seemed another flagrant example of Milton's inconsistency. "Has there been much despair in what we have just been listening to? The speech would almost seem to be incompatible with that. To accept Milton's comment here . . . as if it had a validity equal to that of the speech itself is surely very naïve critical procedure."[9] Yet perhaps the naïveté lies in taking the speech itself at face value. On the surface one sees only the heroic Satan, clothed in the full moral panoply of the conventional epic hero. But one does not need to look far beneath the surface to detect another pattern, and to the theologian this may seem remarkably close to despair. For what else are Satan's refusal

7. Torquato Tasso, *Prose*, ed. Francesco Flora (Milan, 1935), 427–28.
8. Quoted passages of *Paradise Lost* and *Paradise Regained* are from H. C. Beeching (ed.), *The Poetical Works of John Milton* (Oxford Standard Authors; New York, 1935). References in text are to book and lines.
9. Waldock, *"Paradise Lost" and Its Critics*, 78.

to repent and his rejection of grace than conventional signs of reprobation? The "fixt mind" that scorns to "repent or change" can be called heroic constancy; but it may also be diagnosed as "hardening of the heart"—the obduracy of conscience that is commonly symptomatic of a reprobate will. If (as Milton declared elsewhere) "despair . . . takes place only in the reprobate," his comment on Satan's oration seems rather apposite after all.

In most epic and dramatic poetry the author attempts to establish the "real character" of his *personae* at the outset. For Waldock this principle was of fundamental importance; indeed it was the real basis of his quarrel with *Paradise Lost*. The poem does establish Satan's character at the beginning, he argued, and everything Milton says afterwards, either by way of commentary or by actual demonstration, is inconsequential after this first impression. Inevitably the later comments must be of doubtful validity and of inferior authority as evidence. The Satan who soliloquizes on Mount Niphates is not the same Satan who summoned his comrades from the burning lake and held council in Pandaemonium. "It is not merely that the Satan of the first two books re-enters altered," Waldock insisted; "the Satan of the first two books to all intents and purposes *disappears*: I do not think that in any true sense we ever see him again." Nevertheless, "the Satan of the first two books is established once and for all and nothing will avail against him." [10]

In one sense, Waldock's observation is correct. Milton has established Satan's character in the first two books; but it is not precisely the character that Waldock himself accepted as genuine, nor is it inconsistent with the Satan of the later books. According to Aristotle, there are four points at which the author must aim in portraying character. It must be good (that is, not unnecessarily evil); appropriate (to the general class or category to which the individual belongs); "like the reality" (similar, as Renaissance commentators explained, to the individual's character as historical and poetic tradition had already defined it); and, finally, consistent. Moreover, like the fable itself, the characters should meet the requirements of necessity and probability. "[I]n the Characters, just as in the incidents of the play [the right thing is] to endeavour always after the necessary or the probable; so that when-

10. *Ibid.*, 81–82, 85.

ever such-and-such a personage says or does such-and-such a thing, it shall be the probable or necessary outcome of his character; and whenever this incident follows on that, it shall be either the necessary or the probable consequence of it."[11]

As for the alleged disparity between Milton's levels of demonstration and commentary, the latter is, of course, a thoroughly conventional device in epic poetry. More than one Renaissance critic recommends it as a technique for resolving moral ambiguities in the dialogue or action. Tasso, for instance, stands with Plutarch in arguing that the poet is entitled to "interpose his own judgment" and introduce passages of censure or blame. Without such admonitions, the vices he happens to be imitating might easily corrupt his readers. Poetry could be "very dangerous" indeed ("pericolosa molto") if the poet did not point out the path of virtue in "dubious passages" and thus serve as a moral guide.[12]

Milton's commentary hardly seems the ill-advised afterthought Waldock believed it to be—an awkward attempt to "uncreate" the heroic devil the poet had unwittingly created. On the contrary, it fulfills the very function that Renaissance poetic theory demanded of it: to distinguish between appearance and reality, to correct the false opinions that Satan's skillful rhetoric might otherwise impose on the audience's imagination, to expose and neutralize a false rhetorical *ethos* that could perhaps beguile the reader's fantasy as easily as Eve's.

The relationship between commentary and demonstration is, however, only one aspect of the problem of consistency in character. More fundamental is the alleged contrast between the "heroic" Satan of Books I and II and the "degraded" devil of the later books. A notorious example, in Waldock's opinion, is the disparity between Satan's opening addresses and his soliloquy in Book IV.

> O then at last relent: is there no place
> Left for Repentance, none for Pardon left?
> None left but by submission; and that word
> *Disdain* forbids me.
>
> (IV, 79–82)

In point of fact, the *ethos* explicit in this passage bears a striking resemblance to the character implicit in Satan's first address. (In-

---

11. *Aristotle on the Art of Poetry*, 55–57.
12. Tasso, *Prose*, 423.

deed, there are verbal echoes, and these are not, apparently, acci-
dental.) Here are the same refusal to repent and the same disdain,
though arrayed in less sumptuous oratory than before. The soliloquy voices the same despair as the earlier oration and exhibits the
same characteristic *ethos* of the reprobate.

The alleged contradiction between the heroic and degraded
Satans is essentially an illusion. In one sense Satan is already degraded from the moment he first makes his appearance, even
though he does his best to disguise the fact from his fellows and
from himself. His fall is itself a visible and tangible sign of his
degradation in more than one respect: political and moral, physical and metaphysical. Perhaps the most remarkable feature of the
first two books is the skill with which Satan and his fellows seek to
persuade themselves, and one another, that their degradation is a
triumph and their humiliation an exaltation. Certainly, they have
succeeded in persuading more than one critic, dizzied by Satan's
"bad eminence" and dazzled by the barbaric glitter of his throne.
Waldock was not alone in failing to recognize that the Satan of the
first two books is essentially and fundamentally degraded and
that much of the power and beauty of the opening scenes results
from the devil's attempt to mask the fact of his degradation from
himself and from his companions.

The degraded Satan of the later books is by no means a contemptible figure. He is still a heroic image, albeit falsely heroic.
Even in his bestial disguises he bears a significant resemblance to
heroic prototypes, though this time his affinities are less with
Achilles and Agamemnon than with the crafty Ithacan, *polytropos*
Odysseus. His tongue proves more lethal than his gunpowder,
and the masterly oration whereby he seduces Eve would do credit
even to the wily Ulysses. Indeed the question of his heroism is
closely associated with the problem of his rhetorical skill. Besides
the deceptive eloquence that prevails on Eve and links him with
Odysseus, the stirring harangues that kindle new spirit in his
defeated legions associate him with Aeneas, Agamemnon, and
other heroes of the Greco-Trojan cycle. Even more significant,
however, is the classical ideal of the hero as orator. In the *Cratylus,*
Plato had suggested a derivation of *heros* from *eirein* ("to speak")
and interpreted the ancient heroes as "a race of orators and sophists." [13] This suggestion was echoed by Renaissance authors, such

13. *Plato,* trans. H. N. Fowler (9 vols.; Loeb Classical Library; London,
1917–26), VI, 56–57. *Cf.* John M. Steadman, *Milton's Epic Characters: Image and Idol*
(Chapel Hill, 1968), Appendix I.

as Charles Estienne and Torquato Tasso. For many Renaissance readers, moreover, this conception of the orator as hero would have been reinforced by Cicero's quasi-heroic treatment of the rhetorician in his *De Oratore.*

In *Paradise Lost,* Satan conquers a world not by martial force (like the conventional epic hero) but by verbal persuasion. In this respect he resembles the heroes whom Plato had described as "rhetorōn kai sophistōn genos." And, indeed, in the crucial temptation scene Milton explicitly compares him to

> som Orator renound
> In *Athens* or free *Rome,* where Eloquence
> Flourished.
>
> (IX, 670–72)

Against the background of this tradition the portrait of Satan as orator—as rhetorician and as sophist—is just as heroic as the earlier portrait of Satan as martial combatant. Milton has not violated the consistency of his heroic *eidolon* in depicting Satan's alteration from vainglorious warrior to smooth-tongued rhetorician. The archangel still reflects a conventional conception of heroism, which long abuse had generally rendered vicious.

To make Satan "like the reality," Milton must remain as faithful as possible to biblical tradition. The proud rebel who shone like the morning star and vaunted his equality with the Most High, the dragon who warred with Michael and his angels and fell from Heaven, the serpent who lied to Eve in the Garden of Eden, the Adversary who tested the patience of Job, the prince of this world who tempted the Savior in the wilderness—these diverse aspects had long been attached to a single figure, pieced together in a single mosaic, and Milton could not escape the problem of making this composite portrait appear both plausible and consistent. The Lucifer of Isaiah and the dragon of Revelation had warred by force; the serpent of Genesis had triumphed through guile. Milton's task, as a poet committed to Neo-Aristotelian conceptions of epic laws, was to invest his portrait of the archfiend with consistency and verisimilitude, reconciling the contrasting images he found in scriptural tradition and fusing them into a single character. He must make the shift in tactics, the transition from violence to fraud, seem (in Aristotelian terms) "probable or necessary." Probable and necessary, moreover, not only in terms of the sequence of events but also in terms of Satan's character. This was no mean challenge, and he met it admirably.

The opening books, with their martial Satan and the military pageantry of Hell, provide a well-timed transition between the Lucifer image and the serpent of the garden. In Milton's Hell, the legions who warred against the Almighty are scarred, but still intact. And they are still rebellious. Satan has lost neither his pride nor his ambition to reign. Except for the ravages of "spiritual death" (the psychological consequences of his sin), his character is still essentially the same as in his revolt.[14] He is still the biblical Lucifer, though fallen. The chief difference is that he now possesses a richer fuel for his hate and an added incentive for his wrath—revenge. To satisfy his thirst for vengeance he will employ any available tactic that seems expedient; if force is impossible, he will proceed by fraud.

The demonic conclave likewise serves as a transition device. It begins by considering the question of further warfare against Heaven—whether by open force or covert guile. It ends by unanimously acclaiming the enterprise against man, again by the same alternatives, violence or fraud. This project, as the debate demonstrates, is the "probable or necessary" outcome of the logic of events, the only viable course left to the devils and the only one on which they can agree. It is also, under the circumstances, the probable and necessary result of character.

Proleptically, Satan's various disguises—as stripling cherub, as lion, as toad—prepare the way for his more significant disguise in the temptation scene, the serpentine form inevitably imposed on him by biblical tradition. He has committed himself, fairly early in the poem, to a tactic of fraud; eavesdropping has convinced him, not illogically, that this policy offers the best chance of success; and after the encounter with Gabriel, force is clearly out of the question. Once again his actions, especially in the temptation scene, seem the probable and necessary consequences of events and also of his own character.

Milton has obviously taken great pains to make Satan's *ethos* seem both consistent and "like the reality." Besides these transition devices, he employs other, less obvious, means of making the transition from Lucifer to serpent seem plausible. In his account of the angelic war and again in the opening books of *Paradise Lost* he emphasizes the seductive force of Satan's oratory, and also its sophistical character. Even in Heaven, Lucifer is the archtempter,

14. See Milton's *De Doctrina Christiana*, Bk. I, Chap. 12.

the archdeceiver. He does not merely lead his followers; he seduces them. Finally, the poet introduces the element of conscious
deceit onto the very battlefields of Heaven. Concealing his "di-
velish enginry," the cannon, under the pretext of seeking truce,
Lucifer himself becomes the inventor of fraud. This too is a proleptic device; it not only looks forward to Renaissance warfare but
also foreshadows the strategy of guile that Satan must inevitably
employ against Eve.

Ultimately, of course, Satan *is* degraded—"punisht in the
shape he sinn'd"—and his humiliation provoked Waldock's expected rebuke. "The technique of this famous scene is the technique of the comic cartoon. . . . The scene is amusing, and the
writing of it is superb: but about Satan it proves literally nothing
whatever."[15] Actually, Milton has prepared for it rather carefully.
He has deferred Satan's transformation into a dragon from the
actual war in Heaven to the moment of his triumphant return
from Eden. He has rationalized this metamorphosis, moreover,
by linking it specifically with the sentence of judgment already
pronounced on the serpent in the Garden of Eden. Furthermore,
he has foreshadowed this change relatively early in the poem,
through the serpent-woman at Hell-gate, Satan's daughter and
"perfect image." She is his own Sin, and anticipates his own punishment. Although Satan does not realize it when he first reencounters her, he too is doomed to suffer in a similar shape.

The episode of Satan's metamorphosis is meant to surprise—in
fact, it is one of Milton's best attempts at the epic marvelous—but
it is also intended to seem probable and necessary. Knitting together various strands already tightly woven into the texture of
the poem, it provides the final tie between two of the principal
sources of Milton's Satan—the dragon of Revelation and the serpent of Genesis.

The hostile criticism I have examined may perhaps serve, ironically, to augment the poet's own glory. But I have cited it for a
rather different reason. Underlying the specific objections it advances are somewhat larger critical issues, problems that are for
the most part implicit rather than explicit, but which nevertheless
have a direct bearing on the interpretation of Milton's poetry, as
well as the literature of his contemporaries. How can we ascertain

15. Waldock, *"Paradise Lost" and Its Critics*, 91–92.

a literary character's "real" intent? What is to be our standard in attempting to relate his true motives to the arguments he makes in any given speech? How and when should we distinguish between "real" and "apparent" *ethos*, between the character that the poet consciously ascribes to a particular persona and the specious character that the latter may assume in discourse or action as a means of ethical proof?

On the simplest level the problem may be little more than "a knack to know a knave"—the way to distinguish the double-dealer from the plain-dealer. In the average morality play, for instance, there is usually little difficulty in distinguishing virtue from vice; the dramatist normally makes this distinction clear enough at the outset—by the names he assigns his allegorical personae, or by soliloquies and asides that reveal their true "moral purpose." Nor is it difficult to identify the confidence man, or his classical and Renaissance progenitors, in comedy and satire. The dramatist makes the real *ethos* of such a character apparent fairly early in the play; and the audience can recognize and enjoy his subsequent maskings and disguises, the feigned motives and false arguments whereby he "practices to deceive." The reader derives a similar pleasure from the ethical disguises and "quick-change" morality of a character like Ulysses.

Nor is there any great difficulty in distinguishing between real and apparent character in Milton's major temptation scenes. Even the most perverse critics rarely go so far as to take Comus at his word, or to insist that the serpent's arguments in Book IX of *Paradise Lost* are genuine and that his real motives are what he says they are. Nor, for that matter, would they insist on treating the aged rustic whom the Christ of *Paradise Regained* encounters in the wilderness as a bona fide character, whom Milton arbitrarily degrades into a devilish trickster. The reason, of course, is that here we are already aware that the deceiver *is* a deceiver, that the speaker has rhetorically disguised his true motives, just as he has literally disguised himself. We know the confidence man, or Unjust Discourse, for what he is.

On the stage this type of dissembling may be a source of real aesthetic pleasure, not only because it multiplies the possibilities for ironic situations and comments, but also because it builds directly on the fundamental premise of all dramatic performances—impersonation. It extends and enhances the range of dramatic illusion. Not only does the actor himself impersonate another person (historical or fictional, real or allegorical), but the latter in turn—the dramatis persona himself—may impersonate an infinite variety of other characters; and his ability to do so lends variety and surprise to the dramatic performance. When we see Face and Subtle shifting their characters with their garments, when we find Mosca altering his behavior to "lime" one after another fortune seeker and outwit each of several would-be deceivers, when we see Volpone now a moribund invalid, now a mountebank, now an overviolent lover, we delight in the versatility that the actor's complex, many-faceted role affords him.

Judicious readers of *Paradise Lost* may, therefore, find in Satan's tactical disguises—his expedient shifts in tone and manner, his choice of arguments appropriate to each new encounter and each new interlocutor, his assumption of a feigned *ethos* and on occasion an assumed persona—something of the same pleasure they find in following Odysseus' tricks, the ruses of the clever servant of the comic stage, or (in more tragic contexts) the Machiavellian conspiracies of an Edmund or an Iago. Some of the alleged inconsistencies in Satan's character result, in fact, from his versatility. Now hurling scorn and defiance at Sin and Death, now soliciting them with smooth-tongued flattery; now assuming a cherub's form, now hiding his identity under the shape of a toad or snake—he alters his tactics with his situation. His changes in manners and mores are, for the most part, deliberately assumed. Even though they may seem superficially inconsistent, they are, on the whole, firmly rooted in the dominant character traits that he displays throughout the poem: malice, guile, and obdurate hostility to God. His inconsistencies spring in large part from his assumed *ethos* rather than from his essential character.

In distinguishing his real from his feigned intent (as we must do if we are to form a just estimate of his cunning as a strategist and his skill as a rhetorician), we must bear in mind not only the precise circumstances of his speech—its occasion, the nature of his interlocutor, and so on—but also its public or private character. As a rule, his speeches fall roughly into four major categories: soliloquies; conversations with his confidant Beëlzebub; conversations with other persons; and public addresses in council or on the battlefield.

All four types of discourse are conventional in epic and dramatic poetry; but they do not always possess the same value as evidence. In revealing the true motives of his characters, a poet might speak directly in his own person in an epic or through the chorus in a drama. Less direct, but almost as reliable, would be the character's own statement of his motives, either in a formal soliloquy or in an aside; rhetorically, this would serve as a form of inartificial proof. The character's confession to a chosen confidant, in turn, would normally rank next in validity—more authoritative than formal public addresses and conversations with persons other than the principal confidant, but less reliable than the soliloquy and the aside.

Normally an audience could expect to take a soliloquy or a confession to the confidant at face value, inasmuch as both of these devices were thoroughly conventional in both narrative and dramatic exposition. Nevertheless there could be notable exceptions. The speaker might on occasion deliberately deceive his most intimate friend, just as Dido conceals from Anna her intention to commit suicide. Similarly, in *Paradise Lost* one may legitimately wonder how far Satan's conversations, even with Beëlzebub, can be taken literally. Would it be beyond the Father of Lies to deceive even his most trusted confidant?

Let us briefly examine each of these four categories. Satan's principal soliloquies are, on the whole, fairly straightforward expressions of his actual feelings and purposes—his struggle with conscience, his oscillation between wonder at God's creation and the passions (ire, envy, despair) that impel him to destroy it, and finally his fresh committal to revenge. His moral intent is clearly, indeed explicitly, defined; and so, on the whole, are his emotions. Each of his soliloquies is prompted by an act of sight: his vision of the sun ("O thou that with surpassing Glory crown'd" [IV, 32ff.]); his first glimpse of Adam and Eve ("O Hell! what do mine eyes with grief behold" [IV, 358ff.]); the spectacle of their nuptial bliss ("Sight hateful, sight tormenting!" [IV, 505ff.]); his experience of earth's variety and "sweet interchange" through his circumnavigatory flight ("O Earth, how like to Heav'n" [IX, 99ff.]); and finally the "rural sight" of Eve among the roses ("Thoughts, whither have ye led me" [IX, 473ff.]).

The first soliloquy is dominated by despair; it concludes with "All hope excluded," a fresh dedication to Evil as his Good and the means of "Divided Empire with Heav'n's King," and a vague threat to Man and "this new World." The second expresses wonder, grief, and more than a suggestion of pity, but concludes with a more explicit threat against Man and a further evocation of the

theme of "Honour and Empire." In the course of the third soliloquy, dominated by jealousy and envy, Satan hatches his plot ("O
fair foundation laid whereon to build / Thir ruine!"). In its contri-
bution to the development of the plot, this speech performs a
function roughly comparable to that of other conspiratorial soliloquies in Renaissance tragedy. Like the soliloquies of Edmund in
King Lear and Iago in *Othello*, it represents the actual invention of
evil and the inception of a conspiracy.

> Hence I will excite thir minds
> With more desire to know, and to reject
> Envious commands.
>
> (IV, 522–24)

The fourth soliloquy again expresses his "inward grief" and
envy and reaffirms his despair—the futility of hope. Earth's central position in the planetary system reminds him of God, just as
the sun had done in his first soliloquy. Motivated by "Ambition
and Revenge," he seeks heroic glory in destruction, aiming to
spite the Creator by destroying His creation, and advances the
plot by selecting the serpent as his instrument. In the fifth soliloquy his expression of hate is all the stronger for his temporary
distraction by the spectacle of Eve's beauty, a sight that has momentarily disarmed him "Of guile, of hate, of envy, of revenge."
Again he advances the plot by seizing the occasion to tempt Eve in
Adam's absence and to seek her ruin through fraud, "under show
of Love well feign'd."

The soliloquies serve, then, both as ethical and pathetic proof.
They enhance the "passionate" elements in Milton's epic (to echo
his own description of poetry in *Of Education*), and they illuminate Satan's moral intent. They advance the action of the poem by
portraying the internal act (of intellect and will) that precedes the
external, physical act—the ethical decision that prompts the
deed. In each case Satan consciously commits himself anew to
evil; we see him consistently choosing wrongly and thus en-
trenching himself more deeply and inextricably in vice.

Of Satan's four speeches to Beëlzebub as confidant, three occur
in Book I—"If thou beest he" (84ff.); "Fall'n Cherube, to be weak
is miserable" (157ff.); "Is this the Region, this the Soil, the Clime"
(242ff.). The fourth appears in Book V in the account of the angelic
revolt ("Sleepst thou, Companion dear" [670ff.]). In both books
Milton establishes Beëlzebub's status as Satan's close associate

and confidant. He is next to Satan "in power, and next in crime" (I, 79), his "next subordinate" (V, 671). It is to him that Satan communicates his first misgivings about Messiah's vicegerency, his first remarks after the fall into Hell, and his plan to spite the Creator by confounding "the race / Of mankind in one root" (II, 378–85). In Heaven, Satan addresses him as a "Companion dear" with whom he has habitually shared mutual confidence.

> Thou to me thy thoughts
> Wast wont, I mine to thee was wont to impart;
> Both waking we were one; how then can now
> Thy sleep dissent?
>
> (V, 676–79)

After his fall he similarly hails his companion as his long-tried confidant.

> he whom mutual league,
> United thoughts and counsels, equal hope,
> And hazard in the Glorious Enterprize,
> Joynd with me once, now misery hath joynd
> In equal ruin.
>
> (I, 87–91)

Like his soliloquies, Satan's speeches to Beëlzebub advance the plot, but they have less value as ethical and pathetic proof. The "bold words" and vaunts that he utters to his companion not only disguise his real feelings but actually assert the contrary of his real view of the situation. The "deep despair" he experiences inwardly contradicts the "more successful hope" he professes outwardly. This type of tactical falsehood, whereby a military or political leader suppresses his own doubts and misgivings in order to raise the morale of his followers, is nevertheless thoroughly conventional in epic poetry. Aeneas and Odysseus sometimes conceal their fears for similar reasons. So do later commanders in drama as well as in epic; one thinks automatically of Henry V on the eve of Agincourt. In Satan's case, however, there is a subtle difference. He extends the false lure of hope (as we subsequently realize) not simply to rebuild morale and reestablish military discipline but also to persuade his companions to a course that must (as he himself perceives) inevitably aggravate their sufferings and plunge them into still deeper damnation.

His first and second speeches to Beëlzebub advance the primary action of the poem, inasmuch as they reaffirm Satan's persistent opposition to the divine will. The ethical intent he declares

in his second discourse provides the foundation for the strategy
he will subsequently follow in the holy warfare between Heaven
and Hell.

> To do ought good never will be our task,
> But ever to do ill our sole delight,
> As being the contrary to his high will
> Whom we resist.
>
> (I, 159–62)

The same discourse also foreshadows directly the "great consult"
of Book II. Satan seizes the occasion to reassemble his "afflicted
Powers" and "Consult how we may henceforth most offend / Our
Enemy." Once again he appeals, insincerely but expediently, to
the *topos* of hope, but on this occasion he balances it with the
more realistic alternative of despair: "What reinforcement we may
gain from Hope, / If not what resolution from despare."

His third speech to Beëlzebub affirms his ambition to "reign in
Hell," a statement that subsequently proves to be largely sincere;
the same motif recurs, again and again, throughout the poem. As
in the second speech, moreover, Satan again advances the action
by declaring his intention to reassemble his associates. Similarly
he appeals, as before, to the alternative *topoi* of hope and despair:
"With rallied Arms to try what may be yet / Regained in Heaven,
or what more lost in Hell?"

Through his fourth speech to Beëlzebub (in Book V) he in-
fuses, as Milton informs us, "Bad influence into th' unwarie
brest / Of his Associate." He is, therefore, the tempter and se-
ducer of his closest friend. Nevertheless we should not mistake
this evil influence for conscious deception. Although Satan mis-
leads his companion by inducing him to rebel against God, he
does not actually deceive him. Instead, he implicates Beëlzebub
in a deliberate lie designed to deceive his own troops. With
Beëlzebub as his mouthpiece, he tricks his legions into deserting
their post before the divine throne, on the pretext that they have
been commanded to return to the North "to prepare / Fit entertainment" for the Messiah on his royal progress through the angelic hierarchies. Satan does practice deliberate deception in this
speech, but the deceit is directed not so much toward his confidant as toward his soldiers.

Satan's addresses to his confidant are less reliable than his
soliloquies as revelations of his actual feelings and his "moral
purpose." But they are not altogether untrustworthy; however

much they conceal or suppress, they usually betray some significant aspect of his real intent and (much more rarely) of his real emotions.

To the third category belong Satan's dialogues with his offspring Sin and Death (Books II and X) and the semiofficial discourse whereby he concludes a strategic alliance with the powers of the Abyss; his altercations with the faithful angels, Abdiel and Michael, Gabriel, and Ithuriel and Zephon; some of his commands and exhortations in battle; and the conscious deceptions he practices on Uriel and on Eve.

To the fourth category we may assign the formal public harangues he delivers to his council or his assembled troops—such orations as "Princes Potentates" (I, 315ff.); "O Myriads of immortal Spirits" (I, 622ff.); "Powers and Dominions" (II, 11ff.); "O Progeny of Heav'n" (II, 430ff.); "Thrones, Dominations, Princedomes, Vertues, Powers" (V, 772ff.); "O now in danger tri'd" (VI, 418ff.); and "Thrones, Dominations, Princedomes, Vertues, Powers" (X, 460ff.).

The speeches in the third group range from unambiguous statements of his thought and feelings to complex orations whose primary and essential purpose is to deceive. The disdain and fearlessness he expresses when challenged by Death at Hell-gate are genuine; when he declares to Sin that he has never beheld "till now / Sight more detestable then him and thee," he is sincere. The comparative sincerity of these two speeches, however, throws into bolder relief the manifest *in*sincerity of his next discourse, when he greets Sin as his "Dear Daughter" and Death as his "fair Son" and "dear pledge." On this occasion the clear contrast between relative truth and falsehood dramatically accentuates his cleverness and cunning, the rapidity with which the "suttle Fiend" can learn his "lore" and alter the manner and tenor of his discourse; but it also emphasizes the readiness with which he can and will resort to lying and flattery, the rhetorical instruments whereby he will subsequently prevail against Eve. In his next speech, however, his conversation with the powers of the Abyss, his remarks can be taken at face value. In inquiring the whereabouts of the new world, he appeals to the arguments of expediency and honor—the advantage that will accrue to Chaos and Night, the revenge that he himself will achieve. Such arguments as these are, under the circumstances, rhetorically appropriate, but they do not involve conscious deception.

Satan's conversations with persons other than his confidant exhibit, then, much the same variety that we have encountered in his discourse with Beëlzebub. Some of them can be taken largely at face value, whereas others are deliberately deceptive. His exchanges with his enemies range from overt scorn and defiance to delusive flattery; in part at least, they accompany his shift in tactics from violence to covert guile.

Finally, his formal addresses to his council or his assembled troops show something of the same variety that we have encountered in his other speeches. Some of these are deliberately deceptive—a significant fact that has a profound bearing on Milton's characterization of the rebel archangel. We should expect Satan to attempt to deceive his enemies, to lie to Uriel and Gabriel and to Eve, but we should not, as a rule, expect him to deceive—consciously deceive—his own followers and friends. The consolatory deceptions he imposes upon them immediately after their defeat are, of course, thoroughly understandable. The appeal to hope (even though he himself feels despair) is as justifiable in his orations to his legions as in his exhortations to Beëlzebub. It points to bad leadership, however—disastrous leadership—when Satan employs it to persuade his followers to a course of action that is, in the final analysis, hopeless. He himself oscillates significantly between false hope ("high uplifted beyond hope") and despair.

Satan's first public exhortation to his troops is, on the whole, a straightforward appeal to escape the burning lake before God's "pursuers . . . discern / Th' advantage." Concluding appropriately with an exhortation to "Awake, arise, or be for ever fall'n," it employs several types of proof, both pathetic and logical, and varying degrees of validity. Satan plays on his soldiers' fears ("linked Thunderbolts" may "transfix" them "to the bottom of this Gulf") and on their dread of shame (they are slothful, seeking ignoble ease to repose their "wearied virtue" or supinely adoring their conqueror "in this abject posture"). Indirectly he also appeals to hope; he makes the irrevocable loss of Heaven seem merely conditional: "*If* such astonishment as this can seize / Eternal spirits." This argument is probably sophistical, but only if Satan himself has already realized that Heaven can never be regained. The accusations of sloth and abject submission, however, are not so much sophistical as ironical; they are sarcastic jibes designed to abash his hearers and goad them to immediate action. The threat of thunderbolts is a real possibility; of all the arguments advanced in this speech, this is the soundest—both probable and plausible.

The devil's second public speech (immediately after the fallen legions have passed in review, in formal order of battle) advances the action by proposing a "Full Counsel" (to be described in Book II), rejecting the possibility of peace in favor of a policy of continued warfare, and suggesting a "first eruption" against the newly created world. Satan extends to his troops once again, and as he will repeatedly extend in the future, the false hope of regaining Heaven and repossessing "thir native seat." He justifies his own conduct in the previous war that has just terminated in crushing defeat.

His third public address (the speech from the throne that formally opens the debate in parliament) presents greater difficulties than either of these earlier discourses. To what extent does Satan actually believe his "proud imaginations"? Repeatedly he deludes his audience with the illusory hope of recovering Heaven ("I give not Heav'n for lost," and "we now return / To claim our just inheritance of old"), but is he aware that he is deluding them? Does he himself know that the hope he offers his followers is false? On one hand, it is quite possible that for the moment, temporarily relieved of despair, "high uplifted beyond hope," and even aspiring "Beyond thus high," he actually believes his own promise. In this case his argument would be false, but not sophistical; it would be simply the result of his own self-deception rather than an instrument for consciously deceiving others. On the other hand, it is he (as we learn later) who has first devised "and in part propos'd" Beëlzebub's "bold design" to seek an "easier enterprise"—to achieve revenge by attacking God's creation instead of essaying the hopeless enterprise of reconquering Heaven. On the whole, the more likely interpretation seems to be that Satan is deliberately deluding his followers with the hope of regaining Heaven. The difficulties in this passage spring from ambiguities that appear to have been deliberate on Milton's part, unresolved tensions that heighten suspense.

In his fourth public oration Satan once more advances the action by volunteering for the perilous journey through space. By describing the perils of the Abyss, he heightens his own claim to "highest worth"; similarly he gratifies his own "Monarchal pride" by arguing that both hazard and honor are "due alike / To him who Reigns." In risking his own safety in order to seek "Deliverance for us all" and thus earn "high repute," he conforms to a traditional pattern of heroic virtue and its ends and rewards. In this speech there is little actual sophistry, even though such a title as "Terror of Heav'n, though fall'n" comes dangerously close to oxymoron; under the circumstances, such flattery strikes the reader as more than faintly ridiculous.

His fifth public address (in Book V) is, on the other hand, deliberately deceptive. He assembles his troops on the pretense that they and he have been "so commanded to consult / About the great reception of thir King." His insistence that the angels have been "ordain'd to govern, not to serve" contradicts the real nature and function of the angelic orders as "ministering spirits." His claim to equality with the Messiah is false. His argument that "Orders and Degrees / Jar not with liberty" is double-edged; though he employs it to justify his revolt, it can be turned with equal force against his rebellion.

In his sixth public speech (to his "Potentates in Councel" after the first day of battle) there is little evidence of conscious deception. Although several of his conclusions are (as the reader well knows) erroneous, Satan himself does not appear to be aware of the error. He is wrong in valuing "Honour, Dominion, Glorie, and renowne" above Liberty, which he dismisses as "Too mean pretense," but this ethical preference is characteristic of him; he is the classic archetype of the ambitious rebel and "aspiring mind." He minimizes the disadvantage of pain, but amplification and extenuation are, after all, standard rhetorical techniques. (Moreover, Satan turns this disadvantage into an advantage, by seeking a "remedie" in "more valid Armes, / Weapons more violent." As a result he invents the cannon.) The most persistent of his errors in this passage is his rash conclusion about his enemy's capabilities. Inferring wrongly from one day's experience on the battlefield that Jehovah has radically underestimated the rebel forces and grossly overestimated the power of the faithful angels, Satan concludes that God is not omniscient, but fallible.

> Who have sustained one day in doubtful fight,
>
> . . . .
>
> What Heavens Lord had powerfullest to send
> Against us from about his Throne, and judg'd
> Sufficient to subdue us to his will,
> But proves not so.
>
> (VI, 423–28)

The inference is wrong, as is his argument that, having endured one day on the battlefield, the rebels should be able to continue "Eternal dayes."

Similarly, Satan's final public speech (after his successful return to Hell from earth) gives little indication of deliberate sophistry. He does indeed magnify his own exploits, in the hope of greater praise; and, conversely, he extenuates the inevitable penalty he has incurred through the curse pronounced on the serpent: "A World who would not purchase with a bruise, / Or much more grievous pain?" This summary of the curse is, of course, incomplete, but Satan's omission is apparently due largely to ignorance rather than to a conscious desire to deceive. He does not know, apparently, that the other details of the judgment pronounced on the serpent will also be applied directly to himself, and to his companions as accessories. He does not realize that, like the serpent, he too must literally crawl upon his belly and eat the dust. This passage, therefore, is largely devoid of sophistry. On the other hand, when he bids his followers to "enter now into full bliss," he surely knows by his own experience that they can never find either happiness or delight again, much less the plenitude of felicity. Thus the last words he utters in the poem are a conscious sophism.

Thus far we have described Unjust Discourse in isolation. But this is only half the problem. We must now, like Aristophanes, bring Just Discourse upon the stage—that "true eloquence" (as Milton calls her) who is "the daughter of virtue."[16]

In most of his longer poems, Milton gives prominence to the rivalry between these two extremes of rhetoric. The debate between truth and falsehood, right reason and sophistry, appears most clearly in *Paradise Regained*, but it also occupies a prominent position in *Comus* and *Samson Agonistes*. Nor does it play a negligible role in *Paradise Lost*—in Abdiel's debate with Satan, Satan's quarrel with Gabriel, and, indeed, in the crucial temptation scene, when Unjust Discourse triumphs over an Eve "yet sinless."

The element of *dianoia*, in fact, seems to receive a disproportionate emphasis in Milton's epics. In comparison with most heroic poets, he devotes far greater space, and skill, to arming his

16. Milton, *The Reason of Church-Government*, in *Works*, III, 181.

characters with rhetorical arguments for proving or disproving a given point and for persuading or dissuading toward or against a certain course of action. Like Aristotle's "moderns," he makes his personages speak "like rhetoricians." *Paradise Regained* may be "an imitation of an action," but it is also, to an equal or greater extent, a *mimesis* of *dianoia*, an imitation of thought. Before concluding, let us consider some of the reasons for this disproportionate stress on *dianoia*, and therefore on rhetoric, in his heroic poems.

The most obvious factor is Milton's choice of subject. As he tells us, he is not "sedulous by Nature to indite / Warrs, hitherto the onely Argument / Heroic deem'd," and he chooses accordingly the subjects that will enable him to portray spiritual rather than physical conflict. In the crucial battles the antagonists contend not with weapons but with rhetorical arguments, not with swords and spears but with enthymemes and examples. The thrusts that they make or parry are verbal, the confirmations and refutations conventional in logical dispute. The prominent role that *dianoia* plays in Milton's epics (as well as in *Comus* and *Samson Agonistes*) reflects the central position of the so-called temptation motif in his poetic argument and fable. Insofar as he seeks to persuade, the tempter is pursuing a characteristic end of rhetoric. Insofar as the ends to which he persuades are vicious and the arguments he employs are deceptive, his discourse belongs to sophistic, to the art of seeming reason and specious eloquence.

Less obvious, and certainly more complex, are the considerations that underlie Milton's preference for this type of subject. Especially significant in this context are his conception of the nature of heroic virtue and the type of situation or matter that may best exercise, test, or illustrate it. Since wisdom is superior to military valor and patience to active fortitude, a martial subject, however conventional and time-honored, can hardly serve as the best matter for demonstrating the higher virtues. Indeed Milton frequently goes out of his way to demonstrate that military fortitude and the type of combat it involves are not justly heroic. He condemns them as "Brutish" and thus associates them with *feritas*, the diametrical contrary of heroic virtue.[17] It is more godlike, and therefore more truly heroic, to overcome by reason than by

17. See Aristotle's *Nicomachean Ethics*, Bk. VII, Chap. 1, in *The Student's Oxford Aristotle*, trans. W. D. Ross (6 vols.; London, 1942), V.

force. As Abdiel is well aware, the "debate of Truth" is nobler than armed dispute; and "when Reason hath to deal with force" the "contest" is "brutish . . . and foul."

Abdiel is compelled, as we know, to fight with arms as well as words, and his blow staggers his Adversary. The Christ of *Paradise Regained*, however, does not war with weapons but with verbal arguments. His method is persuasion, and this, traditionally, is the proper concern of rhetoric.

> victorious deeds
> Flam'd in my heart, heroic acts, one while
> To rescue *Israel* from the *Roman* yoke,
> Thence to subdue and quell o're all the earth
> Brute violence and proud Tyrannick pow'r,
> Till truth were freed, and equity restor'd:
> Yet held it more humane, more heavenly first
> By winning words to conquer willing hearts,
> And make perswasion do the work of fear.
>
> (I, 215–23)

He prefers, in short, to "try and teach the erring soul" rather than compel it by violence or coerce it by force. Not all of his methods of instruction will be rhetorical, of course. In part he will instruct by an inward light. In part he will teach by his own example—an inductive argument, but essentially nonverbal. But he will also persuade by specifically rhetorical means, by "winning words," by that "true eloquence" whose powers Milton had acknowledged long before, in his *Reason of Church-Government*. "Persuasion," he had declared then, "certainly is a more winning and more manlike way to keep men in obedience than fear." [18]

A third and final consideration is Milton's emphasis on the moral as well as the epistemological value of contraries. From the rhetoricians he had learned that logical contraries appear more clearly, more evidently, by virtue of their opposition. The contrast between good and evil, virtue and vice, truth and falsehood helps to define and distinguish the nature of both. We confirm the true by contrasting it with the false. We apprehend the good by opposing it to evil. We recognize virtue by juxtaposing it with vice. From the moralists, in turn, Milton learned that the matter or subject of virtue and vice are the same, that the same occasion can be the "procatarctic" (external) cause of either good or evil. In both

---

18. Milton, *The Reason of Church-Government*, in *Works*, III, 181.

senses, therefore, ethical as well as epistemological, "trial is by what is contrary." [19]

These principles are partly, if not largely, responsible for the important roles Milton assigns to Just and Unjust Discourse in his temptation scenes. The ordeal of trial tests the understanding as well as the will. By opposing right reason and sophistry, he brings truth and falsehood into clearer opposition, and thus instructs the understanding. At the same time he tests virtue by its contrary vice, and thus exercises the will. In his temptation drama the essential struggle is not limited exclusively to either intellect or will; it is neither purely epistemological nor purely moral. It is both.

19. Milton, *Areopagitica*, in *Works*, IV, 311.

CHAPTER 5

Rhetoric and Character in Paradise Lost

EXCEPT FOR considerations of style, studies of Milton's rhetoric have usually placed primary emphasis on his treatises rather than his epics. Yet the *ars rhetorica* plays a significant role in *Paradise Lost* and an even greater part in *Paradise Regained*. Milton handles rhetorical conventions as effectively in his poetry as in his prose, but with one fundamental difference. In his pamphlets, rhetoric (or logic) is usually the controlling art and hence governs the choice and development of arguments. In his epics and drama, on the other hand, rhetoric is necessarily subservient to poetics.

This fact imposes obvious limitations on any investigation of Milton's rhetoric. To examine the logical or rhetorical elements in his poetry independently of his *ars poetica* is to distort them. "Invention" and "disposition," *ethos* and *pathos, mimesis* and *narratio,* frequently have different meanings for poetics and its sister arts. The argument of a heroic poem is not a rhetorical argument, and its structure differs radically from that of an oration.

Nevertheless, in both theory and practice, Renaissance writers acknowledged the interdependence of poetics with the other "organic arts." For epic and tragedy, thought and diction (*dianoia* and *lexis*) were second in importance only to fable and character (*mythos* and *ethos*). "As for the Thought," Aristotle had declared, "we may assume what is said of it in our Art of Rhetoric, as it belongs more properly to that department of inquiry." In "the speeches of tragedy," *dianoia* "falls under the arts of Politics and

Rhetoric; for the older poets make their personages discourse like statesmen, and the moderns like rhetoricians." Moreover, at least one aspect of *lexis*—"the turns given to the language when spoken"—really "belongs to Elocution and the professors of that art."[1]

Theoretically, then, both thought and diction pertained to the art of rhetoric, or (by Ramist classification) to logic and rhetoric. The Ramists had neatly divided the traditional parts of rhetoric, assigning invention and disposition to logic, and leaving to rhetoric only elocution (*i.e.*, style) and delivery.[2] Thus *lexis* remained within the province of rhetoric while *dianoia* was annexed to the domain of logic.

As a Ramist, Milton must have shared this view, and in the strictest sense he must have regarded thought as pertinent to logic, diction to rhetoric. Yet one should not exaggerate the significance of this distinction. For the purposes of this study it is enough to recognize that Aristotle regarded *dianoia* as the product of rhetorical invention, whereas Milton followed Ramus in assigning the procedures of invention to dialectic.

Accordingly, no analysis of Milton's rhetoric can dispense with his *Ars Logica*. Like other Ramists, he believed that the rhetorician should derive his arguments from the commonplaces of logic; and in practice (though not in theory) the technical differences between the Ramist and Aristotelian classifications tended to disappear. The clenched fist relaxes into the open palm.

In Aristotle's *Poetics*—Milton's authority for the rules of epic and tragedy—he found two guiding principles for his use of rhetoric in dramatic and heroic poetry: (1) the distinction between thought and character and (2) the implications of both for style. The "element of Thought," as Aristotle defined it, is

> the power of saying whatever can be said, or what is appropriate to the occasion. . . . One must not confuse it with Character. Character in a play is that which reveals the moral purpose of the agents, i.e., the sort of thing they seek or avoid, where that is not obvious—hence there is no room for Character in a speech on a purely indifferent subject. Thought, on the other hand, is shown in all they say when proving or disproving some particular point, or enunciat-

1. *Aristotle on the Art of Poetry*, trans. Ingram Bywater (Oxford, 1951), 38, 66–67.

2. *Cf.* Wilbur Samuel Howell, *Logic and Rhetoric in England, 1500–1700* (Princeton, 1956), 165–68, 248; Sister Miriam Joseph, C.S.C., *Shakespeare's Use of the Arts of Language* (New York, 1947), 17.

ing some universal proposition . . . [in] everything to be effected by their language, in every effort to prove or disprove, to arouse emotion (pity, fear, anger,
and the like), or to maximize or minimize things.[3]

From this definition it is clear that *dianoia* includes both logical
and pathetic proof. Similarly, when a speaker in either epic or
tragedy assumes a feigned character or disguises his true motives
in order to win belief and sympathy (as Satan does in tempting
Eve and Christ), we seem justified in classifying this under
dianoia as ethical proof, rather than under *ethos* as an index of
what "the agent" really seeks or avoids. In this respect one may
legitimately distinguish between rhetorical and poetic *ethos*—
though one should not press the distinction too far.

Aristotle's warning against confusing *dianoia* and *ethos*—a distinction so fundamental that he repeats it at several points in the
Poetics—has unfortunately escaped most critics of *Paradise Lost*.
All too often commentators have taken the speakers' remarks at
face value, as an index of character rather than of thought. If the
personality of Satan has been a stumbling block for several generations of critics—Blake, Shelley, Waldock, Peter, Empson, and
others—the reason lies partly in a tendency to mistake *dianoia* for
ethos. Taking the speeches of Books I and II as straightforward
exposition, as a revelation of the real (or poetic) character of the
fallen archangel, many of these writers have dismissed Milton's
own comments and the devil's subsequent remarks as inconsistent. The original outlines of the portrait have, in their opinion,
been distorted by the overpainting. Milton began (they assume)
by sketching a hero; he ended by portraying a villain or a fool.

Usually such writers have explained the contradiction away as
poor draughtsmanship or the result of a conflict between the
poet's conscious and unconscious intents. Yet in reality the inconsistency springs from the mind of the critic rather than the pen of
the artist. It results from the reader's confusion of thought and
character, and it tends to disappear once he has differentiated
Satan's moral intent (what he actually seeks or avoids) from his
arguments. In interpreting the speeches of Milton's personae, one
must distinguish between the revelation of "moral purpose," on
one hand, and the exploitation of rhetorical techniques (*ethos,
pathos, logos*), on the other—the methods the speaker employs to

3. *Aristotle on the Art of Poetry*, 38–39, 66, cf. 35–36.

"prove or disprove," to "arouse emotion," or to win credence from his auditors.

A second stumbling block has been the effect of character and thought on style. Even though critics have correctly stressed the stylistic variations in *Paradise Lost* and called attention to the obviously plainer style of *Paradise Regained*, they have largely ignored the extent to which the choice of a lower style has been dictated by the need for clarity, the degree to which the poet has simplified his diction in order to illuminate the speaker's argument or ethical intent. Theoretically, a plainer, less complex style is requisite for voicing moral purpose or arguing a point. "Elaborate Diction," as Aristotle observes, "is required only in places where there is no action, and no Character or Thought to be revealed. Where there is Character or Thought, on the other hand, an over-ornate Diction tends to obscure them." [4] Since the greater part of *Paradise Regained* and a substantial portion of *Paradise Lost* are devoted entirely to argument or the revelation of moral purpose, Milton had ample occasion for a style simpler, clearer, plainer, and less adorned. To have sustained the predominantly magnificent style of Book I throughout the later books of *Paradise Lost* would have obscured character and thought. It would have been still more of a handicap in the extensive debate scenes of his final epic.

In epic and drama alike, thought is closely interrelated with character and with style. Poetics presupposes a mastery of rhetoric; and the rhetorical arguments employed by Milton's personae are essential and vital to his poetry.

Yet, besides the rhetorical and logical bases of *dianoia* and *lexis*, there were further affinities between poetics and the other organic arts. The Averroistic classification of poetry as a branch of logic survived well into the Renaissance. [5] For Benedetto Varchi, "none can be a poet, who is not a logician; the better logician will be the more excellent poet." Other Renaissance critics— Minturno, Tasso, Sidney—applied to poetry the traditional ends of rhetoric: to teach, delight, and move. Like rhetoric, poetry

---

4. *Ibid.*, 85.
5. John S. Diekhoff, *Milton's "Paradise Lost": A Commentary on the Argument* (New York, 1946), 1–12; J. E. Spingarn, *A History of Literary Criticism in the Renaissance* (New York, 1899), 131ff.

sought to persuade. All three of the organic arts served higher disciplines: ethics, politics, theology. All three pursued a common end—man's beatitude and felicity—by persuading to virtue or dissuading from vice. As Varchi put it, all the sciences "intend and teach man's perfection and beatitude, but variously and by various ways. The Rhetorician through persuasion, the historian through narration, the poet finally through imitation or rather presentation."[6]

Pursuing the same end, the organic arts differed in their means. Whereas rhetoric employed the enthymeme as its principal instrument and logic the syllogism, poetry utilized the example.[7] Yet even in this respect there were significant resemblances. Like poetry, rhetoric made frequent use of example and allegory. Like poetry, it often involved *ethos* and *pathos*, character and emotion. Like poetry, it sometimes resorted to *mimesis*; yet, whereas this was the essence of poetry, in oratory it was merely a minor figure of style.

Finally, however great the difference between heroic poet and orator, the former frequently appealed to the commonplaces of the three major types of oration: deliberative, demonstrative, and judicial. As numerous Renaissance poets and theorists maintained, the heroic poem inspired heroic deeds by narrating them; by arousing admiration for its hero's exploits, it spurred its princely or knightly audience to emulate them. Tasso urges Alfonso d'Este to follow Godfrey's example and lead a new crusade to Jerusalem. Camoëns incites Sebastian to imitate da Gama by conquering new infidel territories for the Cross. In exhorting the reader to "acts of benefit" in war or peace, in persuading him to pursue his felicity through virtue, and in dissuading him from vice through the threat of misery, the heroic poem resembled the deliberative oration, which "urges us either to do or not to do something . . . [and] aims at establishing the expediency

---

6. Benedetto Varchi, *Opere* (2 vols.; Trieste, 1858–59), II, 684–85.

7. Although Varchi and several other Renaissance theorists treat the enthymeme as the principal instrument of rhetoric, Aristotle assigns both the example and the enthymeme to rhetoric as instruments of logical proof; the former is "a rhetorical induction," the latter "a rhetorical syllogism." He does not treat the example as subordinate to the enthymeme. See Aristotle, *Works*, ed. W. D. Ross, trans. W. Rhys Roberts (12 vols.; Oxford, 1908–52), esp. *Rhetorica*, Bk. I, Ch. 2, in vol. XI.

or the harmfulness of a proposed course of action . . . on the ground that it will do good . . . or harm."[8]

The link with demonstrative oratory was even more striking; for the epic—like its allied genre, the panegyric—was patently dedicated to glory. The heroic *tromba* (as critics and poets termed it) was the proverbial trumpet of fame; sounding the praises of its hero, it spread his virtues and achievements throughout the world, conferring an immortality of renown. Its mission, as Tasso phrased it, was to "celebrate heroic virtue and exalt it to the skies."[9] In this respect, the epic resembled the demonstrative oration, which "either praises or censures somebody." The epic poet extolled the merits of his hero; the demonstrative orator "aim[ed] at proving him worthy of honour." Finally, with their common emphasis on the principles of poetic justice, both epic and tragedy showed an affinity with judicial oratory, which "either attacks or defends somebody" and "aim[s] at establishing the justice or injustice of some action."[10]

Although Milton employs all three types of rhetoric, in the context of his epic fable they undergo a sea change. Unlike the orator, he presents them mimetically, through the "imitation of an action." He adapts them to the characteristic method of poetry in general (*mimesis*) and to the requirements of literary genre in particular (the specific demands of the heroic poem). Despite the ethical goals they have in common, poetry and oratory differ in their essential nature and their means; whereas the one is essentially imitative, the other is not. When Milton exploits the topics and methods of deliberative, demonstrative, and judicial oratory, he employs them within the framework of a poetic fiction.[11]

Several modern scholars have emphasized the importance of Milton's rhetorical and logical studies for his verse. Donald L. Clark felt that his poetic dialogue shows the influence of his rhe-

8. *Ibid.*, Bk. I, Chap. 3.

9. Torquato Tasso, *Le prose diverse di Torquato Tasso*, ed. Cesare Guasti (2 vols.; Florence, 1875), I, 165.

10. Aristotle, *Rhetorica*, Bk. I, Chap. 3.

11. For the contents of this paragraph and for other passages in this chapter, I am indebted to Professor Wilbur S. Howell, of Princeton University, who kindly read the original version. For further discussion of rhetoric in epic or drama, see Roland Mushat Frye, "Rhetoric and Poetry in *Julius Caesar*," *Quarterly Journal of Speech*, XXXVII (1951), 41–48.

torical exercises at St. Paul's School. John S. Diekhoff called attention to Milton's use of ethical proof and deliberative rhetoric in
Paradise Lost. Leon Howard analyzed Milton's account of Adam's
fall in terms of Ramist conceptions of the efficient cause.[12] Yet, in
fact, all three of the conventional types of oratory find a place in
Miltonic epic; in varying degrees, they appear not only in the
speeches his characters deliver but also in the broader, more general aspects of his art—in the way he develops his subject and
meets the responsibilities of the heroic poet as a teacher of moral
and religious truth.

Exhortation and "dehortation," praise and blame, accusation
and defense—these are the immediate ends of the traditional
branches of rhetoric, and each of them plays a prominent role in
Paradise Lost. But it is also a complex role. Unless the reader is to
become, like Milton's demonic debaters, hopelessly confused "in
wand'ring mazes lost," he must distinguish between the actual
oratory of the characters themselves and the rhetorical principles
Milton utilizes when speaking *in propria persona*. The studies of
Diekhoff and Howard are, on the whole, concerned with the latter
aspect. These two facets of Milton's rhetoric are closely interrelated, but the distinction between them is fundamental. Milton's
rhetorical tone and strategy will naturally differ according to the
concrete situation and the particular speaker—Adam, Satan,
Christ, or the poet himself.

They will also differ according to the speaker's immediate audience. When Satan addresses Eve or his fallen comrades, when
Belial or Mammon harangues the infernal peers, the poet imitates
a fictitious speech delivered to a fictitious audience within the
poetic fable. Yet Milton also has in mind the effect such feigned
discourses may have on real persons outside the poem. Satan and
Belial intend to persuade the feigned persons who hear them; but
the poet himself intends, by means of his poetic fiction, to move
his own contemporaries. Thus the speeches of Milton's personae
possess a dual character and a dual orientation. They are not only
rhetorical discourses directed to other persons in the plot but also
poetic discourses indirectly addressed by the poet to his readers.

12. D. L. Clark, *John Milton at St. Paul's School: A Study of Ancient Rhetoric in
English Renaissance Education* (New York, 1948), 244; Diekhoff, *Milton's "Paradise
Lost,"* 13–27; Leon Howard, "'The Invention' of Milton's 'Great Argument': A
Study of the Logic of 'God's Ways to Men,'" *Huntington Library Quarterly*, IX (1946),
149–73.

Milton imitates particular orators who employ rhetorical techniques in order to convince an imaginary audience; but by means of such imitations he hopes to persuade his own audience.

To move his readers, the poet can argue through a variety of persons—directly through his own voice or indirectly through his characters. In the latter instance, he achieves what is essentially a poetic imitation of oratory, and this serves a double purpose. In the narrow context of the poetic fiction, the speaker employs rhetorical methods to stir imaginary hearers; in the broader context of actuality, the poet also intends to move his readers.

Such feigned oratory tends to complicate the rhetorical patterns in Milton's epics, since the speaker's arguments and convictions may or may not coincide with those of the poet. Although the Father's discourses are addressed to the angels, Milton obviously intends them to convince his readers. Conversely, though Satan's speeches are designed to produce one effect on the imaginary audience of devils, the poet usually intends them to produce precisely the opposite effect on the "Christian reader." (Indeed, the fact that the devil himself is speaking usually renders the argument suspect.) Within these two extremes, the relationship beteen Milton's arguments and those he assigns to his characters shows considerable range and variety; the degree of similarity or divergence changes with the speaker and the immediate context. Such variations lend additional complexity and subtlety to Milton's poetic exploitation of oratory.

Another factor which complicates still further the poetic image of the orator is his relative sincerity in employing logical, ethical, and pathetic proofs. Thus, in resorting to *ethos* and *pathos,* Satan and Belial frequently disguise their real motives and true feelings; their speeches reveal a feigned intent rather than actual moral purpose. What they pretend to seek or avoid is not what they really desire or shun. On the other hand, the ethical proofs of (let us say) Moloch among the evil spirits and Abdiel among the faithful angels reflect their actual character, their true *ethos.*

That deliberative oratory should form a substantial part of the dialogue in both epics is hardly surprising. First, Milton's choice of argument makes this virtually inevitable. Since both poems deal primarily with spiritual rather than physical warfare, since both center—structurally as well as thematically—on an ordeal of temptation, the poet must necessarily emphasize the techniques proper to this type of rhetoric, the methods of exhortation and dehortation. Insofar as it is verbal (and this it certainly is in Miltonic epic, though it may take other forms in the ordeals of the desert saints), the process of temptation tends to assume the form of dialogue or debate, exploiting the devices of deliberative oratory for confirmation and refutation. It tends to cast the tempter and his opponent in antithetical roles: deceiver and deceived (Satan and Eve) or deceiver and undeceived (Satan and Christ, Satan and Abdiel, Comus and the Lady). On one hand, the tempter resorts to fallacies and false testimony in order to prove his point. On the other hand, the person tempted (if he is successful in resisting his opponent) refutes these specious arguments with sound ones, invalid testimonies with valid, falsehoods with reason and truth.

Second, the infernal council—a legacy from the conventions of classical epic—affords further scope for deliberative oratory. The devils debate the expediency or inexpediency of renewed warfare against Heaven and the question of the most effective means.

Third, another device inherited from classical tradition—the oblique narration of past or future events through the speeches of the characters—affords Milton another opportunity for this type of oratory. The narratives of Raphael and Michael assume, at times, the qualities of deliberative orations; by precept and example they exhort their human auditor to obedience and faith and dissuade him from the contrary vices.

Before examining the actual speeches of Milton's personae, let us consider the rhetorical principles underlying his epic poetry as a whole. Both heroic poems serve as instruments of moral persuasion. Their arguments are deliberative topics—the loss or recovery of beatitude (exemplified by Paradise, "the happy Garden") through vice or virtue (in this case, one man's disobedience or obedience). The principal commonplaces of deliberative oratory—happiness and misery, reward and punishment, good and evil—occupy a central position in both poems, and both works act as positive or negative exempla of virtue and vice and their contrary ends. Through the positive example of Christ and the faithful angels and the negative example of the apostates, Milton exhorts his audience to obedience, patience, and faith and dehorts it from the contrary vices. Adam's example, in turn, serves both purposes; demonstrating the efficacy of repentance

and faith as well as the dire results of sin, it possesses both persuasive and dissuasive force.

In thus transforming the poetic fable into a rhetorical exemplum, Milton follows a pattern already well established in Renaissance poetics. For most theorists and apologists, the poet's
value as moral teacher depended on his role as imitator. By portraying the intrinsic beauty of virtue and the inherent deformity
of vice, he aroused desire or repulsion toward them. By depicting
their contrary rewards, he induced his reader to pursue the one
and shun the other. Milton himself is no stranger to these principles, and he conforms to both. He makes Satan contrast his own
diminished luster with the beauty of the unfallen angels ("Virtue
in her shape how lovely"), and he utilizes both the allegory of Sin
and Death and the transformation scene of Book X to exemplify
even more dramatically the essential deformity of evil. In like
manner, he contrasts the contrary rewards of righteousness and
unrighteousness. Logically, both techniques utilize the commonplaces of cause or effect and illustrate the peculiar value of
dissentaneous arguments. "[E]ach is equally argued by the other;
yet by their dissent they more evidently appear." [13]

Since poetry was, for most of Milton's contemporaries, an art
that teaches by example, it is not surprising that he treats both the
epic argument and the epic fable as an exemplum. Yet Milton also
employs other rhetorical methods of persuasion. Diekhoff noted
the value of the autobiographical passages in *Paradise Lost* as ethical proof. Pathetic proof appears in the effort to arouse admiration
or ridicule, pity or fear. The first two of these "affections" are
especially significant as means of magnifying or diminishing the
subject. When Milton consciously evokes wonder at a divine miracle or deliberately overwhelms the fallen angels with ridicule, he
is exploiting the emotional force of poetry as a means of pathetic
proof. Finally, the fact that his argument is based on Scripture
gives it additional rhetorical force. His exemplum possesses the
authority not only of history but of the word of God. It rests on
divine testimony.

The characters in both epics similarly employ conventional
methods of rhetorical proof and the commonplaces of delibera-

13. Milton, *Art of Logic*, in Frank Allen Patterson (ed.), *The Works of John Milton*
(18 vols.; New York, 1931–38), XI, 99ff., hereinafter cited as *Works*. Cf. *Of True
Religion*, in *Works*, VI, 178: "In *Logic* they teach, that contraries laid together more
evidently appear."

tive oratory, but they make more extensive use of the enthymeme than does Milton himself writing *in propria persona*. In *Paradise Regained* the second temptation exhibits a structural pattern long familiar in ethical treatises on the nature of happiness and the supreme good. Christ successively rejects the secular versions of the *triplex vita* that his Adversary proposes, and instead restores the true paradisal felicity to man.[14] Satan employs both hortatory and dehortatory arguments; he seeks not only to persuade his opponent to accept a worldly kingdom but also to dissuade him from the Messianic path of suffering and humiliation by threatening dangers and adversity. In the infernal council of *Paradise Lost* the devils appeal to the deliberative topics of happiness and misery, good and evil. Raphael's account of the revolt of the angels serves as a rhetorical exemplum; the contrary fates of Satan and Abdiel illustrate "the terrible reward of disobedience" and the contrary rewards of obedience. This is a deliberative argument designed to persuade Adam to remain loyal and to dehort him from recapitulating Satan's crime. Michael's prophecy utilizes antithetical examples of righteousness and unrighteousness drawn from human history in order to strengthen Adam's patience and faith, to inspire him to obey his Creator, and to persuade him to rely on Providence and divine grace. In tempting Eve, Satan appeals to false testimony, arguing fallaciously from his own example; he himself (he claims) has partaken of the forbidden fruit and lived. In *Paradise Regained* both of the principal speakers make extensive use of the rhetorical example, appealing to a host of worthies—Hagar and Ishmael, Elijah and Job, Gideon and Jephtha, David and Socrates, Cincinnatus and Fabricius, Curius and Regulus, Alexander and Scipio, Pompey and Julius Caesar. As means of logical proof, all of these exempla serve the ends of deliberative oratory.[15]

Moreover, in both epics Satan utilizes pathetic and ethical proof. Feigning "Zeal of Right," pretending "Love to Man and indignation at his wrong," he exhorts Eve with passionate vehemence, arguing the injustice of the divine decree that bars her from the food of divinity. At Hell-gate he flatters Sin into unlocking the portals by heaping terms of endearment on both of his monstrous offspring and asserting his intent to procure their freedom. To acquire the information he needs from Chaos, he

14. See Howard Schultz, *Milton and Forbidden Knowledge* (New York, 1955), 225.
15. Aristotle, *Rhetorica*, Bk. I, Chap. 2, Bk. II, Chap. 20.

affects a concern for the latter's kingdom. In *Paradise Regained* his appeal to transform the stones into bread fits his assumed character as a starving desert dweller. When this disguise is detected, he represents himself as a servant of God ("For what he bids I do"), a lover and admirer of virtue, and less a "foe to all mankind" than a "Copartner," who lends them aid and advice and has lost all feeling of hatred or envy. When accused of lying, he pleads the compulsion of misery; even though a liar, he delights in discourse of truth. When his antagonist warns him "that my rising is thy fall," he pretends to be "Sollicitous for the advent of Christ's kingdom."

> I would be at the worst; worst is my Port,
> . . . .
> The end I would attain, my final good.
> (III, 209–11)[16]

These pretended motives are all rhetorical devices. Far from reflecting Satan's true character, they disguise his real intent. They are rather the ethical proofs of rhetoric than the *ethos* of Aristotle's *Poetics*.[17] Satan employs pathetic proof in the same way by appealing to his auditor's emotions, attempting to stir pity for himself, to awaken despair and distrust, to play on the hero's patriotism, ambition, and religious zeal.

Divine and human testimony figure prominently in this later epic.[18] In contrast to Satan's false arguments, based frequently on human testimony or the misuse of Scripture, Christ counters with divine testimony, founded on the word of God. This opposition becomes explicit in the first temptation.

> is it not written
> . . . .
> Man lives not by Bread only, but each Word
> Proceeding from the mouth of God . . . ?
> (*PR*, I, 347–50)

16. Quotations from *Paradise Lost, Paradise Regained, Comus*, and other poems by Milton are from Milton's *Paradise Lost*, ed. Merritt Y. Hughes (New York, 1935), and *Paradise Regained, the Minor Poems, and Samson Agonistes*, ed. Merritt Y. Hughes (Garden City, N.Y., 1937).

17. Since Satan's motives are feigned, these "ethical proofs" do not reveal true "moral purpose" (poetic *ethos*). They do, however, contribute indirectly to the latter, inasmuch as their obvious falsity helps to establish Satan's character as the archetypal liar and the infernal prototype of the sophist and unscrupulous rhetorician.

18. Milton, *Art of Logic*, in *Works*, XI, 284ff.

And it is underlined by a further antithesis between Satan's lying oracles and Christ's role as God's "living Oracle . . . to teach his final will." Satan's treatment of the biblical prophecies concerning the Messiah is ambivalent. On occasion he employs them as an argument to urge Christ to employ worldly means to establish his kingdom. At other times he treats them as a negative argument, stressing the ominous and threatening elements in these predictions.[19] Sometimes he casts doubt on them, arguing that they are contingent on the secular means he proposes. Nevertheless, whatever aspects Satan chooses to emphasize for the sake of the argument, he consistently distorts these prophecies; he consistently interprets them in terms of a worldly rather than a spiritual kingdom, and he consistently seeks to deter his opponent from the Messianic path of humiliation foreshadowed in the "Law and the Prophets." Christ, on the other hand, remains constant to the Messianic *ethos* as defined by Scripture. He counters Satan's allurements with biblical texts, and his final rebuttal is a quotation from Deuteronomy.[20] He does not merely outargue the devil; he also confounds him with divine testimony.

In both *Paradise Lost* and *Paradise Regained*, however, the principal oratorical tool of the speakers is the enthymeme, the rhetorical counterpart of the logical syllogism. Satan derives his enthymemes from many commonplaces. When he tempts Eve to transgress, he combines the argument of cause and effect with a "consentany argument" from the lesser to the greater. If the tree of knowledge could bestow rational discourse on a beast of the field, it can surely, by "proportion meet," transform a woman into a goddess.[21] This argument from analogy rests, of course, on false testimony, since the serpent has never tasted the fruit and possesses the power of speech only through demonic agency. But since Eve is unaware of the fraud, she accepts the evidence of her senses and mistakes the diabolical wonder for a true miracle; accordingly, the devil's argument seems plausible.[22] In persuad-

---

19. *Cf. Paradise Regained*, I, 259ff., III, 185ff., etc. Although Satan pretends to find the prophecies of suffering and adversity in the stars and in the tempest he himself has sent, they are (as his opponent already knows) present in Scripture.

20. *Paradise Regained*, III, 387, 409ff., 427ff., 436ff., IV, 147ff., 176ff., 321ff., etc.

21. Milton, *Art of Logic*, in *Works*, XI, 461; Aristotle, *Rhetorica*, Bk. I, Chap. 2, Bk. II, Chap. 22; Milton, *Works*, XI, 179ff., 193ff.

22. The devil's false miracles are examples of infernal testimony; for instances of the latter, see Miriam Joseph, *Shakespeare's Use of the Arts of Language*, 309.

ing his followers to rebel against Messiah, Satan argues from the commonplace of nobility, ingeniously deriving his argument from the angelic titles themselves and drawing the sophistical inference that the Son's vicegerency infringes natural and inalienable rights.[23] In tempting Christ, he exploits (as Howard Schultz has pointed out) the commonplaces of the voluptuous, active, and contemplative lives—"aught / By me propos'd in life contemplative, / Or active, tended on by glory or fame" (*PR*, IV, 369–71).

Even when Satan's arguments are not based on outright lies or false testimony, they usually involve sophistical fallacies, notably the fallacies of equivocation and *secundum quid*.[24] In seducing Eve, he plays on the ambiguity of the word *die*—plausibly, since she is herself ignorant of the full meaning of the term.

> So ye shall die perhaps, by putting off
> Human, to put on Gods, death to be wisht,
> Though threat'n'd, which no worse than this can bring.
> (*PL*, IX, 713–15)

This type of sophistical argument enables Satan to minimize or extenuate the basis of the contrary argument (the threat of death as the penalty for tasting the fruit) and to maximize the topic of its desirability. In exhorting his followers to rebel, the inference he draws from their "magnific Titles"—that these "assert / Our being ordain'd to govern, not to serve" (*PL*, V, 801–802)—is also sophistical. It is based on the fallacies of *secundum quid* and *ignoratio elenchi*, since "the affirmation and the denial are not concerned with the same point" and "the contrarietie is not perfect."[25] Although Satan treats "governing" and "serving" as contraries, their apparent contradiction is illusory, for they do not refer to the same objects. Governing others under a monarch is perfectly compatible with serving him. Indeed (as Milton's readers well knew), it was the basis of the historical feudal order, as well as the foundation of the hierarchical order of Heaven.

23. *Cf.* Milton, *Art of Logic*, in *Works*, XI, 218ff., on the argument from *notatio*.

24. *Cf. ibid.*, 476ff., on "homonymy or equivocation"; and A. Wolf, *Textbook of Logic* (2nd ed., rev.; New York, 1962), 281, on *A dicto secundum quid ad dictum simpliciter*.

25. *Cf.* Milton, *Art of Logic*, in *Works*, XI, 382ff; see Miriam Joseph, *Shakespeare's Use of the Arts of Language*, 371; and Aristotle, *De Sophisticis Elenchis*, in Ross (ed.), *Works*, Bk. I, Chap. 6.

PACIFIC UNIVERSITY LIBRARY
FOREST GROVE, OREGON

Satan similarly dismisses the doctrine of creation with a sophistry.

> who saw
> When this creation was? remember'st thou
> Thy making . . . ?
> We know no time when we were not as now;
> Know none before us.
>
>   (*PL*, V, 856–60)

Once again, the premise does not prove the conclusion—that the angels were not created but "self-begot, self-rais'd." Since the creature could not be present throughout his own creation and thus could not possibly see or remember it, this objection is invalid. It involves the fallacies of *ignoratio elenchi* and "false cause."[26]

Similar falsehoods and fallacies characterize Satan's speeches in Book I. The exclamation "fardest from him is best" might be valid if he were not referring to God himself, the Supreme Good. The statement "Whom reason hath equall'd, force hath made supreme / Above his equals" is an untruth based on the denial of divine omniscience. The proud boast that he "brings / A mind not to be chang'd by Place or Time" ignores the psychological ravages of spiritual death.

In *Paradise Regained* fallacies and equivocations remain the devil's principal weapons. He urges wealth, but not the virtue without which wealth itself is impotent, and hence commits the fallacy of false cause. He offers honor, but not the true glory of Heaven. He proposes arms, but these are actually evidence of human weakness; they prove the contrary of his argument. He offers kingdoms and learning, but these are no more than temporal power and the vain wisdom of the world. In most cases the fallacy results from the disparity between their meaning and value in the eyes of the world and in the eyes of God, between earthly and fleshly power or wisdom and their heavenly and spiritual counterparts. Glory, dominion, learning are ambiguous terms; they have a spiritual as well as a carnal significance, and these meanings are usually at variance. Hence the dialogue takes the form of proposition and refutation, statement and analysis, thesis and antithesis, assertion and objection. Satan

26. *Cf.* Milton, *Art of Logic,* in *Works,* XI, 380ff., on the fallacy of "non-cause as cause."

offers worldly ends, means, and rewards; the Messiah counters by exposing their falsity and contrasting them with their celestial analogues—the true values, the archetypal meanings. Rhetorically, the development of this dialogue hinges on the equivocal nature of Satan's allurements—their diverse, and indeed contrary, meanings for the spirit and the flesh.

Thus, in exhorting Christ to seek glory, Satan appeals to the example of the greatest conquerors of antiquity. His antagonist replies by defining earthly glory as the praise of the injudicious rabble and contrasting it with the true glory of Heaven, by dismissing the ideal of conquest as inglorious, and by condemning these "Benefactors" as malefactors. From the same premise, he draws the contrary conclusion. When Satan counters with another fallacy (based on analogy and *secundum quid*), arguing that since God the Father seeks glory, his Son should do the same, Christ replies by emphasizing the essential distinctions between primary and secondary ends and between God and man.[27] God does not seek "glory as prime end," and fallen man does not merit glory, but its contrary—"condemnation, ignominy, and shame." Similarly, when Satan offers Greek learning and wisdom, his opponent refutes him by condemning them as false wisdom. "Alas! what can they teach, and not mislead; / Ignorant of themselves, of God much more" (*PR*, IV, 309–10). By distinguishing between divine and earthly wisdom—true and false learning—Christ turns his Adversary's argument into its contrary.

In these temptation scenes, Satan consistently plays the role of the primeval liar and archsophist. He beguiles his companions "with calumnious Art of counterfeited truth." He seduces Eve with "glozing lies," overt flattery, and "persuasive words." (It is significant that Milton compares him to "some Orator renown'd / In *Athens* or free *Rome*.") He tempts the Messiah with "soothing words" and "persuasive Rhetoric."

Satan's eloquence represents an abuse of both logic and rhetoric; but it is nevertheless firmly rooted in classical tradition, and Milton himself had already attacked a similar misuse of rhetorical principles. Plato had stigmatized rhetoric as the art of flattery and *eidolon* of politics; he had condemned sophistry as a technique of

27. On "distinguishing" in replying to an opponent in debate or disputation, see Miriam Joseph, *Shakespeare's Use of the Arts of Language*, 379.

equivocation and illusion.[28] Satan himself brands the "Idolisms" and "Paradoxes" of classical Greece as "Error." The Lady of *Comus* despises the "dazzling fence" of her tempter's "Wit and gay Rhetoric," contrasting it with the "flame of sacred vehemence." In his pamphlets Milton scoffs at "the despicable trifles" of the rhetoricians, the "wretched bottlefuls of rhetoric paint and fustian dye," and "the rhetoric of the devil" and the apostate Julian.[29] When the hero of *Paradise Regained* scorns the "swelling Epithetes" of Greek poetry as mere "varnish on a Harlots cheek," he is echoing a familiar charge against the colors of rhetoric—that they are merely external ornament, mere fucus and "rhetorical cosmetic."[30]

Nevertheless, the devil's sophistries and rhetorical gambits do not go unchallenged. Just as Protagoras and Gorgias met their match in Socrates, so Satan must stand "confuted and convinc't / Of his weak arguing, and fallacious drift" (III, 3–4). Christ outreasons him. Abdiel refutes his heresies. Gabriel maneuvers him into contradicting himself. His falsehoods and fallacies demand a rebuttal, and in all of these debates we find his opponents making considerable use of objections and both ostensive and refutative enthymemes.[31]

In rebutting Satan's arguments, his adversaries usually follow a standard method of debate and disputation. They refute his points one by one and generally follow roughly the same order.[32] Thus Gabriel begins by countering Satan's opening jibe ("thou hadst . . . th' esteem of wise") and then challenges his second point ("Lives there who loves his pain?"). Similarly, Abdiel opens his speech by taking up Satan's first topic, the divine "Decree" appointing Messiah vicegerent, and then replies to an argument

28. Plato, *Gorgias* (London, 1925), 313–23.

29. Milton, *Prolusion #7*, in *Works*, XII, 277; *First Defence*, in *Works*, VII, 43; *Works*, VIII, 291.

30. *Cf.* Milton, *First Defence*, in *Works*, VII, 225, 343. For classical application of the term *fucus* to rhetorical ornament, see *Thesaurus Linguae Latinae* (10 vols. to date; Leipzig, 1900–), *s.v. fucus*. The word not only carries the sense of "rouge" or "paint for the complexion" but also implies "pretence, disguise, deceit, dissimulation."

31. On objections, see Aristotle's *Rhetorica*, Bk. II, Chap. 25; on ostensive, refutative, and apparent enthymemes, see *ibid.*, Bk. III, Chap. 17, Bk. II, Chaps. 22–24.

32. *Cf.* Miriam Joseph, *Shakespeare's Use of the Arts of Language*, 379, on this feature of disputation; and Aristotle, *Rhetorica*, Bk. III, Chap. 17.

the devil had advanced later in the same speech—the injustice of "assum[ing] Monarchy over . . . equals." In the first temptation of *Paradise Regained*, the Messiah begins with his opponent's final point (the devil's pain and grief), but then proceeds to answer his previous arguments in their original sequence: (1) the devil's boasted release from Hell, (2) his leave to enter Heaven itself, (3) his service to God through tempting Job and inspiring Ahab's "flattering Prophets" with lies, and finally, (4) his prophetic role in the Gentile oracles. Again, after the vision of the Parthian empire, Christ first passes judgment on the spectacle itself ("Much ostentation vain of fleshly arm"), and then refutes his Adversary's points in order: (1) Satan's argument that "prediction . . . supposes means," (2) his "politic maxims" concerning the expediency of choosing the Parthian empire rather than the Roman, and (3) his exhortation to deliver "thy brethren, those ten Tribes" of Israel. Subsequently, in countering Satan's exhortation to choose the Roman empire, Christ follows the same method, replying in order to the arguments of civil magnificence, the international embassies, the vicious character and vulnerability of the emperor, the opportunity to free "A victor people . . . from servile yoke," and the final threat that, without Roman power, his tenure on "David's Throne" will be either brief or impossible.

Similarly, in rejecting Satan's offer of the wisdom of Greece, the Messiah tends to follow the sequence of his Adversary's arguments, but with minor variations. After introducing the chief topic ("The *Gentiles* also know, and write, and teach"), the devil had developed it by appealing to the poetry, oratory, and philosophy of Athens and their value for the education of a king. In rebuttal, Christ answers Satan's first argument, the value of Gentile knowledge, and then takes up his opponent's fourth point (philosophy), finally replying to the remaining topics in order. Moreover, he discusses the philosophical schools of Greece in the same order as his opponent, except for introducing a reference to Pyrrhonism.

In these speeches, as in other debate scenes such as the infernal council in *Paradise Lost*, the rebuttal usually refutes the opponent's arguments in the sequence in which they were first proposed. But this order is not observed strictly, nor is there generally an attempt to answer every point raised by the preceding speaker. Nevertheless, the structural development of argument and counterargument, speech and counterspeech, remains roughly parallel; and as a result the dialogue acquires something of the formality of an oratorical disputation or debate.

These adversaries of Satan exhibit an altogether different rhetorical ideal from that of their opponent. As Aristotle had pointed out, rhetoric can be both used and abused. As an instrument of persuasion, it can exhort either to virtue or to vice. The unscrupulous rhetorician, he explains, stands in the same relationship to the conscientious orator as the sophist to the logician.[33] (Milton makes a similar distinction between "ignorant and libidinous poetasters" who instill "vicious principles" and true poets who exhort to virtue.)[34] In both epics, as in *Comus*, the tempter and the tempted embody opposing conceptions of the rhetorician, comparable to the moral antithesis between sophist and logician. Whereas Comus and Satan abuse the art of rhetoric, their opponents—the Lady, Abdiel, and Christ—represent the true and valid use of eloquence.[35] They exemplify its principal characteristics in their oratory, and Milton himself points out its distinctive attributes in his prose.

Unlike its specious counterpart, this ideal rhetoric is sincere— and often divinely inspired. It aims at truth rather than deception. Instead of the studied art of superficial adornment, it relies on the spontaneous eloquence of inner conviction or supernatural inspiration. The Lady's "sacred vehemence" is inspired by her theme, "the sage and serious doctrine of Virginity."[36] Her opponent himself observes that "Her words [are] set off by som superior power." In contrast to Satan's simulated passion—the "shew of Zeal and Love" that beguiles Eve—Abdiel, the "fervent angel," bears witness to the truth with unaffected eloquence and unsimulated emotion—"a flame of zeale severe." This type of eloquence also characterizes the isolated "just men" who defend the truth against a corrupt world and devote their powers of persuasion to exhorting their wicked contemporaries to repent.

Moreover, this "sacred eloquence" proves indispensable for

33. *Cf.* Aristotle, *Rhetorica*, Bk. I, Chap. 1.

34. *Cf.* Ida Langdon, *Milton's Theory of Poetry and Fine Art* (New Haven, 1924); and Diekhoff, *Milton's "Paradise Lost,"* 1–12.

35. For parallels between Comus and Satan as tempters, see *Paradise Lost,* ed. Merritt Y. Hughes (New York, 1935), 290.

36. Nevertheless, though this topic inspires the Lady, she never reveals the doctrine. She asserts its truth instead of demonstrating it. Her remarks on the subject (ll. 780–99) involve ethical and pathetic rather than logical proof.

Christ's ministry of redemption. It serves as a principal means for establishing and expanding his spiritual kingdom. Persuasion and instruction, the functions of the good orator and teacher, belong to his "prophetic" role as mediator.[37] They are, he maintains, nobler and more effective instruments of government than force; it is

> more humane, more heavenly first
> By winning words to conquer willing hearts,
> *And make perswasion do the work of fear;*
> At least to try, and teach the erring Soul
> Not wilfully mis-doing, but unaware
> Misled.
>
> (*PR*, I, 221–26, italics mine)

Hence, in rejecting "Riches and Realms," the Son demonstrates his preference for persuasion rather than violence. He chooses to advance his spiritual empire, the Church, by teaching and exhortation, by word and by his own example (I, 473ff.).

Milton himself held strong views on this subject, and his prose tracts dwell at length on the superiority of persuasion to force in church and state alike. Christian perfection should not "be forced upon us by compulsion and penal laws, but must be produced, if at all, by exhortation and Christian admonition." In "all wise apprehensions the perswasive power in man to win others to goodnesse by instruction is greater, and more divine, then the compulsive power to restraine men from being evill by terrour of the Law." Hence "Christ left *Moses* to be the Law-giver, but himselfe came downe amongst us to bee a teacher." The "great art" in government is "to discern in what the law is to bid restraint and punishment, and in what things perswasion only is to work." Since the law cannot remedy "inward vices" by "outward constraint," it must leave them to "conscience and perswasion."[38]

Thus for Milton sacred eloquence is an essential tool of the Christian minister. The "Churchmans office" is "to exhort" and to "teach men the Christian faith." The "provinces of teaching and of exhortation . . . are both alike assigned to the pastor, no less than to the teacher so called; the functions are twofold, but the office and the agent are one." The same dual functions also be-

37. See Milton, *De Doctrina Christiana*, Bk. I, Chap. 15.
38. Milton, *De Doctrina Christiana*, in *Works*, XV, 159; *Animadversions*, in *Works*, III, 165; *Tetrachordon*, in *Works*, IV, 157; *Areopagitica*, in *Works*, IV, 318–19.

long to the poet. In proposing "wise and artfull recitations" for "instructing and bettering the Nation," Milton suggests that they be held not only in pulpits but also "after another persuasive method, at set and solemn Paneguries, in Theaters, porches, or what other place."[39]

What are the salient features of this Christian rhetoric? As Milton describes them in his prose or verse, they consist primarily in the speaker's own virtue, in truth, and in clarity. "True eloquence" is "the daughter of virtue," he quotes Plato as saying, and it is nothing other than "the serious and hearty love of truth." No orator can "be truly eloquent" who is not "a good man," for the "most eloquent" art "approaches neerest to nature," and "they express nature best, who in their lives least wander from her safe leading, which may be call'd regenerate reason." Milton himself "boast[s] of no other eloquence than that persuasion which is inherent in truth itself."[40] These two qualities are, for him, the only valid foundation for ethical and logical proof. They are also the most effective.

Finally, true eloquence demands clarity. When Christ rejects the "Arts and Eloquence" of Athens, he contrasts them with the "majestic unaffected stile" of the Hebrew prophets, whose plainer discourse, largely stripped of superficial adornment, can teach the "rules of Civil Government" more effectively than "all the Oratory of *Greece* and *Rome*."

> In them [the prophets] is plainest taught, and easiest learnt,
> What makes a Nation happy, and keeps it so,
> What ruins Kingdoms, and lays Cities flat.
>
> (*PR*, IV, 361–63)

The classical orators (as Plato himself observed) presented the mere *eidolon* of politics; the Hebrew prophets (as Milton argues) expressed the idea.

In renouncing profane rhetoric for sacred eloquence, the hero of *Paradise Regained* attacks classical eloquence on three grounds. First, it cannot teach without misleading, for Greek learning at best is ignorant of the truth and can teach only the "false resemblance" of wisdom. Second, what it does teach it teaches badly.

39. Milton, *Of Reformation*, in *Works*, III, 40; *De Doctrina Christiana*, in *Works*, XVI, 239; *Reason of Church-Government*, in *Works*, III, 240.

40. Milton, *Reason of Church-Government*, in *Works*, III, 181; *An Apology*, in *Works*, III, 287, 363; *Second Defence*, in *Works*, VIII, 105.

Not only does it contain little of profit, but it celebrates vice as virtue. Finally, it makes its appeal primarily through extrinsic ornament rather than through plain truth.

Since this scene has often been misinterpreted as puritanical obscurantism—a revulsion against the classical studies that had delighted Milton's youth and dominated his scheme of education—we must emphasize its limited scope and its actual function in the drama of temptation. The chief issue at this point in the dialogue is the choice of rhetorical technique. The essential question for the speakers is not so much the value of classical studies as the type of eloquence Christ must employ in his chosen role as teacher in establishing his kingdom through instruction and exhortation. The scene develops logically out of the preceding temptations. Acknowledging Christ's preference for ruling by persuasion rather than by force, Satan alters his tactics to cope with this new turn. Hence he presents Greek learning less as an end in itself than as a means to an end, as an instrument of persuasion.

> And with the *Gentiles* much thou must converse,
> Ruling them by perswasion as thou mean'st,
> Without thir learning how wilt thou with them,
> Or they with thee hold conversation meet?
> How wilt thou reason with them, how refute
> Thir Idolisms, Traditions, Paradoxes?
>
> (*PR*, IV, 229–34)

When the Messiah rejects classical eloquence for biblical plainness, he conforms to a pattern that Milton's contemporaries regarded as historical. For the Reformation, the plainness and simplicity of Scripture were proverbial, especially the sayings attributed to Jesus in the Gospels. In style and diction these seemed to have been intentionally adapted to the capacities of an unlearned and even an illiterate audience. Christ's rejection of Greek rhetoric is consistent with the type of plain, unaffected eloquence the Scriptures reported him as using. No sound critic could possibly argue that the Messiah spoke like Isocrates or Gorgias, Cicero or Demosthenes. His attitude toward Hellenic eloquence, as Milton describes it, fits historical fact and conforms to the principle of decorum.

Milton is not condemning the classics per se so much as he is censuring the use of classical rhetoric for "evangellic perswasion." [41] One may, with plausibility, interpret the Son's rejection of classical rhetoric as an attack on the pulpit eloquence of his day or a condemnation of the viewpoint that led Cardinal Bembo to prefer the style of Cicero to that of the Bible. But it would be a mistake to construe the Messiah's plainness as Milton's unqualified dismissal of Hellenic civilization.

Since this Christian oratory is based largely on virtue and truth, it differs radically from its Satanic counterpart. Insofar as the speech itself reflects the moral character of the speaker, it serves as ethical proof. Yet, in contrast to the oratory of Satan and Belial, this is not merely a rhetorical device. Whereas Satan assumes a false character to acquire greater plausibility, the ethical proofs of Christ and Abdiel, Gabriel and Michael are based on their real character. In these cases, the disparity between rhetorical and poetic *ethos*—so marked in Satan and Belial—tends to disappear. [42]

Another result of the confrontation of these contrasting rhetorical modes is epistemological. It tends to reduce the dialogue to a clear-cut debate between truth and falsehood. Abdiel, the witness (or martyr) to truth, refutes Satan's lies. The argument of *Paradise Regained* proclaims "the Tempter foil'd / In all his wiles," and the nature of the spiritual duel is summed up in the final line of Book III: "So fares it when with truth falsehood contends."

Nor is it surprising that Milton's epics borrow freely from the conventions of demonstrative oratory. A literary genre traditionally devoted to praising heroic virtue could hardly dispense with the branch of rhetoric specifically concerned with praise and dispraise, honor and shame. The temptation motif itself, so central to the plot of both poems, has rhetorical force; by subjecting the hero's virtue or vice, strength or frailty, to trial, it demonstrates his true worth. By testing his merits, it proves them worthy of praise or shame.

This consideration, moreover, was one of the factors that led Milton to prefer the theme of spiritual combat to that of physical warfare. The latter is not only subject to the vagaries of fortune,

41. Milton, *History of Britain*, in *Works*, X, 322.
42. Among the devils this disparity occurs primarily in the more sophisticated orators; it does not appear in the simpler oratory of Moloch in *Paradise Lost* or in the speeches of Belial in *Paradise Regained*. In both of the latter instances ethical proof is based on real rather than assumed character.

but at best can merely demonstrate the hero's physical strength and military skill. It does not prove his piety, nor does it provide the best test of his prudence or wisdom.[43]

Spiritual warfare, on the other hand, tests and proves higher virtues. In *Paradise Regained*, after the champion has demonstrated his "wisdom" against "hellish wiles," he leaves

> his Victorious Field
> Against the Spiritual Foe . . .
> By *proof* the undoubted Son of God.
> (I, 9–11, italics mine)

The ordeal of temptation is designed "To shew him worthy of his birth divine / And high prediction" (I, 141–42), just as Job's trials had served "To prove him, and illustrate his high worth" (I, 370). In *Comus* the tempter's efforts "to try" the Lady's virtue end by confirming it more clearly. In such cases temptation serves as a demonstrative argument; by testing virtue the ordeal proves it worthy of praise.

In *Paradise Lost* temptation performs the same function in the case of Abdiel, who alone among Satan's followers resists the latter's sophistries and bears witness to the truth. But in the central episode, Satan's temptation of Eve and her seduction of Adam, it does precisely the opposite. Here temptation demonstrates weakness rather than strength, vice rather than virtue, serving as an argument for shame rather than praise.

This is a striking innovation in the heroic tradition, but Milton knew what he was doing. The example of Adam—created perfect, without tincture of original sin—serves as an argument from the greater to the less. If unfallen man fell into sin, despite his pristine perfection, despite his possession of a will and intellect uncorrupted by sin and spiritual death, how much less can fallen man avoid sinning! How much less can he hope, by his own unaided efforts, to triumph over evil! Adam's example thus functions as a deliberate argument, persuading his fallen descendants to rely not on their own merits but on divine grace. By stressing human frailty on one hand, and the value of repentance and faith on the other, the poem exhorts its reader to trust in divine mercy and Providence.

43. The basic issue is that of the proper *matter* of the various virtues and vices. See Aristotle's *Nicomachean Ethics*, in *The Student's Oxford Aristotle*, trans. W. D. Ross (6 vols.; London, 1942), V; and Milton's *De Doctrina Christiana*, Bk. II.

But this example also functions as a demonstrative argument; by illustrating man's frailty, by proving his demerit, it inculcates a sense of shame. In *Paradise Lost* the glory and honor belong primarily to God and his Messiah; the virtues and "acts of benefit" that Milton celebrates—the Son's victory over the rebels, his creation of the world, his redemption of man—are, for the most part, divine virtues and divine acts. The chief action on the human plane, conversely, is a crime. Instead of glory, it incurs shame; in place of honor, dishonor.

In thus emphasizing the antithesis between divine merit and human demerit, Milton radically alters the traditional character of the heroic poem. But he is not content simply to take "Man's First Disobedience" as his epic argument and the archetypal sinner as his epic person. Instead, he underlines his point by altering the conventional character of the epic machinery. Investing Satan with qualities of an epic hero and his activities with attributes of an epic enterprise, Milton develops his infernal machines in a quasi-heroic manner that, in effect, judges and condemns practically the entire heroic tradition. Satan acts like a conventional epic hero, but his exploits are crimes, his apparent heroism is brutishness, and his final rewards are not the glory and honor he expects (the conventional guerdon of an epic hero), but ignominy and shame. Satan's example, like Adam's, serves both as a deliberative and demonstrative argument. Conversely, Milton develops his divine machinery heroically, treating the Son as a heroic archetype whose exploits demonstrate his divine virtues and win divine honors as their merited reward.

Milton's treatment of demonstrative topics is, however, far more complex than is customary in heroic poetry or demonstrative rhetoric. Virtue and vice, merit and demerit, praise and shame, have opposite meanings in the eyes of the world and the sight of God. Abdiel incurs scorn and reproach from Satan and his legions, but wins praise from God and the faithful angels. The fallen world heaps contumely on the isolated just men, but God rewards them with fame in Heaven. The corrupt world judges amiss. Fallen Eve praises Adam's decision to die with her as a "glorious trial" of heroic love. Fallen Adam extols his wife's judgment and taste. In a deliberate parody of Father and Son, Sin and Death glorify their parent with a "Monument of merit," and he in turn honors them by making them his vicegerents on earth. Satan praises the exploits of his legions while they honor him as a god.

The fallen world rewards virtue with scorn and infamy with fame; Heaven, on the contrary, requites the world's heroes with shame and the objects of the world's contempt with glory.

The conventional topics of demonstrative oratory dominate the dialogue of *Paradise Regained*, but here Milton normally develops them as deliberative arguments. Satan exploits them primarily to persuade the hero to seek secular ends and means. Yet the poet does at times treat these topics demonstratively, often through divine testimony. At the beginning of the poem John the Baptist bears witness to Christ as "his worthier," and the Spirit of God pronounces him "his beloved Son." In the celestial council the Father emphasizes his "merit" and "consummate virtue" while the angelic chorus sings a hymn of praise. Moreover, in both infernal councils Satan acknowledges Jesus' worth. The poem ends with "Heavenly Anthems" celebrating his victories. At such points the poem approaches the techniques of demonstrative rhetoric.

If judicial rhetoric plays a much more prominent part in *Paradise Lost* than in most heroic poems, the reason lies partly in Milton's choice of argument ("Man's First Disobedience" and its condign punishment) and partly in his avowed intent to "assert eternal Providence / And justifie the wayes of God to men" (I, 25–26). In the former instance Milton is, on the whole, pleading the case for the prosecution; in the latter he holds the brief for the defense. In both, he appropriately makes use of the branch of rhetoric specifically concerned with defense and accusation, justice and injustice, the law and the causes of evil. The principal topics in his argument—crime and punishment, extenuating circumstances and degree of guilt, justice and mercy—belong properly to judicial oratory. The celestial council of Book III (as recent scholarship has pointed out), follows a judicial or legalistic interpretation of the Incarnation.[44] Father and Son debate the issues of mercy and justice. The Father "clears his own Justice and Widsom" by arguing that he had "created Man free and able enough to have withstood the Tempter" (III, Argument). He justifies the differences in his treatment of fallen angel and fallen man by arguing that the latter "fell not of his own malice, as did *Satan*, but by him seduc't."

44. See C. A. Patrides, "Milton and the Protestant Theory of the Atonement," *PMLA*, LXXIV (1959), 7–13.

In order "to render Man inexcusable," he "sends *Raphael* to admonish him of his obedience, of his free estate, of his enemy near
at hand" (V, Argument). After the Fall he dispatches the Son to
pass "the mortal sentence" on man's "transgression"—a sign that
he intends "Mercy colleague with Justice." The final books describe the execution of this sentence. Sin and Death wreak havoc
in the universe. Michael expels Adam and Eve from the garden;
his prophecy is heavily weighted with judicial topics—the Law
and the Gospel, the Old and New Covenants, God's judgments
and promises, the dire consequences of Adam's crime, divine justice and mercy, "supernal Grace contending / With sinfulness of
Men." Similarly, Raphael's speech traces the beginning of Satan's
disobedience and its punishment. The allegory of Sin and Death
illustrates the origin, nature, and punishment of evil. In the transformation scene of Book X, divine justice punishes Satan "in the
shape he sinn'd" according to the doom pronounced on the serpent; his companions share his punishment as accessories. From
the opening lines to the final verse, from the statement of the
argument to the expulsion from Paradise, from angelic prehistory
to the Last Judgment, the poem is concerned, in fable and episodes alike, with sin and its punishment or remission.

No other heroic poem has provided so full or so detailed an
anatomy of the causes and effects of sin. Defending divine justice
by placing the blame squarely on man and his tempter, Milton
follows the Ramist theologians in their complex analysis of the
causal structure of the Fall. In the opening section of the poem he
raises the question of impulsive cause:[45]

> say first what cause
> Mov'd our Grand Parents . . .
> . . . to fall off
> From thir Creator . . .
>
> . . . .
> Th' infernal Serpent; he it was.
>
>   (*PL*, I, 27–34)

In the celestial council of Book III, Milton takes pains to refute the
possible charge that God is the author or efficient cause of sin.[46]
This had long been a stumbling block for divine apologists in

---

45. See Howard, "'The Invention' of Milton's 'Great Argument,'" for a fuller
discussion of this point.
46. See Milton, *Art of Logic*, in *Works*, XI, 28ff., on "procreant causes."

theological controversies on predestination and foreknowledge, and in the *De Doctrina Christiana*, Milton had taken pains to answer it.

Reformed theologians were acutely sensitive to this problem. To regard God as the "author of sin" seemed blasphemous, but the tenor of their doctrines—their emphasis on general and special Providence, their views on predestination, the severe limitations they placed on the human will after the Fall—laid them open to this charge. Calvin's followers might vehemently deny it, but his Roman Catholic opponents continued to accuse him of this doctrine. Arminians leveled the same objection against orthodox Calvinism.[47] Although Milton shared the more liberal Arminian views on predestination and free will, he was painfully aware of the problem, and indeed his remarks on the subject in the *De Doctrina Christiana* and the divorce tracts indicate a concern to clear the Deity of this possible accusation.[48] In *Paradise Lost* he makes the vindication of divine justice a principal objective.

To demonstrate that God is not the author of sin, Milton attempts to prove that the blame lies with the sinner himself, through his abuse of free will. Adam and Eve are "Authors to themselves in all / Both what they judge and what they choose" (III, 122–23). The "fault" is their own, for they were created free, "nor can justly accuse / Thir maker, or thir making, or thir Fate" (III, 112–13). Michael makes an analogous point when he brands Satan as author of evil.[49] Satan himself exonerates the divine justice and confesses his own responsibility for his revolt; endowed with free will, he is guilty on the same grounds that subsequently incriminate Adam and Eve.

> Hadst thou the same free Will and Power to stand?
> Thou hadst: whom has thou then or what to accuse,
> But Heav'ns free Love dealt equally to all?
>
> (IV, 66–68)

47. *Cf.* A. W. Harrison, *The Beginnings of Arminianism to the Synod of Dort* (London, 1926), 37, 62–63, and *passim;* and Milton, *Of True Religion*, in *Works*, VI, 169.

48. See Milton, *De Doctrina Christiana*, Bk. I, Chaps. 3, 4, 12; Milton, *Doctrine and Discipline of Divorce*, in *Works*, III, 440, 442; *Tetrachordon*, in *Works*, IV, 157; Maurice Kelley, *This Great Argument* (Princeton, 1941); and Merritt Y. Hughes, "The Filiations of Milton's Celestial Dialogue," in *Ten Perspectives on Milton* (New Haven, 1965), 104–35. In *The Doctrine and Discipline of Divorce* (*Works*, III, 440), Milton observes that "the Jesuits, and that sect among us which is nam'd of *Arminius,* are wont to charge us of making God the author of sinne."

49. See *Paradise Lost*, II, 381, 864, and X, 236, 356.

Finally, the self-accusations of Adam and Eve shift the blame from God's justice to themselves. Adam confesses that his "punishment" is "justly" at God's "Will" and that "his doom is fair."

> Him after all Disputes
> Forc't I absolve: all my evasions vain
> And reasonings . . . lead me still
> But to my own conviction: first and last
> On mee, mee only, as the source and spring
> Of all corruption, all the blame lights due.
>   (X, 828–33)

Eve, in turn, blames herself as "sole cause" of Adam's "woe": "both have sinn'd, but thou / Against God only, I against God and thee" (X, 930–31).

In thus fixing the responsibility for sin on the creature rather than the Creator, Milton relies partly on "artificial" arguments (logical demonstration), but also on "inartificial" arguments, such as the sinner's own confession (a form of "human testimony").[50] In *Samson Agonistes*, Milton employs the same techniques in proving that "Just are the ways of God, / And justifiable to men."

> Appoint not heavenly disposition, Father,
> Nothing of all these evils hath befall'n me
> But justly; I myself have brought them on,
> Sole Author I, sole cause.
>   (SA, 373–76)

Thus all three of the "kinds of speaking" (as Milton refers to them in his First Prolusion)—"whether demonstrative or deliberative or judicial—occur in his poetry. They link the oratory of *Paradise Lost* and its sister epic with pre-Ramist rhetorical traditions.[51]

In neglecting the rhetorical techniques that underlie the speeches in *Paradise Lost*—and, more particularly, in blurring the distinc-

---

50. For confession as testimony, see Aristotle, *Rhetorica*, Bk. I, Chap. 15; and Miriam Joseph, *Shakespeare's Use of the Arts of Language*, 309.

51. Milton, *Works*, XII, 119. Although Milton's *Ars Logica* does not discuss the traditional three kinds of oratory, it leans heavily on Cicero and Aristotle as well as on Ramus. There is no inconsistency in this combination of Ramist and traditional rhetoric, since Ramus regarded himself as a purifier and restorer of Aristotelian doctrine rather than as an opponent. Milton's commitment to the Ramist reorganization of logic and rhetoric did not mean a decisive break with Aristotelian and Ciceronian tradition.

tion between *ethos* and *dianoia*—critics have usually done scant justice to Milton's methods of characterization. In the case of Satan, they have mistaken thought for character and rhetorical for poetic *ethos*. In the case of Milton's God, they have emphasized the unpleasant impressions left by his discourse without considering the particular rhetorical ends it was intended to serve.

Although there is indeed a striking difference in tone between Satan's orations in the first book and his soliloquy on Mount Niphates, this does not spring (as critics have often argued) from inconsistency in character, but rather from different rhetorical functions. The dissimilarity is, on the whole, less ethical than rhetorical. Although the orations and the soliloquy do exhibit profound contrasts in *dianoia* and in rhetorical *ethos*, the poetic *ethos* (the revelation of Satan's moral purpose) is essentially the same.

Moreover, though Satan's opening speech is heroic in tone whereas his soliloquy is tragic, both reveal the same character traits and the same motives. Both concern the same theological concepts (repentance and grace) and the same psychological affections ("disdain" and "dread of shame"). Both reveal the same moral defect—the obdurate and unrepentant will that, in Milton's *De Doctrina Christiana*, characterizes the unregenerate sinner and the reprobate.[52] On the first occasion Satan boasts that he *will* not (or *does* not) "repent" or "sue for grace"; on the second, he laments that he *cannot*. In the former case he disguises his refusal to repent as heroic constancy and a voluntary choice; in the latter he recognizes it as a vice and a tragic necessity. In this first oration Satan hails his rebellion as a heroic exploit, a "Glorious Enterprize"; in his later speech he condemns it as sin, the fruit of malice, pride, and "worse Ambition." In the former he depicts his hate and "study of revenge" as heroic qualities, facets of an indomitable courage. In the latter he sees them as the only alternative left him, since "true reconcilement" is impossible. The pretense of an "unconquerable will" turns out, in reality, to be no more than *servum arbitrium*, the "bondage of the will." Satan is enslaved to his own evil.

The following speeches of Satan in *Paradise Lost* involve a similar fusion of character and thought, real and assumed *ethos*. In Satan's deliberate choice of evil,

52. See Milton, *De Doctrina Christiana*, Bk. I, Chap. 4.

> To do aught good never will be our task,
> But ever to do ill our sole delight,
> As being the contrary to his high will
> Whom we resist;
>
> $\qquad\qquad\qquad$ (I, 159–62)

and in his monarchal ambitions,

> Here we may reign secure, and in my choice
> To reign is worth ambition though in Hell,
> $\qquad\qquad$ (I, 261–62)

he reveals his true motives; and they are practically identical with those that conclude his soliloquy on Mount Niphates:

> Evil be thou my Good; by thee at least
> Divided Empire with Heav'ns King I hold
> By thee, and more than half perhaps will reign.
> $\qquad\qquad$ (IV, 110–12)

All three of these speeches reveal essentially the same *ethos*, but rhetorically they are poles apart. In the former instance Satan presents these motives heroically and couples them with courage and hope. In the latter case, however, "all hope is excluded"; they spring from despair.

Yet if despair is explicit in the soliloquy, it is nevertheless implicit in Satan's first oration. There is no real contradiction between the two in *ethos*, and Milton's reference to the speaker's despair is apposite. In both speeches Milton has delineated the characteristic moral traits of the hardened and unrepentant sinner. One of the latter's distinctive attributes, a quality unique to him, is despair. As the *De Doctrina Christiana* observes, this "takes place only in the reprobate." [53]

But if Satan's despair is consistent both with the *ethos* of his first speech and with the later development of his character, so is his "vaunting." An even more exaggerated boasting marks his speeches in Heaven, earlier in time but later in the poetic narrative. One of the problems Milton faced in depicting the fallen archangel was to preserve some degree of continuity with his character before his exile from Heaven; another problem was to foreshadow the particular traits he would later display in seducing Eve. Before his expulsion he envies Messiah's glory; after his fall he envies the native glory of man. Satan's ambition, desire of glory and empire, and affectation of deity remain after his expul-

53. See *ibid.*, Bk. II, Chap. 3.

sion from Heaven; they link the fallen angel with the unfallen rebel. On the other hand, his unwavering hatred, his pursuit of revenge, his commitment to evil, his attempt to frustrate the divine will—motives that dominate his first orations in the poem—lead directly to his assault on man. The boasts he utters to Beëlzebub and his fallen legions are, in a sense, echoes of his vaunts in Heaven.

Moreover, these motives are consistent with the character of Lucifer as represented in Isaiah 14. According to Aristotle's *Poetics*, character should be "like the reality." [54] The poet (as commentators explained) should represent a person's *ethos* as historical and literary tradition had depicted it. For most of Milton's contemporaries, Lucifer's distinctive traits appeared in his extravagant but empty boasts to "exalt his throne above the stars of God" and to "be like the most High." This passage not only revealed the ambition and pride that would subsequently become proverbial but also fixed his character as the braggart. Commentators emphasized his "vaunting" or "glorying" (*gloriatio*) and compared him to the boastful Thraso. [55] Milton follows this aspect of biblical tradition, both in his account of the rebellion itself and in his description of Satan's behavior after his fall. In his "vaunting aloud" and "glorying" in his own strength, the devil conforms to the pattern already established in Isaiah.

The speeches of the Father in Books III and V of *Paradise Lost* have antagonized more than one generation of readers. Some have blamed Milton's theology, others his personal piety, and still others his craftsmanship and literary tact. Yet, though they have differed as to the cause, most of them have agreed in treating the Father's oratory as essentially a problem of characterization, a matter of *ethos*. Nevertheless, it is equally, if not primarily, a problem of *dianoia*. Much of the responsibility lies with Milton's rhetorical methods.

Aside from the limitations imposed by literary genre (whether pagan or Christian, the divine machinery in a heroic poem must necessarily be anthropomorphic), Milton faced certain major rhetorical problems that resulted from his avowed intent to "assert

54. *Aristotle on the Art of Poetry*, 56.

55. See *Biblia Sacra*, ed. F. Junius, trans. and annotated by Immanuel Tremellius and Franciscus Junius (London, 1593), especially the note on Isaiah 14 : 13; and Haymo of Halberstadt, *Patrologia Latina*, J.-P. Migne (comp.), CXVI (Paris, 1879), col. 792.

eternal Providence / And justifie the wayes of God to men" (I, 25–26). This purpose involved him in judicial rhetoric. It was directly responsible for the passages in which the Father attempts to clear "his own Justice and Wisdom from all imputation" (III, Argument). It required that the poet emphasize Jehovah's principal decrees, especially predestination.[56] It compelled him to stress not only the divine law that Adam and Eve transgress but also the sentence of condemnation passed on them and the actual infliction of punishment. These legalistic aspects of Providence may seem repugnant to a modern audience, but they derive largely from Milton's commitment to judicial rhetoric. Paradoxically, the features that have antagonized his readers result from his attempt to demonstrate that his God is both merciful and just.

Nearly all the arguments Milton assigns to the Father are theological commonplaces, and had the poet presented them through another speaker they might have left a different impression. When ascribed to God himself, when presented in anthropomorphic terms, these arguments inevitably invite comparison with human justice, and the analogy is hardly fair to Jehovah. As Aristotle had observed, a speaker cannot make certain assertions about himself or his opponent without exciting dislike or seeming "abusive or ill-bred," and "such remarks, therefore, [should be put] into the mouth of some third person."[57] The responsibility for the unfavorable effect the Father's speeches have sometimes produced on the reader is due to a combination of two factors. Taken alone, neither Milton's anthropomorphic technique nor his arguments in defense of divine justice should have prejudiced his audience against his God. The difficulty arises from the fact that it is Jehovah himself who is advancing these arguments, that it is the speaker himself who praises his own virtues and casts blame and reproach on his adversaries. When he employs the terminology and arguments of theologians, he can hardly avoid looking like a "school-divine."

Yet one cannot really censure either Milton's theology or his craftsmanship. Within the framework of the heroic tradition, it was conventional to present the divine decrees directly, through the mouth of Jove or Jehovah himself. Homer and Virgil had set the precedent, and poets as orthodox as Tasso and Vida had fol-

56. Milton, *De Doctrina Christiana*, Bk. I, Chaps. 3, 4.
57. Aristotle, *Rhetorica*, Bk. III, Chap. 17.

lowed it. Indeed, their portraits of the Christian God are, if anything, more anthropomorphic than Milton's.

The topics of judicial rhetoric are largely responsible for the unfortunate impression sometimes left by the Father's oratory.[58] As with other passages in *Paradise Lost*, critics have mistaken rhetorical techniques for methods of characterization and *dianoia* for *ethos*.

In both of Milton's epics there is a striking disproportion between fable and thought, *mythos* and *dianoia*. For Aristotle, the former is the very "life and soul"of the poem; for Milton, action sometimes yields to dialogue. In *Paradise Regained*, for example, thought tends to take precedence over fable. If, like other heroic poems, this epic arouses "passion or admiration," it evokes them as much by "the wily subtleties and refluxes of man's thoughts from within" as by "the changes of that which is called fortune from without."[59] To arouse wonder or marvel—the characteristic affection of the heroic poem—this epic relies more on rhetorical argument, on *dianoia*, than on action.

On the whole, this disproportion reflects Milton's preference for spiritual rather than physical warfare. The Book of Job, that biblical epic of spiritual combat and heroic temptation, exhibited a similar imbalance between action and dialogue.[60] Moreover, the concept of patience and "Heroic Martyrdom" as a "better fortitude" inevitably affected the relationship of fable and thought. The patient witness (martyr) to truth tends to suffer rather than act; unlike most epic heroes he is not the agent of violent deeds but is their victim. In his case the heroic ordeal is less action than passion. And since the contest of reason is superior to that of force, he defends truth primarily through argument rather than by the sword, by "sacred eloquence" rather than force of arms, by thought rather than deed.

58. In condemning the Father's "self-*justifying* soliloquies," A. J. A. Waldock (*"Paradise Lost" and Its Critics* [Cambridge, 1947], 99) overlooks their affinities with judicial rhetoric, as does F. E. Hutchinson (*Milton and the English Mind* [London, 1949], 124–25), who objects that Milton makes "the Almighty *argue like a lawyer*" (italics mine).

59. *Aristotle on the Art of Poetry*, 38; Langdon, *Milton's Theory of Poetry and Fine Art*, 220; Milton, *Reason of Church-Government*.

60. See Charles W. Jones, "Milton's Brief Epic," *Studies in Philology*, XLIV (1947), 209–27; Barbara Kiefer Lewalski, *Milton's Brief Epic: The Genre, Meaning, and Art of "Paradise Regained"* (Providence, R.I., 1966).

Like *dianoia*, *ethos* assumes far greater importance in Milton's epics than in most heroic poetry. Like the *Odyssey*, these are "stories of character," but, unlike Homer's poem, they place much greater emphasis on character than on action.[61]

This emphasis is not without its implications for style. In the speeches of both epics, the critic must not merely distinguish between real and assumed *ethos* and between character and thought. He must also consider their bearing on levels of discourse. In employing a plainer style for *Paradise Regained*, Milton was following Aristotle's principles as well as the rhetorical tenets expressed in his own prose. Truth, he believed, does not require adornment; it argues most effectively of itself. Presented with clarity and perspicuity, it offers per se the soundest proofs and the most effective arguments. Since this epic demonstrates the hero's moral character and intellectual powers primarily through argument, and since the poem consists largely of dialogue and the expression of *ethos* and *dianoia*, it naturally demands a style suitable for revealing character and thought—a style lucid, plain, perspicuous, unaffected, and unadorned. Such a style was completely in character, and since it was consistent with the simplicity of Christ's discourse in the Gospels, it seemed "like the reality." Moreover, because it was best adapted to teaching, this style furthered Christ's ministry of redemption. Since it was "low" (the *stylus humilis*), it befitted his humiliation.

61. *Aristotle on the Art of Poetry*, 81.

PART III

Greatness of Mind: Samson Agonistes and Paradise Regained

Oh how comely it is and how reviving
To the Spirits of just men long opprest!
When God into the hands of thir deliverer
Puts invincible might
To quell the mighty of the Earth, th' oppressour,
The brute and boist'rous force of violent men

. . . .

He all thir Ammunition
And feats of War defeats
With plain Heroic magnitude of mind
And celestial vigour arm'd

. . . .

*   But patience is more oft the exercise*
Of Saints, the trial of thir fortitude,
Making them each his own Deliverer,
And Victor over all
That tyrannie or fortune can inflict.

—Milton, Samson Agonistes

CHAPTER 6

Heroes and Orators: Dialectical Process in Milton's Major Poetry

ALL THREE of Milton's major poems center on the themes of man's fall and restoration; and whether considered separately or ensemble, all three are themselves exemplars and agents of a literary instauration and revolution. They achieve not only the revival and restoration of the classical poetic genres but also a significant revaluation and reorientation. And the poet accomplishes his *coup de main* (and *coup d'état*) largely through a process of radical asceticism and renunciation: the qualified rejection of the conventional heroic argument of warfare and its displacement (in whole or in part) by the ordeal of spiritual combat. This involves, with few exceptions, the substitution of dialectical process for the carnage of the battlefield or the dazzling farce of swordplay, and of right reason (or its specious counterfeit) for martial valor. In *Paradise Lost*, the Adversary conquers a world by false premises and defective syllogisms; in *Paradise Regained* the same antagonist is decisively vanquished by wisdom rather than by force. Milton's Christ condemns the military might of Parthia as merely the vain ostentation of "fleshly arm": an argument of weakness rather than strength. For Milton's Abdiel on the battlefield of Heaven, the contest seems brutish and foul when reason must contend with force. In his *Second Defense*, writing *in propria persona*, Milton himself professes to defend by reason the cause that his countrymen had hitherto defended by arms.[1]

1. John Milton, *Complete Poems and Major Prose*, ed. Merritt Y. Hughes (New York, 1957), 819: "Thus with the better part of my frame I contributed as much as possible to the good of my country and to the success of the glorious cause in

The wars of truth are both epistemological and moral, engaging both the intellect and the will (whether fallen or regenerate), and in portraying them Milton deliberately exploits the methods of dialectics. In action or in contemplation, in doing or in suffering, his principal heroes face the problem of discriminating between truth and error; and the criterion by which they are ultimately judged is, as a rule, the norm of the patient witness or martyr defending the Truth and undergoing humiliation or overt violence in the cause of Truth. As instruments of persuasion or refutation, rhetoric and logic accordingly play a prominent, and at times a central, role in all of his major poems; and the ideal of the hero is closely linked (though not positively identified) with that of the orator. The close association between these ideals in his poetry is, in a significant degree, a testimony to the strength of the humanist tradition, even though humanism itself is ultimately weighed in the balance and found wanting. But one must not weight the scales prematurely, and the temptation of Greek *paideia* merits a chapter to itself.

In a divided Europe, torn by the wars of religion and by national and civil conflicts, humanists like Erasmus had pleaded the cause of peace, the superiority of spiritual and moral combat to the feats of the battlefield, and the efficacy of rational persuasion as an alternative to violence. Committed to the patriotic ideal of the orator as an active participant in the political life of his nation, yet also to the principles of a *pietas literata*, they offered a more humane, more peaceful means of achieving civil and spiritual happiness and the "public good."[2] The man of learning and eloquence might embody a higher mode of heroism than the national warrior or the crusader.

Yet the role of the orator-hero also belongs to Satan. In both of Milton's epics the issue of world dominion is fought not by arms

---

which we were engaged; and I thought that if God willed the success of such glorious achievements, it was equally agreeable to his will that there should be others by whom those achievements should be recorded with dignity and elegance, and that the truth, which had been defended by arms, should also be defended by reason; which is the best and only legitimate means of defending it."

2. See Joseph Anthony Wittreich, Jr., "'The Crown of Eloquence': The Figure of the Orator in Milton's Prose Works," in Michael Lieb and John T. Shawcross (eds.), *Achievements of the Left Hand: Essays on the Prose of John Milton* (Amherst, 1974), 3–54; William Harrison Woodward, *Studies in Education during the Age of*

but by words, and in both poems the devil inverts and parodies this motif. In *Paradise Lost* he conquers by persuasion rather than by force. In *Paradise Regained* he relies primarily on his "persuasive Rhetoric," and it is only after this has failed that he resorts to the "work of fear." In both instances he is playing a part ironically reminiscent of classical and Renaissance ideals: the rhetor as patriot, exploiting the techniques of persuasion in the interests of the state and as an instrument of public polity. Unfortunately the polity is that of Hell, and its state religion is devil worship. But the political functions of oratory are clearly exhibited in the debate in Pandaemonium; and in tempting Eve, Satan affects "Zeal for right" like the great orators of free Greece and Rome.

This equivocal use of the means of persuasion, serving divine or diabolical ends, is characteristic of contemporary attitudes toward rhetoric as the instrument of truth or falsehood. In *Paradise Regained* the moral intent or *ethos* of the two contestants is sharply contrasted, polarized as a conflict between truth and falsehood, heavenly wisdom and "hellish wiles." Accordingly the poem provides models for both the use and the abuse of dialectic and rhetoric, for the association and dissociation of discourse and truth.

A comparable polarization underlies the debate between Comus and the Lady in Milton's Ludlow masque; and this opposition is apparent not only in the contrasting *ethos* (or moral purpose) of the two disputants and in the truth or fallacy of the arguments they advance, but also in the quality of their language and style. The Lady's plainer, soberer discourse, stripped of the "dear wit," levity, and sensuous ornament of her adversary, nevertheless possesses a "sacred vehemence," an intrinsic purity appropriate to the virtue she presents and the truth from which she argues.

In *Samson Agonistes* and in *Comus,* and in both epics, the debates serve the ends of dialectic by bringing truth and falsehood into direct confrontation and thus proving and establishing the truth. Yet it is not only the epistemological opposition between true and false that is thus illuminated; the moral qualities of the contestants emerge more clearly through this confrontation, and also the profanation or consecration of discourse.

In both epics, and also in the masque, the tempter's role is the conventional part of the Adversary in Scripture and of the vices and devils of the morality plays. His office is to beguile and entrap the soul, thereby preserving and extending his own kingdom. It is an office of persuasion, and in literature at least, much of the technique of seduction is achieved through rhetorical means.

In visual representations of temptation, emphasis on the silent rhetoric of some enticing or fearful object is almost inevitable. In poetry this stress on the actual persuasive power of the object itself is also common, but because of the nature of the medium, it is generally complemented or replaced by seductive or threatening language, the rhetoric of exhortation or dehortation. In the drama the tempter's command, and perversion, of rhetoric may be a principal feature not only for illustrating his character and determining his role in the plot but in shaping the structure of the dramatic action. In an epic centered on the temptation ordeal, like *Paradise Lost* and *Paradise Regained,* the rhetoric of seduction will likewise assume central importance; moreover, in *Paradise Lost* it acquires specifically heroic overtones inasmuch as the poet has deliberately assimilated his tempter to an illusory but traditional paradigm of the epic hero. For an *eidolon* of heroic virtue, characterized by many of the "splendid vices" of ancient pagan heroes, the garment of a specious oratory is also appropriate. It belongs to the decorum of illusion and falsehood.

In *Paradise Regained* it is Satan who is inevitably dependent on the art of rhetoric, since it is his office to persuade to evil. The discourse of the Son, on the other hand, would appear to belong primarily to dialectic rather than to rhetoric. Unlike Satan, he does not have to think of the rhetorical effectiveness of his arguments on the mind or will or emotions of his opponent. He is not endeavoring to convince or persuade his infernal Adversary, but simply to refute the latter's arguments—and, in refuting them, to achieve a clearer idea of the best means for fulfilling his divine mission. In the course of his ordeal in the wilderness, the right way becomes more evident through contrast with its diabolically proposed alternatives.

In the temptation of the kingdoms of the world, the principal issue is the nature of Christ's monarchy and the best means of establishing and maintaining it. The offer of a secular kingdom— and of secular and temporal goods as a means of achieving it— serves to define and emphasize the spiritual nature of Christ's kingdom, the Church, and the imperative of utilizing spiritual instead of secular means to support and govern it.[3] The separation of church and state, the distinction between civil and ecclesiastical jurisdiction, had long been one of Milton's most cherished convictions. He had argued it polemically in his prose, and now adapts it simultaneously to the polemical conventions of the debate genre and the polemical context of heroic poetry. Presented as an issue for debate, it is part of a mortal duel between two supreme "heads of state"—the prince of this world and the Son of God, anointed universal king. In this poem the dialectical methods of debate and the adaptation of the motif of heroic combat (such as the monomachy of David and Goliath) to the motif of temptation cooperate to bring into bolder contrast the distinction between church and state, the antithesis between heavenly and earthly dominions. The true nature of the kingdom of Heaven appears more clearly through contrast with the kingdoms of this world.

As critics are well aware, the dialectical process, in one form or another, is of fundamental importance for Milton's poetic strategy. It underlies the thematic and narrative structures of both of his epics, and it conditions not only his imitation of thought (*dianoia*) but his *mimesis* of action, character, and passion as well. It is equally significant for his poetry considered as "passionate epic" and as "logical epic." In a temptation drama, centered on purification by trial and trial by contraries, the dialectical process is virtually inevitable; but it is also apparent in Milton's treatment of epic machinery and of the complex relationships—complementary or parodic, analogous or antithetical—among the principal personae. Moreover, insofar as it brings contraries into dynamic opposition, it generates a series of tensions within the poems themselves; these tensions, in large part, are responsible for many of the features, in style and structure, that some of our own contemporaries associate with the baroque.

3. Howard Schultz, *Milton and Forbidden Knowledge* (New York, 1955). In *The Reason of Church-Government*, Milton had similarly placed the reformation of the church in a dialectical context: "For if there were no opposition, where were the trial of an unfeigned goodness and magnanimity?" Elemental and mixed things "cannot suffer any change of one kind or quality into another without the struggle of contrarieties." The "reforming of the church . . . is never brought to effect without the fierce encounter of truth and falsehood together" (*Complete Poems and Major Prose*, 662).

Poetics is not logic or rhetoric, though all three were sometimes confused with one another both in theory and in practice.[4] As Milton himself recognized, the poet had his own methods, distinct from those of the logician and the orator. Nevertheless he could and often did borrow from both of the latter arts, especially in composing the speeches of his personae. In his *Poetics*, Aristotle had referred the reader to rhetoric for further instruction on *dianoia*; and behind the art of rhetoric (particularly after the Ramist reforms) lay the art of dialectics or logic. The same critic had also insisted on the logical construction and development of the plot. Action should seem the probable or necessary result of character; and the connection of incidents, and the tragic reversal itself, should likewise conform to probability and necessity. The tragic hero passes "by a series of probable or necessary stages from misfortune to happiness, or from happiness to misfortune." Tragic incidents produce the greatest effect on the mind when they "occur unexpectedly and at the same time in consequence of one another." Discovery and *peripeteia* should "arise out of the structure of the Plot itself, so as to be the consequence, necessary or probable, of the antecedents." Dramatic structure or narrative structure must seem logical.[5]

In these passages Aristotle was primarily concerned with causality, with the probable or necessary effects of character on action, and with the logical nexus of incidents leading to the catastrophe. Nevertheless, logical structure and narrative structure do not usually coincide, even though there may be a close relationship between them. Nor does logical progression proceed in the same manner or at the same pace as narrative progression. One should not look, therefore, for a strict observance of logical principles in Milton's poetic but one should not overlook the freer, more general, and less constricted treatment of causality in his images of both character and action. In *Paradise Lost* these are closely associated with his vindication of divine justice and Providence and are manifested chiefly in his careful motivation of the Fall.

In his anatomy of the causes underlying the fall of man, Milton placed primary emphasis on man's own free will; and the same emphasis is apparent in his treatment of both disjunctive and

4. Tasso regarded poetry as a subdivision of dialectics or logic. See Allan H. Gilbert (ed.), *Literary Criticism: Plato to Dryden* (2nd ed.; Detroit, 1962), 473–77.
5. *Aristotle on the Art of Poetry*, trans. Ingram Bywater (Oxford, 1945), 41–46.

hypothetical modes of reasoning. Man and angel alike are confronted with moral imperatives (either A or B) and with contingencies (if A, then B; if A_1, then B_1). Both are closely associated, moreover, with the motif of temptation and trial. The alternatives are clearly presented: obedience *or* disobedience; life *or* death, beatitude *or* misery, liberty *or* bondage, God *or* Satan, Heaven *or* Hell. *If* one partakes of the forbidden fruit, *then* one must certainly die. *If* one rejects God's anointed vicegerent, *then* one must likewise be rejected by Heaven. *If* one repents and believes, *then* one will be saved. In the temptation scene Eve is confronted with a clear-cut choice between believing God *or* Satan. And in the principal machining persons and the nominal protagonist of *Paradise Lost*, Milton has depicted the spiritual paradigms between which fallen men will be compelled to choose: between the likeness of the First Adam and that of the Second; between the Satanic archetype and the divine archetype manifested in the Son.

The dialectical pattern in *Paradise Lost*, and the significance of both disjunctive and hypothetical modes in the moral drama, are enhanced by Milton's essentially Arminian interpretation of the doctrine of predestination. Since the decree is contingent, allowing scope for man's free will and voluntary choice even in his fallen condition—with the important proviso that he not reject divine grace—there can be a real, not merely a token, choice between such alternatives; and it is operative not only for the fallen protoplasts themselves but for the *Christianus lector*.

In *Paradise Lost*, as in many of Milton's other poems, the moral and dialectical drama involves more than a clash of concepts and conceits (such as the taunts and fleers that the contending angels exchange), more than alternative patterns of heroic virtue, and more than a positive choice between good and evil. It also involves the epistemological warfare between truth and falsehood, grappling in deadly conflict through the verses of *Paradise Lost* and *Paradise Regained* as well as through the pages of *Areopagitica*. For the sake of decorum, the devil must be given his due; masquerading as verity, falsehood must wear a plausible disguise, the superficial semblance of truth. Yet, if the reader is not to be beguiled and ensnared himself, the disguise must be exposed, and naked vice revealed in its true deformity. For these purposes, the poet's own moral commentaries (sometimes presented as epiphonemas) or the counterarguments of truth's own warriors may prove sufficient; but in many instances, in other Renaissance epics besides *Paradise Lost*, the undisguising may be more violent and more dramatic: an act of recognition that is also a public judgment. The logical outcome of the action must be an act of poetic justice.

In Renaissance literature such exposures, real or metaphorical, were not uncommon. In intrigue-plots, comic or tragic, the schemers are finally exposed and punished. In Renaissance allegorical poetry, heavily influenced by the tradition of a moralized Ovid, transformations into gods or metamorphoses into stones and trees and beasts represented a judgment of virtues or vices. The satirist commonly regarded his office as one of exposure: "abuses stripped and whipped." In Ariosto's romance-epic, illusions vanish before the ring of reason, and the enchanters themselves are exposed in their weakness or deformity. Atlante is revealed as a frail old man; Alcina as a repulsive hag. Stripped of her finery, Spenser's Duessa is exposed as "a loathly, wrinckled hag," filthy and misshapen.

> Such is the face of falshood, such the sight
> Of fowle *Duessa*, when her borrowed light
> Is laid away, and counterfesaunce knowne.
> (*The Faerie Queene*,
> Book I, canto viii, stanza 49)

In *Paradise Lost* the moral deformity of evil is exhibited through the device of the metamorphosis and, appropriately, Satan himself is compelled to recognize the ugliness of his own sin ("Now in thine eye so foul, once deem'd so fair / In Heav'n"). In giving birth to Death, the fruit of her own incest with Satan, Sin is grotesquely changed into an emblem of the evil she incarnates: simultaneously fair and foul, human and bestial, alluring and deadly; a hellhound gnawed by remorse. Satan undergoes a comparable transformation, punished in the very shape in which he had sinned, through the sudden intervention of divine justice. These metamorphoses of Sin and Satan into dragon forms—and the indeterminate shape of their firstborn, Death—are symbolic representations of their true nature, seen under the aspect of eternity.

In most of these instances, the motifs of transformation and exposure possess epistemological as well as moral significance. They unmask the liar, the hypocrite, the pretender (and it is significant that Satan is a "pretender" to the throne of Heaven in more than one sense); and they also reveal the essential nature of the vice or vices they expose.

As in *Lycidas*, the final word belongs to the "all-judging" Deity himself, who pronounces "lastly" on each deed. The ultimate criteria of good and evil, truth and falsehood, are the divine will and divine judgment. The God of *Paradise Lost* is not only the supreme power but the supreme wisdom, creating by the Word and destroying by the Word. His insight is both the norm and determinant of truth. And just as his will is fate, his wisdom is, in a sense, reality. He has merely to know and to judge evil or falsehood in order to confound it.

The dialectical process is apparent both in the interplay of ideas and through the movement of events: the contrasting patterns of creation and destruction, degeneration and regeneration; the contrary strategies of Heaven and Hell; the moral opposition between reason and passion, love and hate, ambition and humility, obedience and disobedience; the distinctions between internal and external liberty, inward and outward happiness, the earthly and heavenly paradises and the "paradise within." It appears in the contrast between Adam's act of "exceeding love" in resolving to die with Eve and the Messiah's voluntary resolve to die for mankind; in the antithesis between Satan's grudging incarnation in the serpent and the Son's willingness to humble himself by assuming flesh; in the opposition between worldly or diabolical tyranny and the true spiritual king; between the realities of Heaven and their counterfeit imitations in Hell; in analogies between the infernal and celestial councils; in the parodic imitation of the relationship between Father, Son, and Spirit by the infernal triad (Satan, Sin, and Death); in parallels between Satan's expedition into Chaos and to the world and those of the Son; and in the contrasting merits of Christ and Satan, rivals to the throne of Heaven and to spiritual dominion over mankind. The dialectical pattern is also implicit not only in the contrasting actions of Christ and Satan but in the separate actions that they perform. Satan first seeks dominion through force, and loses; subsequently by fraud, and (momentarily at least) triumphs. Christ's first *aristeia* is an act of destruction; his second, an act of creation, but of physical creation, the creation of nature. His third is also an act of creation, but of spiritual re-creation, the renovation of man's corrupted nature through grace. His first advent is in humility; his second in power.

Finally, the dialectical process is also operative in human history, in the struggle between the elect and the reprobate, the righteous few and the ungodly multitude, the true church and the world. The panorama of human history, as Michael represents it, displays essentially the same recurrent pattern:

> good with bad
> Expect to hear, supernal Grace contending
> With sinfulness of Men.

In the poetic microcosm, and the greater world, the same opposing forces are at work, and the same contradictions are apparent. A sort of proto-Hegelian dialectic is operative in the poetic action as in history itself.

The implications of the dialectics of temptation in Milton's poetry extend far beyond their immediate contexts in the wilderness: the desert of *Paradise Regained*, the garden of *Paradise Lost*, the "leavy Labyrinth" of *Comus*. Through meditation or debate the confrontation of good and evil results not only in a clearer knowledge of both but also in purification. By distinguishing and separating the false from the true, and rejecting the evil, the work of purification and renovation both in the human soul and in the universe is begun. Trial by contraries, as Milton delineates it in *Areopagitica*, purifies the individual, the human microcosm, in mind and will.

But the principle of purification through separation operates also on a cosmic level. Heaven is purified by the separation and expulsion of the evil angels: a divine analogue of the process of domestic purification that follows Odysseus' homecoming to Ithaca. At the Second Coming the son will

> dissolve
> *Satan* with his perverted World, then raise
> From the conflagrant mass, purg'd and refin'd,
> New Heav'ns, new Earth
>
> (*PL*, XII, 546–49)

Sin and Death serve as God's

> Hell-hounds, to lick up the draff and filth
> Which man's polluting Sin with taint hath shed
> On what was pure
>
> (*PL*, X, 630–32)

and are destined to be ultimately slain by the Son:

> Then Heav'n and Earth renew'd shall be made pure
> To sanctity that shall receive no stain.
>
> (*PL*, X, 638–39)

And in *Comus*, the Elder Brother asserts the inviolability of virtue
and its immunity to the contagion of evil:

> Yea even that which mischief meant most harm
> Shall in the happy trial prove most glory.
> But evil on itself shall back recoil,
> And mix no more with goodness, when at last
> Gather'd like scum, and settl'd to itself,
> It shall be in eternal restless change
> Self-fed and self-consum'd.
>
> (ll. 590–96)

Both the little world of man and ultimately the larger world are to
be restored to their pristine purity and holiness through a process of spiritual dialectics, by isolating the good and destroying
the evil elements in their nature.

The purification of the hero or heroine is a prominent motif in
several of Milton's longer poems. Central to all four are the dialectics of temptation, though the situation is significantly different in *Paradise Lost*. Adam and Eve are corrupted, not purified, by
trial. In their case the test of virtue results in the contamination of
original purity rather than in the purification of a native impurity:
the inherited defilement of original sin. In *Paradise Regained* the
temptation scenes conclude not only with the moral rejection of
evil but with the downfall of the tempter. In *Comus* the trial of the
Lady's virtue is followed by the banishment of the contrary vice
and by a purification ritual. In this respect *Paradise Lost* again follows a different pattern; it concludes with the expulsion not of the
tempter but of his victims. No longer pure, they are no longer
worthy of Paradise:

> But longer in that Paradise to dwell,
> The Law I gave to Nature him forbids:
> Those pure immortal Elements that know
> No gross, no unharmonious mixture foul,
> Eject him tainted now, and purge him off
> As a distemper, gross to air as gross.
>
> (XI, 48–53)

In a temptation drama the dramatic emphasis must, almost inevitably, be divided between the tempter and the tempted,

regardless of whether the test or trial is a "good" or "evil" temptation or whether it concludes triumphantly or ignominiously for
the tempted.[6] In Milton's poetry it ends successfully for the Lady
in *Comus*, for the Christ of *Paradise Regained*, and for Samson, just
as it had finished victoriously for the hero in the Book of Job,
traditionally regarded as a divinely inspired model for the poetry
of temptation. For the protagonists of *Paradise Lost*, on the other
hand, the trial concludes ignominiously, demonstrating the
frailty of human virtue even in its pristine perfection. The victory
belongs, though only temporarily, to the tempter; and one of the
underlying ironies in the poem is that throughout the action the
tempter is himself divinely tempted, repeatedly exposed to one
opportunity after another in order that he may entrench himself
more deeply in evil and through the "dynamics of evil" further
the execution of a divine plan.

In this kind of drama (or epic), whatever other specific virtues
are tested, the trial is—again almost inevitably—a trial of patience and constancy. The role of the victim is essentially passive,
though the trial may involve alternative courses of action, oppor-
tunites for action or contemplation, or a choice between action
and ignoble idleness. Insofar as he is confronted with alternative
or contrary possibilities between which he must decide, the emphasis falls primarily not on external action but on the action of
the mind and will. In these circumstances *mythos* is assimilated to
ethos and *dianoia*. The hero must endure and decide, and the initiative, the active role, belongs primarily to the tempter. In
Milton's Ludlow masque and in *Paradise Regained* this role is concentrated in a single figure: in Comus himself or in Satan. In *Paradise Lost* the burden of temptation again falls on Satan, though he
enlists the irrational serpent and Eve herself as his instruments.
In *Samson Agonistes* the tempter's role is diffused among several
dramatis personae—though if the poet had so elected, he could
have represented them as Satanic instruments, agents of the
single author of all ill.

In a successful temptation, where virtue emerges triumphant
and the tempter is "foiled again" (like the villainous creditor in a
Victorian melodrama)—a denouement more conventional in fiction than in the theater of this world—the devil is usually exposed

6. See Milton's *De Doctrina Christiana*, Bk. I, Chap. 7, on this topic.

as a dunce, more fool than hero. In the Book of Job he is defeated, though we do not witness his chagrin. In the morality plays he is usually foiled, and sometimes left with the additional burden of a final soliloquy voicing his frustration and despair. In Goethe's *Faust*, partly modeled both on Job and on the morality theater, he is twice defeated at the moment of apparent triumph; the tragedies of the condemnation of Margaret and the damnation of Faust conclude as comedies of salvation: *gerichtet, gerettet*. This pattern is more closely observed in Milton's brief epic, though obliquely shadowed in the longer poem, through the comically appropriate judgment that befalls Satan and his legions on his triumphant return to Hell.

In both epics Milton accommodates the tempter's role to the requirements of epic decorum; but in *Paradise Lost* it is felicitously complicated by a clever (and in many respects novel) fusion of a variety of roles conventional in epic or in drama. With the traditional office of the tempter as delineated in the Book of Job, in saints' legends, and in the moralities, Milton has combined the roles of the hero-as-villain and the hero-as-orator, the epic antagonist and the conquering destroyers of the secular martial epic, and the infernal machinery of the Renaissance heroic tradition. As a result he is able simultaneously to discredit the conventional martial heroism as essentially diabolical, to invest the role of epic antagonist with theological significance, to represent the act of temptation itself as a heroic enterprise—the evil *aristeia* or "pernicious best" of the archetypal world conqueror and world destroyer—and to endow a conventional machining person with attributes of a conventional epic hero.

The power of the Satanic image in this poem results in large part from ambivalence: from the ambiguities consequent upon the skillful combination of a wide variety of diverse literary and theological conventions. To separate the diverse elements that compose the Satanic *eidolon* belongs primarily to the power that could divide the flames, discriminating light and heat: an act of judgment reflected not only in the qualities of Milton's hellfire but in the decisive intrusion of judgment in Book X. But the poet has also left the burden of discrimination to his readers. The "problem of Satan," as an earlier generation of critics regarded it, resulted largely from the poet's conscious artistry: from the deliberate techniques whereby he invested the familiar office of the tempter and the epic machines with the no less familiar attributes of epic heroism.

The elements of the Satanic image were, for the most part, well established in both literary and theological tradition. Taken separately, they constituted a kind of diabolical decorum, endowing Milton's image with more than the shadow of probability and verisimilitude. In combination they may seem paradoxical to the point of contradiction: an innovation not only on epic tradition but on conventional representations of the devil. The elements of the marvelous and the sublime that early critics found in this fully constructed *eidolon* were in large part a response to the surprising novelty of the Satanic image as Milton chose to develop it. To an audience familiar with classical and Renaissance heroic poetry, as well as to some of our own near-contemporaries, Satan's thought and character bore an embarrassing likeness to those of the conventional epic hero and an impressive resemblance to the much-lauded virtues of the ancients. In the context of the humanist tradition one might easily forget that the latter had been repeatedly discredited by theologians as often little more than "splendid vices"; and against the background of epic tradition one might (as some have done) confuse Milton's heroic idol with conventional pattern heroes. One might overlook the inherent absurdity of a godlike devil—a deliberate oxymoron—and the elements of heroic derring-do, not unmixed with ambition and pride, latent in the angelic rebel of the Apocalypse and in the Old Testament Lucifer. In actuality, as Addison recognized, Milton took pains to reveal the moral evil that perverted Satan's heroic gifts of intellect, strength, and will and to expose as brutishness the kind of misdirected heroism that he exemplified. Although surprising to the point of paradox, it was not illogical that, in a heroic poem where the initiative must inevitably belong to the fallen archangel and tempter, the adversary and antagonist of both God and man should be clothed in at least the external trappings of conventional epic heroism.

To recapitulate a point that one has already discussed elsewhere, Milton has depicted Satan's role in the ruin of mankind as an epic enterprise, observing the decorum of heroic poetry and achieving an impressive (though not entirely unprecedented) innovation in the familiar epic treatment of machining persons. On this point Milton had been anticipated by the author of *Genesis B*, though it is doubtful that he was aware, and certain that most of his audience were completely unaware, of this analogue.

In the majority of epics that made use of machines—divine or infernal councils, emissaries from Heaven or from the underworld, warring divinities or combating angels—the epic action is divinely proposed and eventually executed in spite of the counteraction of hostile deities or devils. In classical epic, the action normally springs from the will of Zeus; it is abetted by deities friendly to the hero and his side, and opposed by hostile gods or goddesses. In some instances, the latter may enlist the aid of infernal powers, as Juno stirs up the Furies against Aeneas, driving Turnus, king of the Rutulians—the counterhero of the poem, and as a second Achilles a foil to the superior heroic virtues concentrated in Aeneas—to war and the Latian queen Amata to raving madness. In Camoëns' *Lusiads* the hostile divinity is Bacchus, former conqueror of India, who is jealous of the Portuguese expedition under Vasco da Gama; the Portuguese on the other hand are (inconsistently) assisted by the pagan Venus and the providential care of the Christian God. In Tasso's *Jerusalem Delivered* the action is initiated by God himself, and opposed by the powers of Hell.

Although infernal councils are numerous in heroic poetry, they do not as a rule initiate the epic enterprise. Instead, they normally serve as His Majesty's disloyal opposition, endeavoring to frustrate actions ordained by Heaven and proposing counter-strategies. What they usually initiate are the delaying actions, setting up obstacles and stumbling blocks in the ordained path of the epic hero. Nevertheless, there are significant instances in which the powers of the underworld do take a positive, albeit destructive, role in setting events in motion. In Claudian's *Against Rufinus*, in *Genesis B,* and in Vida's *Christiad* the initiative belongs to Hell.[7] An example nearer home, however, occurs in Milton's brief poem on the Gunpowder Plot, *In Quintum Novembris.* Alternatively described as an epyllion and as a mock-epic, the poem opens with the firm establishment of peace and the "inviolable league" between England and Scotland under the rule of James I, and immediately turns to the activities of "the cruel tyrant" of

7. See Milton, *Complete Poems and Major Prose,* 382, 484, on the demonic council in Vida and Tasso; see John Milton, *Paradise Lost,* ed. Merritt Y. Hughes (New York, 1935), 20*n,* for the infernal council in Claudian's *Rape of Proserpina* and *Against Rufinus.*

Acheron. Enraged by the sight of a wealthy and peaceful land devoted to the worship of the true God, a nation "alone rebellious against me," the devil vows revenge, seeks out the sleeping pope and inspires him with the design of the Gunpowder Plot. The latter in turn enlists the aid of the infernal twins, Murder and Treason. Meanwhile God himself laughs at these "vain undertakings," takes upon himself "the defence of his people's cause," and entrusts the goddess Fame with the responsibility for divulging the conspiracy. The poem concludes felicitously with thanksgivings and public rejoicings.[8]

In structuring this somewhat bigoted little epic of sectarian nationalism, Milton relied almost entirely on the resources of divine and infernal machinery and personification allegory. For all its brevity the poem displays in miniature, or indeed in embryo, the techniques he would employ on a more ambitious scale in *Paradise Lost* and *Paradise Regained*.[9] The divine honors bestowed on the Messiah provoke Satan's initial revolt; he holds a council of war; God laughs at his vain designs and ultimately defeats them. The favors bestowed on mankind similarly arouse Satan's envy and hate; he again summons a council of war and plots a course of action; this in turn is countered by the strategy of grace and redemption set forth in the divine council; the devil will succeed in seducing man, but his victory will be as vain as it is temporary. The divine honors publicly accorded the Messiah at his baptism stimulate Satan's envy and goad him into action; he holds yet another council of war, which is immediately counterpointed by a divine council revealing the divine strategy underlying the temptation of the Son and predicting the latter's victory and Satan's defeat. In the words of the angelic chorus:

> The Father knows the Son; therefore secure
> Ventures his filial Virtue, though untried.
> .   .   .   .
> Be frustrate, all ye stratagems of Hell,
> And devilish machinations come to nought.
> (*PR*, I, 176–81)

In both of these epics Satan is performing his traditional office as God's antagonist and rival, and endeavoring to frustrate the

8. Milton, *Complete Poems and Major Prose*, 15–21.

9. For discussion of recent criticism of *In Quintum Novembris*, see Douglas Bush (ed.), *A Variorum Commentary on the Poems of John Milton* (3 vols. to date; New York, 1970–   ).

decrees of divine Providence. But in both it is he who initiates the
epic enterprise, and in both the enterprise itself is presented simultaneously as an act of further rebellion against the divine
monarchy and in terms of the temptation and seduction of man.
The act of temptation is depicted as an epic action, and the role of
the tempter is assimilated to that of an epic hero. It is a false heroism, to be sure, but in the commonwealth of Hell he is the
patriotic defender of his people. In his own eyes and in those
of his fellows he is a national hero. Milton's Dalila enjoys a similar reputation—equally vain and far briefer—among her own
countrymen.

The studiedly "heroic" qualities of Milton's epic Adversary set
him apart from the majority of the scheming devils of Renaissance epic tradition. As epic machines, these may indeed display
many of the features of a more primitive heroic code—constancy
in the pursuit of revenge, envy and ambition and pride, a spurious magnanimity and a reckless courage—but the figures themselves are often grotesque to the point of absurdity. Milton has
retained many of these traditional motives, but has assimilated
them to the *ethos* of the classical hero. There are conventional heroic elements in the devils of *Genesis B,* but these result in large
part from a different poetic tradition. The Old English epic tradition was essentially a heroic tradition; and, in substituting biblical subject matter for that of the Germanic heroic age, poets retained much of the vocabulary and *ethos* of the native heroic
tradition, representing Christ and his apostles and the devil and
his angels alike as a Germanic prince surrounded by a comitatus
of loyal athelings. In *Genesis B* the prince of Hell remains immo-
bile, a caitiff in fetters; and a loyal thane, faithful to the primitive
heroic code, must undertake the seduction of man as a mission of
revenge. The heroic attributes of the tempter spring naturally, if
not inevitably, from the inherited epic tradition.
    Milton, on the other hand, is writing in a different epic tradi-
tion, in which the devil, and whatever heroic qualities he might
possess, had been depicted as grotesque, rendered ludicrous by
moral and physical deformity; the heroic attributes of his devil
appear accordingly as a daring innovation. The poet has deliberately enhanced the heroic stature of his archfiend by emphasizing
not only Satan's affinities with traditional epic heroes but also the
points in which the devil actually surpasses them. He excels them

in stature, in strength, and in daring. He surpasses his peers in cunning, in courage, and in merit; he alone dares undertake the perilous journey through primeval chaos to the newly created world. His stature is further enhanced by the distinction, deliberately emphasized by the poet, between the aristocratic few, who compose the infernal house of peers, and the plebeian multitude.

Literary and pictorial tradition, to be sure, offered the Renaissance poet a variety of models for depicting the temptation crisis without actually bringing the devil himself into the scene. Of classical models, the most influential would appear to have been the Judgment of Paris, the Choice of Hercules, and the myths associated with Circe and the Sirens. The first of these—the myth of the Trojan shepherd-prince confronted by three rival goddesses contending for a beauty prize and offering bribes appropriate to their character and jurisdiction—had been allegorized in terms of a choice among the three principal modes of life discussed in Aristotle's *Ethics*: active, contemplative, and voluptuous. As Howard Schultz pointed out, this schema underlies the hierarchy of secular values set forth in Milton's representation of the temptation of the kingdoms in *Paradise Regained*.[10] Instead of distributing the role of tempter among three different figures, he concentrated it in the single figure of the infernal monarch of this world.

In Prodicus' description of Hercules' Choice, the youthful hero, meditating in the wilderness on his future career and the choice between "the path through virtue or the path through vice," encounters two female figures, personifications of virtue and vice. These offer to guide him by "the most pleasant and most easy way" to a felicity that is in fact illusory, or by "labour and care" to true happiness.[11] Behind this fable lay a still older version

10. Schultz, *Milton and Forbidden Knowledge*.

11. See Erwin Panofsky, *Hercules am Scheidewege und andere antike Bildstoffe in der neueren Kunst*, Studien der Bibliothek Warburg, XVIII (Leipzig, 1930); Panofsky, *Studies in Iconology: Humanistic Themes in the Art of the Renaissance* (New York, 1939); John M. Steadman, *Milton's Epic Characters: Image and Idol* (Chapel Hill, 1968), 124–27. In his academic prolusions, Milton applied the crossroads metaphor to the scholastic curriculum at Cambridge, apparently combining it with the motif of true and false education set forth in the *Tabula Cebetis*. The controversies of the schoolmen "have brought endless discord into the schools, which has marvellously impeded the scholars' happy progress." The "unhappy reader is in a quandary, as if at a crossroads, uncertain which way to turn and which road to take. . . . So, at last the reader is obliged to imitate the long suffering of Ceres and go searching with a lighted torch for truth through the whole wide world, and find

of the crossroads motif—the tradition of the Pythagorean Y, associated with the choice of routes that the soul must make after
death and in the underworld; it had also been elaborated symbolically in terms of the soul's metaphorical journey through this
world and in this life. In antiquity the various elements in this
tradition were sometimes isolated and developed separately. In
Virgil's account of Aeneas' descent to the underworld, the hero
is instructed to avoid the sinister path to Tartarus and to follow
the right path leading to the Elysian Fields. The rival ladies of
Hercules' Choice, in turn, reappear in the dream of the youthful
Scipio as Virtue and Pleasure.

In medieval and Renaissance tradition, the motif of the Pythagorean Y, along with the symbolism of right and left, were frequently assimilated to biblical metaphors of the two paths: the
ways of the righteous and the ungodly (Psalm 1:6), the ways of
life and death (Jer. 21:8; cf. Deut. 30:19), the "strait" and "wide"
gates and the "narrow" and "broad" ways leading to life or to
destruction. In some instances the moral alternatives are personified, but in many cases the temptation consists almost entirely in
the outward appearance of the two paths themselves: initially
smooth and inviting, or rough and forbidding. In the course of his
journey the symbolic traveler—adolescent lover or apprentice-
hero, wayfaring pilgrim or wandering knight—may simply come
to a fork in the road where he must choose between alternative

---

it nowhere" (*Complete Poems and Major Prose*, 606). In his treatise *Of Education*, he
proposes to "conduct ye to a hillside, where I will point ye out the right path of a
virtuous and noble education; laborious indeed at the first ascent, but else so
smooth, so green, so full of goodly prospect and melodious sounds on every side,
that the harp of Orpheus was not more charming" (*Complete Poems and Major Prose*,
632). In one of his sonnets ("Lady that in the prime of earliest youth," in *Complete
Poems and Major Prose*, 141), he has (as Hughes suggests) apparently adapted not
only the biblical metaphor of the two paths but a motif from the *Tabula Cebetis*:

> Lady that in the prime of earliest youth,
> Wisely hast shunn'd the broad way and the green,
> And with those few art eminently seen
> That labor up the Hill of Heav'nly Truth.

In *The Reason of Church-Government* he also made use of the image of the path of
virtue: "whereas the paths of honesty and good life appear now rugged and difficult, though they be indeed easy and pleasant, they would then appear to all men
both easy and pleasant, though they were rugged and difficult indeed" (*Complete
Poems and Major Prose*, 670). For fuller discussion of Milton's use of these themes
and images, see Chapter 7 herein.

gateways. Sometimes the latter bear inscriptions indicating their identity. And in erotic fantasies like the *Hypnerotomachia Poliphili*, the youthful pilgrim is apt to select the primrose path of pleasure instead of a life of strenuous action and contemplation.

The crossroads motif, with its choice between two or three alternative routes, might also be combined with motifs derived from the Circe myth and the fable of the Sirens; but the latter usually enjoy an independent life of their own, either *in propria persona* or as Mata Hari types: beautiful infidels, seductive fays, enchantresses endowed with genuine or magical beauty. The malignant fays of Boiardo's romance-epic, the *Orlando Inamorato*, belong to this category, along with Ariosto's Alcina and Tasso's Armida, Spenser's Duessa and Acrasia; Milton exploits aspects of this tradition in his characterization of Dalila. In this tradition the temptress may play a more prominent role than does Pleasure or Vice in the tradition of Hercules' Choice, or Aphrodite in the tradition of the Judgment of Paris. Moreover, their characterization is frequently based not only on a mixture of myth and romance but also on the allegorical interpretations that mythographers had extracted from the fables of Circe and the Sirens: the enticements of sensual pleasure and (more narrowly) the allurements of the meretrix or harlot. In Renaissance epic, the Circean seductress may act on her own initiative without outside intervention, but in other cases she may be prompted and assisted by the archtempter himself. Thus Armida's activities are instigated and abetted by the powers of Hell, and Duessa in turn is aided by Archimago, a type of Satan.

Such figures normally play a much more active and more sustained part in the development of the plot than do the personified Vice or Pleasure of Hercules' Choice and Scipio's Dream; and their benevolent rivals—Ariosto's Logistilla, Spenser's Una and the Palmer, Tasso's Hermit, and others—may assume a correspondingly greater role than does Prodicus' Virtue. They may also acquire functions analogous to those of the good and evil daimons of Neoplatonic tradition (which Milton exploits for his supernatural machinery in his Ludlow masque) and the Bonus Angelus and Malus Angelus of the morality tradition. Most of these conventional schemas are, in varying degrees, operative in *Paradise Lost* or in *Paradise Regained*. Nevertheless the poet's primary emphasis in both cases falls on the heroic elaboration of the tempter's role as set forth in Genesis, in the Book of Job, and in the Gospels of Luke and Matthew.

In *Paradise Lost*, Milton has deliberately concentrated the power and authority of Hell into one heroic figure and invested him with an active role in the plotting and execution of the epic action. On the other hand, he has dispersed the divine opposition to Satan among a variety of personae: God the Father, who initiates the counteraction but does not himself engage in activity; the Son, who intercedes for mankind and fulfills the divine decrees but does not act independently of the Father's will; a variety of angelic opponents, Uriel, Gabriel, Zephon and Ithuriel, and (indirectly) Raphael and Michael; and the human protagonists, Adam and Eve. The role of the Malus Angelus is thus initiated and performed by Satan alone. The office of the Bonus Angelus, however, though initiated by God himself, is performed by several angels. The dramatic emphasis falls, accordingly, almost inevitably on one diabolical figure—the "mighty Paramount" who seems, virtually from the outset, "Alone th' Antagonist of Heav'n."

CHAPTER 7

Paradise Regained: The Crossroads Motif and the Ordeal of Initial Choice

AS THE hero of *Paradise Regained* enters the wilderness to be tempted, he reflects on the earlier aspirations of his boyhood and young manhood.

> victorious deeds
> Flam'd in my heart, heroic acts; one while
> To rescue *Israel* from the *Roman* yoke,
> Then to subdue and quell o'er all the earth
> Brute violence and proud Tyrannic pow'r,
> Till truth were freed, and equity restor'd:
> Yet held it more humane, more heavenly, first
> By winning words to conquer willing hearts,
> And make persuasion do the work of fear;
> At least to try, and teach the erring Soul.
>
> (I, 215–24)

The speaker is Milton's "Most perfect *Hero*," who will ultimately be "tried in heaviest plight / Of labours huge and hard, too hard for human wight"—the Passion—and whose temptations in the wilderness involve "deeds / Above Heroic." In this passage Milton evokes an idealized image of the martial hero not uncommon in Renaissance epic poetry: warrior and conqueror, deliverer of his people, queller of tyrants, restorer of justice and truth. The deliverance of Israel as heroic enterprise might suggest to the poet's first readers an analogy with Tasso's epic devoted to the liberation of Jerusalem and the Holy Sepulcher; yet it would also contain ecclesiastical implications. In the context of the English

194

Reformation, the allusion to Israel might be taken as a reference to the holy community; its rescue from the yoke of Rome might readily be applied to the church.

The hero of the epic of recovered Paradise exemplifies a higher heroism, however, than that of the warrior and ultimately achieves a loftier, more spiritual deliverance. He will conquer the souls of men rather than their bodies; he will employ words instead of arms, discourse instead of force, and persuasion rather than fear. Ultimately he will in large part transcend discourse itself, illuminating and persuading the soul from within.

Like the heroes of Milton's other major poems, he transcends not only the conventional heroic patterns but also the ordinary nature of man; like Adam and Samson, he is in the fullest sense of the word an "extraordinary" hero. The protagonist of *Samson Agonistes* is the strongest of mortal men, endowed with miraculous force. The epic person of *Paradise Lost* is unfallen man in his original perfection. The hero of *Paradise Regained* (unlike the heroic demigods of classical myth) is uniquely God and man; and the uniqueness of his nature, the "mystery of godliness," is implicit in the very terms in which he describes his earlier heroic ambitions. To eschew force for persuasion is "more humane, more heavenly"; it suggests the condign *ethos,* the moral decorum appropriate for an epic hero who is also a theanthropos, a union of the human and the divine.

Both the military ideal and the nonviolent mode of persuasion and instruction recur as Satanic lures in the temptation of the kingdoms, and significantly the hero of Milton's brief epic rejects both. He refuses the poetry, the oratory, and the philosophy of Athens just as he had earlier dismissed the armed might of Parthia and the imperial authority of Rome. The "power and wisdom" of God does not require these things from the world. A "living Oracle" expressly sent from Heaven would presumably learn little from the moral teachers of pagan Greece; and, not surprisingly, he prefers the prophets and poets of Scripture: an eloquence and wisdom divinely inspired. Although (like many Renaissance humanists) he prefers persuasion to force, he does not need to acquire the art of persuasion from the *ars rhetorica* or the *ars poetica* of the Gentiles.

As an epic of *paideia*—the education of the prince, the spiritual warrior, the future teacher—*Paradise Regained* offers suggestive points of contrast as well as analogies with humanistic educational ideals. In this debate between the incarnate Logos and the prince of darkness, the *studia humaniora* appear not only superfluous but fundamentally erroneous; the view of human nature they embody is as mistaken and as misleading as their conceptions of the divine nature. The classical studies of the great Renaissance schoolmasters—the curricula of Vittorino da Feltre and Guarino of Verona, the programs of Sturmius and Erasmus and Agricola, the course of authors at St. Paul's School and at Milton's utopian academy—would have been notably out of place at this school in the desert wilderness. Here the once and future king masters the principles of his vocation through debate and meditation: by reflection, divine inspiration, and disputation with his clever Adversary. The topics considered and the questions raised may be suggested from without, but the answers are from above or from within.[1] Underlying this drama of the mind is the antithesis between true and false education; and as in *The Tablet of Cebes*, the true *paideia* appears in clearer definition through its juxtaposition with the false.

Recent interpretations of *Paradise Regained* have emphasized two related aspects of the hero's ordeal. It is preliminary, and it is also traditional—an initiation into spiritual combat in preparation for the protagonist's public career, and at the same time a familiar heroic motif. According to Frank Kermode, "The action . . . concerns the primary heroic crisis, the emergence of the hero from seclusion." In Arnold Stein's opinion, the "exercise in the wilderness is, formally, for the purpose of laying down the first rudiments of the 'great warfare,'" but it is also the "most important preparation for war, the preliminary self-conquest of the successful soldier or captain of men"; Christ "has been teaching himself as preparation for his end of teaching the world."[2] Yet

1. See Louis L. Martz, *The Paradise Within: Studies in Vaughan, Traherne, and Milton* (New Haven, 1964), 171–201; Martz, "*Paradise Regained*: The Meditative Combat," *ELH*, XXVII (1960), 223–47; Barbara Kiefer Lewalski, *Milton's Brief Epic: The Genre, Meaning, and Art of "Paradise Regained"* (Providence, R.I., 1966); Merritt Y. Hughes, "The Christ of *Paradise Regained* and the Renaissance Heroic Tradition," *Studies in Philology*, XXXV (1938), 254–77; Frank Kermode, "Milton's Hero," *Review of English Studies*, n.s., IV (1953), 317–30; Arnold Stein, *Heroic Knowledge: An Interpretation of "Paradise Regained" and "Samson Agonistes"* (Minneapolis, 1957); E. M. W. Tillyard, "The Christ of *Paradise Regained*," in his *Studies in Milton* (London, 1951), 100–106; A. S. P. Woodhouse, "Theme and Pattern in *Paradise Regained*," *University of Toronto Quarterly*, XXV (1956), 167–82.

2. Kermode, "Milton's Hero," 321; Stein, *Heroic Knowledge*, 11, 133.

there is a further, additional sense in which Christ's temptation represents both a "preparation for his end" and a "primary heroic crisis." Like other heroes and princes—Hercules, Paris, Scipio, Solomon, and the "true wayfaring Christian" of *Areopagitica*—he is involved in an ordeal of initial choice.[3] Standing metaphorically "at the crossroads," he must choose, at the beginning of his public career, the way of life he is to follow to the end. The moral dilemma that confronts him recalls a complex of interrelated traditions: Hercules' Choice, the Judgment of Paris, the Pythagorean Y, the role of Mercury as wayfarers' guide, and the motifs of the labyrinth and the *selva oscura*. In this chapter I shall consider three aspects of these traditions in relation to *Paradise Regained*: the ordeal of initial choice as a conventional heroic motif; the rational analysis of ends and means; and the relative merits of the active and contemplative lives.

In the final lines of Milton's epic, the angelic chorus bids the Messiah to "enter" on his "glorious work" and "begin to save mankind." This brings to a close the meditations that had engaged him for the greater part of his ordeal.

> How best the mighty work he might begin
> Of Saviour to mankind, and which way first
> Publish his God-like office now mature.
> (I, 186–88)

> How to begin, how to accomplish best
> His end of being on Earth, and mission high.
> (II, 113–14)

These reflections on how to "enter, and begin" his career are reminiscent not only of Prodicus' Hercules, who is "hesitating by what road [he] should enter upon life," but also of a host of other young men approaching maturity.[4] According to the commentary on Junius' emblem of Hercules ("Bivium virtutis & vitij"), Paris had faced a similar crisis at adolescence.

---

3. The first edition reads "wayfaring." Hughes prefers the reading "warfaring." See John Milton, *Complete Poems and Major Prose*, ed. Merritt Y. Hughes (New York, 1957), 728*n*, on the "true wayfaring Christian" in *Areopagitica*. All quotations from Milton's poetry in this chapter are based on the Hughes edition. See also Hughes (ed.), *John Milton: Prose Selections* (New York, 1947), 233.

4. E. L. Hawkins (ed.), *A Literal Translation of Xenophon's Memorabilia of Socrates, Book II* (2nd ed.; Oxford, 1902), 13–17. For the tradition of Hercules' Choice and its variants, see Erwin Panofsky, *Hercules am Scheidewege und andere*

All things extend to the institution and choice of life, which is proposed to us by God the magistrate of souls or by nature when we arrive at maturity. For at that most apt time one chooses to enter some certain way of life. The judgment of Paris is nothing other than the adolescent's choice in pursuing this or that institution of life. Either right reason leads him to the love of true goods, (that is, the love of the life of Pallas), or else the madness of the passions of the mind seduces him to the life of Venus and he is seized with admiration for a beautiful form.[5]

Moreover, as Renaissance commentators observed, the tradition of Hercules' Choice between virtue and vice had been broadened to include a wider range of values and personalities: Lucian's hesitation between Statuaria and Doctrina, Poggio's representation of Industria and Pigritia, Saint Gregory Nazianzen's dream of Sanctimonia and Temperantia, Stobaeus' comparison between Riches and Virtue, Philo Judaeus' personifications of Virtus and Voluptas.[6]

With Silius Italicus' *Punica*, this motif had become a part of the epic tradition; for in this poem the youthful Scipio beholds a vision of Virtue and Pleasure while he is reflecting on the Punic War. "In Book 15 of the Punic War Silius Italicus elegantly transfers this fable to Scipio. While Scipio was thinking about war in Africa (Silius feigns) there appeared to him Virtue on the right

---

antike Bildstoffe in der neueren Kunst, Studien der Bibliothek Warburg, XVIII (Leipzig, 1930). See especially 42–52 on Prodicus and Xenophon; 53ff. on Sebastian Brant and Saint Basil; 68–83 on Silius Italicus; 45–46 on Hesiod's *Works and Days* (ll. 287ff.); 48–50, 64, 98 on Dio Chrysostom; 50 on *The Tablet of Cebes*; 99 on the Judgment of Paris; 173–80 on Titian; and 44, 65–68 on the Pythagorean Y. See also Panofsky, *Studies in Iconology: Humanistic Themes in the Art of the Renaissance* (New York, 1939). For the application of this motif to *Paradise Regained*, see *Paradise Regained, the Minor Poems and Samson Agonistes*, ed. Merritt Y. Hughes (New York, 1937), 477*n*; John M. Steadman, *Milton's Epic Characters: Image and Idol* (Chapel Hill, 1968), 124–27. In *The Infernal Triad: The Flesh, the World, and the Devil in Spenser and Milton* (Princeton, 1974), Patrick Cullen has noted the adaptation of the crossroads motif in the writings of Deguilleville, Hawes, and Cartigny (pp. 5, 10, 14). In *The Pilgrimage of the Life of Man*, the Pilgrim must choose between the broad and easy way and the narrow, difficult path. In *The Pastime of Pleasure*, Graunde Amoure is confronted at the crossroads with a choice between the active and contemplative lives. In *The Wandering Knight*, the knight and his guide Dame Folly encounter two ladies, Virtue and Voluptuousness, at the crossroads.

    5. *Hadriani Junii Emblemata* (Leiden, 1596), Emblem no. 44.

    6. *Hadriani Junii Emblemata*; Panofsky, *Hercules am Scheidewege*; cf. *Opus aureum et scholasticum, in quo continetur Pythagorae carmina aurea . . . & aliorum poemata*, ed. Michael Neander of Sorau (2 vols; Leipzig, 1577); *Herakles ek deuterou ton Apomnemoneumaton Sokratous*, in *Opus aureum*, I.

and Pleasure (Voluptas) on the left, each uttering a speech effective for persuasion."[7] Centuries afterward, DuBartas' *Second Weeke* applied the Hercules-Paris dilemma to the theme of kingship. Representing Solomon's dream (1 Kings 3:5–15) as a choice between four beautiful women—Glory, Wealth, Health, and Wisdom—he described in detail the young king's criticism of the three inferior rewards. In rejecting Glory, DuBartas' Solomon (like Milton's Christ) objects that

> the long Custom of inhumane Slaughter,
> Transformes in time the myldest Conquerors
> To Tigers, Panthers, Lions, Bears, and Boars.

Nevertheless, because Solomon has chosen wisdom in preference to the other values, God promises him the fruition of all four.[8]

Like Paris, the protagonist of Francesco Colonna's *Hypnerotomachia Poliphili* must choose between three alternatives, and like Paris he chooses unwisely.[9] At the bidding of Queen Eleutherillida (freedom), her handmaids Logistica and Thelemia (reason and will) accompany the youthful Poliphilus (or "lover of many") to the three gates of Queene Telosia (end or goal). The three gates are labeled respectively Theodoxia (glory of God), Cosmodoxia (glory of the world), and Erototrophos (love). In spite of Logistica's warnings, he selects the third.

In the "Cambridge Songs," a poem on the Pythagorean Y presents the choice between the two ways of virtue and vice as a crisis which confronts the "age of youth" ("juventutis etas") at the conclusion of childhood and beginning of adolescence. "The Greek letter Y contains an I below but branches into two parts above. It is an appropriate similitude of human life. For simple childhood does not easily know whether to subject the mind to vice or virtue. The age of youth offers us a crossroads."[10]

Although the ordeal of initial choice was usually represented either through the crossroads image or through contrasting female figures, it could also be expressed in terms of the wilder-

---

7. *Hadriani Junii Emblemata; cf.* Panofsky, *Hercules am Scheidewege.*

8. See Josuah Sylvester, *Du Bartas His Divine Weekes and Workes* (London, 1621), *Second Weeke.*

9. See Francesco Colonna, *Hypnerotomachia Poliphili* (Venice, 1499); and the 1592 English translation by R.D. [Robert Dallyngton(?)], *The Strife of Love in a Dream*, ed. Andrew Lang (London, 1890).

10. See F. J. E. Raby, *A History of Secular Latin Poetry in the Middle Ages* (2 vols.; Oxford, 1934), I, 298.

ness. Thus, according to Dante's *Convivio*, "The adolescent who enters into the wandering wood of this life would not know how to keep the right path if it were not shown him by his elders. Nor would their indications avail if he were not obedient to their commandments, and therefore obedience was necessary for this age."[11]

Alessandro Vellutello identified this "selva erronea" with the "selva oscura" of the *Inferno* (I, 2), in which Dante had lost his way ("la diritta via"). "By the forest (*selva*) the poet means the same wood that he had treated in his *Convivio*. He calls it the wandering wood (*Selva erronea*) in which man enters at the age of adolescence. One should note that, as *selva* properly denotes any thick multitude of trees, so the poet means by *selva* any thick multitude of what things soever."[12]

In Valvasone's *La Caccia*, the young Arthur faces a similar crisis. While hunting in "una gran selva," he loses his way ("si ritrovò smartito [*sic*], & lasso"), but he soon beholds on his right hand "a rocky mountain which contained a hidden cave." The notes by Olimpio Marcucci not only explain this passage in terms of Hercules' Choice but also call attention to the problem of "primo ingresso."

> The right hand (*destra manno*) alludes to the story of Hercules. At his left hand there was a pleasant way which led to delights; at his right hand a rough and thorny way which led to virtue. Hercules chose the latter and left the former. These two ways—one of delight, the other of virtue—were designated by the letter of Pythagoras [the letter Y]. . . . The mountain, the stones, and the cave are thus the difficulties which one encounters on first entrance to the sciences. The delightful plain, which extends around them, figures delights. Our reason leaves these pleasures and enters through difficulties to understand the secrets of nature.[13]

The problem that confronts the hero of *Paradise Regained* is, then, a conventional crisis of adolescence: the dilemma of the young man considering how to begin and enter upon his course of life, and meditating on what way precisely to follow. In describing the biblical temptation, Milton has adapted the familiar classical motif of the crossroads to a Palestinian setting; and the ordeal

---

11. *The Convivio of Dante Alighieri*, trans. Philip H. Wicksteed (London, 1940), 350–51.

12. Alessandro Vellutello, *La Comedia di Dante* (Venice, 1544), on *Inferno*, Canto I.

13. Erasmo da Valvasone, *La Caccia* (Venice, 1602), fol. 155.

of initial choice which his hero undergoes is comparable to that of other princes and heroes—Scipio, Arthur, and Solomon.

Milton's hero is concerned not only with the problem of commencement ("how to begin") but also with the specific question of ends and means ("how to accomplish best / His end of being on Earth, and mission high"). In this respect he again resembles the conventional wayfarer at the crossroads. Like the latter, he is confronted with a choice between two paths: the short and easy road of vice and the long and difficult way of virtue. And, like the latter, he must base his decision on a rational analysis of the paths themselves and the ends to which they lead.

When Satan contrasts the "short time" and "ease" with which his "offer'd aid" would have set Christ "On David's Throne; or Throne of all the world" with the hard assays "Of dangers, and adversities and pains" that the latter must otherwise undergo in order to obtain "*Israel's* Scepter," he is following the conventional characterization of the two ways of classical tradition. According to Hesiod, "it is possible *easily* to meet with vice even in abundance, the road is smooth, and it dwells *very near*. But the immortal gods have placed sweat in front of virtue; and the path is *long and steep* to her, and *rough* at first; but when you have arrived at the summit then indeed it becomes easy, though it was *difficult*" (italics mine). In Prodicus' narrative of Hercules' Choice, Vice promises to lead the young man to happiness "by the most pleasant and most easy way," contrasting it with the "difficult and long . . . road" of Virtue.[14] The two paths are similarly characterized in the pseudo-Virgilian epigram on the Pythagorean Y. "The forked letter [Y] of Pythagoras shows the figure of human life. For the steep way of virtue seeks the path on the right. This offers at first a difficult approach to the beholders, but it gives rest to the weary on its highest summit. The broad way appears to offer an easy journey; but the final end precipitates the travellers and rolls them through steep rocks."[15]

In the later development of this tradition, the two ways became partly identified with biblical parallels: notably Jeremiah 21:8 ("Behold, I set before you the way of life, and the way of death") and Matthew 7:13–14 ("Enter ye in at the strait gate: for wide

14. Hawkins (ed.), *Xenophon's Memorabilia*, 12–15.
15. Valvasone, *La Caccia*, fol. 155.

is the gate, and broad is the way, that leadeth to destruction, and . . . strait is the gate, and narrow is the way, which leadeth unto life"). In Christoff Murer's illustration of Hercules' Choice, the two allegorical women (Virtue and Vice) are labeled "VIA VI-TAE" and "VIA MORTIS."[16] Costalius' emblem of Hercules represents the path of pleasure as "spacious at its entrance," but its end is death: "Et sur la fin cachant la mort obscure." Conversely, the path of virtue, "rude & Terrible" at the beginning, ends on level ground, promising "entire recompense for the ills suffered on the first part of the way."[17] For Lactantius, the two ways of virtue and vice lead respectively to Heaven and Hell, and he adapts Virgil's account of the two paths (*Aeneid*, VI) to this intent. "Thus one is the way of virtue and the good, which conducts not into the Elysian fields (as poets say) but to the very citadel of the world. But the left concerns the punishments of evil and leads to impious Tartarus."[18] In the Pythagorean sequence in the "Cambridge Songs," the two ways of the classical motif are identified with those of Matthew 7:13–14. Whereas the broad path of vice ends in the torments of Hell, the "narrow path" of virtue leads to the joys of Heaven: "at the end, rich in happiness, extend the eternal joys of sweet life."[19]

In the Talmud, the parable of the crossroads is introduced to explain Deuteronomy 11:26 ("Behold, I set before you this day a blessing and a curse") and 30:15 ("See, I have set before thee this day life and good, and death and evil").

> You see this path that its beginning is plain and for two or three steps you walk in comfort, but at its end you meet with thorns. You also see the other path the beginning of which is thorny; for two or three steps you walk through thorns, but in the end you come to a straight road. . . . You see the wicked prospering; for two or three days they prosper in this world, but in the end they will be thrust out. You also see the righteous in trouble; for two or three days they suffer in this world, but in the end they will have occasion for rejoicing.

Genesis 3:22 ("Behold, the man is become as one of us, to know good and evil") is also interpreted in terms of the two ways. "The

16. Panofsky, *Hercules am Scheidewege*, pl. 25.

17. Pierre Cousteau (Petrus Costalius), *Pegma cum narrationibus philosophicis* (Lyons, 1555), 125.

18. Lucius Caecilius Firmianus Lactantius, *Patrologia Latina*, J.-P. Migne (comp.), VI (Paris, 1844), col. 644.

19. Raby, *History of Secular Latin Poetry*, 298–99.

All-present has set before him two ways, the way of life and the way of death; but he chose for himself the latter path." [20]

Besides the biblical antithesis between the ways of life and death, the motif of Hercules' Choice was extended to include further ethical contrasts significant for Milton's epic: the choice between kingship and tyranny, and between earthly and heavenly beatitude. Thus Neander observed that in Dio Chrysostom's First Oration *De Regno*, "Mercury leads Hercules to a very high mountain, and there he shows the boy two women, Kingship and Tyranny." [21] In Panofsky's opinion, Titian's painting generally known as "Sacred and Profane Love" closely resembles Cesare Ripa's representations of "Felicità Eterna" and "Felicità Breve." Panofsky further noted that in a Byzantine miniature, Saint Basil stands between "Worldly Happiness" and "Heavenly Life." [22] Moreover, in *Areopagitica*, Milton had already adapted the theme of Hercules' Choice to the motif of Christian warfare and the contrasting ends of immortality and "earthly bliss." Like Hercules, the "true wayfaring Christian" must "apprehend and consider vice with all her baits and seeming pleasures, and yet abstain, and yet distinguish, and yet prefer that which is truly better"; like Hercules, he must know and reject "the utmost that vice promises to her followers." Just as the reward of true virtue is to be attained through labors and difficulties, so the "immortal garland is to be run for, not without dust and heat." [23] Thus Spenser's Sir Guyon has been conducted "through the cave of Marmon, and the bower of earthly bliss," in order that he "might see and know, and yet abstain." [24]

In exploiting the crossroads motif, Milton has retained several of its most significant antitheses: the way of life and the way of death, true and false kingship, eternal and transitory felicity, celestial and secular bliss. The short and easy path that Satan pro-

20. Abraham Cohen (ed.), *Everyman's Talmud* (New York, 1949), 99–100.

21. Cf. *Opus aureum*, on Hercules and Dio Chrysostom; see also Panofsky, *Hercules am Scheidewege*.

22. Panofsky, *Studies in Iconology*, 150–54.

23. J. A. St. John (ed.), *The Prose Works of John Milton* (Bohn's Standard Library; 5 vols.; London, 1848–53), II, 68; cf. Milton, *Complete Poems and Major Prose*, ed. Merritt Y. Hughes (New York, 1957), 728n, for references to Phil. 3:14, 2 Tim. 4:8, and James 1:12.

24. St. John (ed.), *Prose Works of Milton*, II, 68; cf. James Holly Hanford, "The Temptation Motive in Milton," *Studies in Philology*, XV (1918), 176–94.

poses retains its conventional significance as the *via mortis*. As the way of vice, it leads to spiritual death. Inasmuch as its rewards are earthly and therefore transitory, they terminate with death. The military conquerors are themselves overcome by their "Conqueror Death" and receive "Violent or shameful death [as] thir due reward." Conversely, the hard and difficult path that Christ elects to follow will culminate in eternal life. Although it leads "even to the death," it is paradoxically the true *via vitae*. It is through the way of "many a hard assay," through "Humiliation and strong Sufferance" that the Messiah must "conquer Sin and Death"; and his choice of this *via dextra* ("righthand way") is appropriately rewarded by symbolic fruition of eternal life: "Fruits fetcht from the tree of life, / And from the fount of life Ambrosial drink." Like Prodicus' Hercules, Milton's Christ chooses the hard way of virtue in preference to the easy way of vice, the *via vitae* instead of the *via mortis*. Like the Hercules of Dio Chrysostom, he differentiates true kingship from tyranny. Finally, as in medieval and Renaissance adaptations of the crossroads motif, he is faced with a clear-cut choice between the carnal and the spiritual, the secular and the celestial, the temporal and the eternal.[25]

Besides developing the contrast between the short and easy way and the long and difficult path of the crossroads tradition, Milton also made use of certain allied motifs, such as the labyrinth and the *selva oscura*. As Arnold Stein justly observed, such a metaphor as "Wand'ring this woody maze" is an image of "profound, labyrinthine self-search."[26] Both Christ and Hercules are tempted in the desert; and the wilderness of *Paradise Regained*, like that of Dante's *Commedia*, is a *selva oscura*. As a conventional symbol of "variety and multitude," the forest provides an appropriate symbolic setting for the "multitude of thoughts" that assail Milton's solitary hero, and for the variety of alternatives available to him: an external correlative of intellectual and spiritual process.[27]

In addition to the crisis of initial choice, and the antithesis be-

25. *Cf.* also Francis Quarles' personification of Flesh and Spirit as two female figures; John M. Steadman, "The Iconographical Background of Quarles' 'Flesh' and 'Spirit,'" *Art Bulletin*, XXXIX (1957), 231–32; *cf. Opus aureum*, on Hercules and Dio Chrysostom.

26. Stein, *Heroic Knowledge*, 53; *cf.* 9, 129.

27. *Cf.* Vellutello, *La Comedia di Dante*, on *Inferno*, Canto I. See also Thomas E. Maresca, *Three English Epics: Studies of "Troilus and Criseyde," "The Faerie Queene," and "Paradise Lost"* (Lincoln, Neb., 1979), on the *selva* motif.

tween the hard and the easy way, *Paradise Regained* exploits yet another aspect of the crossroads tradition. The criteria that the hero employs in choosing his way—right reason and revelation—are those which had conventionally guided the wayfarer at the crossroads and the traveler in the labyrinth.

Alciati's emblem of Mercury "in trivio" (no. 8) brings together, for instance, several conventional elements that recur later in *Paradise Regained*: the mountain, the choice of way, and divine guidance. "At the crossroads there is a mount of stones. Over-topping this is the mutilated effigy of a god as far as the breast. This is the tomb of Mercury. Traveller, hang up garlands of flowers to the god who will show you the right way. All of us are at the crossroads, and in this path of life we err unless God himself shows us the way." Claude Mignault's commentary on this emblem suggests further affinities with Milton's epic: "Here by the name of Mercury, messenger of the gods, we understand either the sacred scriptures (which open the divine will to us), or else prophets and doctors, announcers of the sacred and celestial oracle, from whom it is necessary to receive the orthodox way and knowledge of eternal salvation."[28] Similarly, in *Paradise Regained* (I, 260–64) it is through revolving "The Law of Prophets, search-ing what was writ / Concerning the Messiah, to our Scribes / Known partly" that Milton's Christ has learned that he must in-deed choose the hard and difficult path: "my way must lie / Through many a hard assay even to the death."

Second, according to Mignault, the blindness and ignorance of the human understanding (Eph. 4:18) make it imperative that the wayfarer seek knowledge of the way from God himself.[29] Simi-larly, Milton's Christ contrasts the ignorance of the Gentiles ("Alas! what can they teach, and not mislead; / Ignorant of them-selves, of God much more" [IV, 309–310]) with the divine revela-tion of the Law and the Prophets.

> But herein to our Prophets far beneath,
> As men divinely taught, and better teaching
> The solid rules of Civil Government.
>
> . . . .
>
> In them is plainest taught, and easiest learnt,
> What makes a Nation happy, and keeps it so,

28. *Omnia Andreae Alciati V. C. Emblemata: cum commentariis . . . per Claudium Minoem Divionensem* (Antwerp, 1581), 51, 52.
29. *Ibid.*, 52.

> What ruins Kingdoms, and lays Cities flat;
> These only, with our Law, best form a King.
> (IV, 356–64)

Finally, in Mignault as in Milton, the office of wisdom in teaching the true way is related to the crisis of initial choice, the problem of entering upon a certain way or mode of life. "It seems that this emblem can refer (not badly) to the kind and institution of each life. Since entering into it is difficult, there is need for some Mercury—that is, some perceptor or doctor who will teach the way." [30]

Much the same kind of interpretation had been applied to the labyrinth as a moral and epistemological symbol. In Claude Paradin's *Heroicall Devises*, the "simbole of the Labirinth . . . may perchance signifie, that we are lead by the grace of God to finde the way that leadeth to eternall life, the same giving the thread as it were of his holy precepts into our hands, which when we have once taken hold of, and do follow, we turne away from the dangerous wandrings, and feareful by wayes of this world." [31] Similarly, the *Emblemes* of Francis Quarles includes an illustration of the labyrinth, with an angel guiding the wayfarer onward by a thread—a Christian variant on the myth of Theseus and Ariadne. The accompanying verses identify this maze as the world itself ("The world's a Lab'rinth") and the true path with divine guidance ("Great God, . . . Thou art my Path; direct my steps aright"). The religious significance of the way is further developed by a text from Psalm 119:5 ("Oh that my wayes were directed to keep thy Statutes") and by a quotation from Saint Augustine's *Soliloquies* ("O Lord, who art the Light, the Way, the Truth, the Life; . . . The way, without which there is wandring; The Truth, without which there is errour; Life, without which there is death"). [32]

Like the wayfarers confronted by the alternatives of the crossroads and the ambiguities of the labyrinth, the hero of *Paradise Regained* distinguishes the true path from the false through reason and revelation. Like many spiritual travelers, he learns the right way from the Scriptures; and like the first wanderers, Adam and Eve, he relies upon Providence as his guide: "Who brought

30. *Ibid.*

31. *The Heroicall Devises of M. Claudius Paradin . . . Whereunto are added the Lord Gabriel Symeons and others*, trans. P.S. (London, 1591), 118–19.

32. Francis Quarles, *Emblemes* (London, 1639), 189; the emblem is reproduced in Rosemary Freeman, *English Emblem Books* (London, 1948.)

me hither / Will bring me hence, no other Guide I seek" and "For what concerns my Knowledge God reveals" (I, 335–36, 293). In one respect, however, he is unique; he does not merely choose his way, but he is himself "the way, the truth, and the life" (John 14:6). Since he is himself the truth (the "living Oracle" sent by God "Into the World, to teach his final will"), the "ways of truth"—however "Hard . . . and rough to walk"—are not extrinsic but intrinsic to him: essential to and inseparable from his nature and his office. He is himself the *via vitae*: "the way . . . and the life."

Although this wilderness ordeal is essentially a crisis of initial choice, the imagery of the labyrinth and of Paradise lost and regained suggests a further, more comprehensive meaning. Both the labyrinth and the wilderness were conventional symbols for the world. And the ordeal that Milton's hero undergoes in the desert is, in a sense, an epitome of the future redemption of mankind: a prophetic miniature of the act of salvation to be accomplished in the years to come, when the Messianic hero will "bring back / Through the world's wilderness long wander'd man / Safe to eternal Paradise of rest" (*PL*, XII, 312–14).

As the crossroads motif could involve a choice between two, three, or more kinds of life, it could be applied not only to the clear-cut alternatives of virtue and vice but also to the conventional distinction between the active, contemplative, and voluptuous lives. There are only two alternatives in Hercules' case, but a choice among three different possibilities in the instance of the youthful Paris or the young Poliphilus. In presenting Satan's offer of an earthly kingdom, Milton exploits the motif of the *triplex vita*—proceeding from the rewards of the voluptuous life to those of the active life, and finally to those of the *vita contemplativa*.[33]

The background of the Choice of Hercules and the Judgment of

33. For an analysis of Satan's lures in terms of the voluptuary, active, and contemplative lives, see Howard Schultz, *Milton and Forbidden Knowledge* (New York, 1955), 225–26. Renaissance commentaries recognized in Hercules' Choice the same sort of youthful crisis that Paris had faced on Mount Ida. The explanation of Junius' Emblem no. 44 of Hercules ("Bivium virtutis & vitij") not only cites Prodicus' story but proceeds to point the analogy with Paris. *Cf.* Natale Conti on the Judgment of Paris in *Natalis Comitis Mythologiae* (Geneva, 1641), 664, 670. Juno offers the Trojan shepherd dominion over Europe and Asia ("Asiae Europaeque imperium"). Pallas proposes to make him wiser than all the Greeks ("omnibus Graecis sapientiorem"). Venus offers him the most beautiful of all women

Paris is not without significance for a problem that engaged both Tillyard and Hughes as well as later scholars: the relation between action and contemplation, and between action and passion, in *Paradise Regained*. In Milton's brief epic, Hughes detected a long-standing concern "over the conflict of the contemplative with the active ideal: and an affinity with Renaissance debates over their relative superiority. Tillyard agreed that the poem "deals with a theme . . . which had long been present in Milton's mind," but believed that Milton had unduly emphasized "the passive virtues." Kermode stressed the importance of the analogy between Milton's Christ and Scipio as "the true exemplar of the nice balance of active and contemplative." Woodhouse maintained that "passion (in its root meaning) is the prevailing note" in *Paradise Regained* and that it is "passion, not contemplation, that is opposed to action, for Christ . . . rejects two temptations which are contemplative in character, as well as a whole series that involve action." Stein regarded the wilderness ordeal as essentially a preparation for heroic action. "[A]ll the preparation was preparation to act in the world, to act God's will and love in the world. All of the hero's descent into the self and all of the antagonist's offers of transcendence have clearly recognized, and reiterated, this end of being on earth: action." [34]

Underlying these apparent divergences is an element of common truth which may perhaps be seen more clearly against the background of the crossroads motif and its allied traditions. Like other ordeals of initial choice, the central event in *Paradise Regained* is contemplative in character. The hero does not act; he meditates. [35] The fable depicts an internal process of the understanding and will rather than the accomplishment of an external action; and the hero's *aristeia* (so far as we can judge it) belongs not to the battlefield but to the mind. Both the argument of Milton's epic and its mode of presentation involve reflection rather than deeds; and the poem is less an "imitation of an action" than an imitation of thought.

("mulierum omnium pulcherrimam"). In brief, "Iuno regnum, sapientiam Pallas, pulcherrimam mulierum Venus adpromitteret."

34. Tillyard, "The Christ of *Paradise Regained*," 105; Hughes, "The Christ of *Paradise Regained*," 254–77; Tillyard, "The Christ of *Paradise Regained*," 105–106; Kermode, "Milton's Hero," 320; Woodhouse, "Theme and Pattern in *Paradise Regained*," 168; Stein, *Heroic Knowledge*, 134.

35. Martz, "*Paradise Regained*: The Meditative Combat."

Nevertheless, the contemplative nature of this ordeal does not provide sufficient grounds for some of the inferences that have been drawn from it: that Milton's Christ embodies the contemplative rather than the active ideal of heroism; that Milton himself regarded contemplation as superior to action; or even that the epic itself is concerned with the relationship between action and contemplation. As the crisis of initial choice was traditionally reflective in nature, the quality of the hero is *a fortiori* to be found rather in the objects of his contemplation and in his assessment and evaluation of them, than in the contemplative nature of his ordeal. Although Paris and Poliphilus contemplate the different rewards offered by the *triplex vita*, neither of them is in fact a contemplative hero. On the contrary, both youths reject the *vita activa* and the *vita contemplativa* for the voluptuous life: the life of pleasure and (more specifically) of amatory delight. Similarly, though Hercules likewise undergoes an ordeal of solitary reflection, the heroic ideal that he exemplifies belongs primarily to the type of active valor.

The predominance of the contemplative and meditative element in *Paradise Regained* is, then, a conventional characteristic of the ordeal of initial choice. It does not in itself prove that Milton's Christ is a contemplative hero or that either the poet or his hero prefers the life of contemplation to that of action. Like other young men confronted with a career decision, Milton's hero contemplates the various modes of life and their rewards—specifically, various rewards offered by the *vita voluptaria*, the *vita activa*, and the *vita contemplativa*—but he does not positively choose the last of these in preference to the others. Instead, he rejects Satan's version of the "life contemplative" just as decisively as he has hitherto refused the devil's offers of the life of pleasure and the apparent goods of the active life.

Again, though Milton's Christ rejects "temptations which are contemplative in character" as well as others "that involve action," he does not fully repudiate either the active or the contemplative modes of heroism. Instead he repudiates Satan's essentially secular version of them: "aught / By me propos'd in life contemplative, / Or active, tended on by glory or fame" (IV, 369–71). This renunciation of the worldly aspects of the "threefold life" (the conventional *triplex vita*) gives additional emphasis to the spiritual means and celestial ends that he does not renounce. He rejects the worldly delights of the banquet scene, but he does not decline the heavenly delights of the angelic banquet: the spiritual pleasures of the new "*Eden* rais'd in the waste wilderness." He refuses the wisdom of the world, the arts and sciences of the Gentiles, but he consistently extols the heavenly wisdom accessible through the Hebrew tradition. He dismisses the kingdoms of the world and their power and glory, but he does not scorn the kingdom of Heaven, its spiritual power, and its heavenly glory. In all three branches of the *triplex vita*—active, contemplative, and voluptuous—he decisively rejects the secular, but decisively affirms the celestial.[36] As Frank Kermode rightly observed, *Paradise Regained* is "concerned . . . to establish the heavenly nature of the rewards which supersede the earthly recompense of the old heroes."[37] The basic antithesis in Milton's epic is not between the active and contemplative lives, but between worldly and heavenly ends and means.

Finally, the pattern of rejection is not only inseparable from the "drama of knowledge," that epistemological agon rightly emphasized by Stein, Kermode, and other critics. It is also the means by which Milton progressively demonstrates his hero's superlative excellence. Each new test provides additional evidence of the intellectual and moral superiority of this "perfect hero" to all other heroes and kings. Each rung of the "ethical ladder" (or to adapt Satan's metaphor, each step up Virtue's hill) raises him head and shoulders above yet another category of his fellowmen.[38] As each new temptation calls forth a further demonstration of his "godliness," this progressive proof of his essential "likeness to God" leads gradually but inevitably to the final manifestation of his unique nature ("True Image of the Father") in the temple episode and the angelic banquet that concludes it. In rejecting the entire complex of secular values, Milton's hero demonstrates his heavenly character, as opposed to the earthy nature of the First Adam. This Second and greater Adam is "the Lord from Heaven," and he reveals his essentially heavenly nature by refusing the offer of the world.

36. *Cf.* Schultz, *Milton and Forbidden Knowledge*, 225–26.
37. Kermode, "Milton's Hero," 329.
38. For the image of virtue's hill and the hill of truth, see A. S. P. Woodhouse and Douglas Bush (eds.) *A Variorum Commentary on the Poems of John Milton* (3 vols. to date; New York, 1970–), II, 381; *ibid.*, III, ed. Walter MacKellar (New York, 1975), 100–101; and Paul R. Sellin's essay, "The Proper Dating of Donne's 'Satire III,'" *Huntington Library Quarterly*, XLIII (1980), 275–312.

The knowledge-rejection pattern underlying Milton's presentation of the second temptation thus serves two purposes. First, it represents, in Christ's moral dialectic and successive acts of choice, the reorientation of the human understanding and will toward the "chief good." Second, it represents the restoration and regeneration of the divine image in the human soul through the agency of Christ the mediator. In the final analysis, however, these functions are almost identical. The *summum bonum* (or highest good) and the divine image are inseparable. "Our beginning, regeneration, and happiest end," Milton maintains, is "likeness to God, which in one word we call godliness." Moreover, it is through regeneration after God's "own image" that the understanding is renewed to "prove what is that good will of God," and the will restored "to its former liberty."

As Logos, as "the great mystery of godliness," Milton's Christ is the perfect archetype of the divine image and exhibits its essential characteristics in their perfection: "Truth, Wisdome, Sanctitude severe and pure, / Severe, but in true filial freedom plac't." If the "dialectical drama" of *Paradise Regained* emphasizes the hero's righteousness, knowledge, and holiness, it is largely because these are the basic attributes of divine resemblance. As Milton presents it, the second temptation is in its major outlines a moral demonstration of the essential features of the divine image. The hero proves his divine sonship by demonstrating his spiritual "likeness to God"; and this demonstration leads directly and logically to the final revelations of the temple episode and the angelic banquet, where he is hailed as true image of the Father.

The rejection motif is thus an essential element in Milton's delineation of the divine image. The act of rejection establishes the hero's knowledge, his "righteousnesse and true holiness," and his "filial freedom": all of which are characteristic of the divine image renewed in the "new man." This detailed analysis and refusal of the ends and means that Satan proposes is, moreover, a comprehensive and continuous anatomy of "the body of sin": a dissection, so to speak, of "the old man with his deeds," which a regenerated humanity is to "put off" in the process of its renovation. Milton is not content simply to dismiss the old hero for the new. He goes deeper still, and his pattern of rejection is ultimately founded on the pattern of regeneration. For his pattern of the new hero, he chooses the archetype of the new man—the Son of God and "True Image of the Father"; and the old hero he dismisses is, in the final analysis, the old man. The rejection of the image of the *vetus homo* is essential for the manifestation of the image of the *homo novus*. The central action of *Paradise Regained* is thus a simultaneous process of ceremonial divesture and investure, "putting off" the garments of the First Adam and "putting on" those of the Second Adam. Representing the process of man's gradual renewal in knowledge after the image of the Creator, it is essentially the imitation of an internal, invisible operation of the spirit: a paradigm of regeneration.

CHAPTER 8

Satanic Paideia: The Devil as Humanist

THE CENTRAL temptation in *Paradise Regained* concludes quietly but climactically with the bait of Athenian learning. One of the salient features of the course of studies that Satan
proposes is its predominantly philosophical and philological
character. The devil is offering much the same kind of training
that Horace had recommended for the poet and that Quintilian
and Cicero had proposed for the orator: the study of Greek literary masterpieces and arts of discourse, and a knowledge of
Hellenic philosophy. Indeed it conforms fairly closely to the type
of education that Cicero himself had received—a pedagogical
ideal shared by many other Roman orators and statesmen, by
various fathers of the church, and by a substantial number of Renaissance educators.

Its exclusively Hellenic character is worthy of note. There is no
suggestion that a mastery of Latin eloquence would be helpful to
the future king; and on this point Milton parts company with a
large proportion of Renaissance humanists. Accustomed to reading the ancients either for style or for *eruditio,* or for both, many of
them venerated the learning of the Greeks as comprising virtually
the entire range of knowledge necessary for or available to man.[1]
Consequently the advancement of the arts and sciences (and

1. See William Harrison Woodward, *Studies in Education during the Age of the
Renaissance, 1400–1600,* ed. Lawrence Stone (New York, 1967); Woodward,
Desiderius Erasmus Concerning the Aim and Method of Education (Cambridge, 1904);
Woodward, *Vittorino da Feltre and Other Humanist Educators* (Cambridge, 1905).

of society itself) depended in large measure on retrieving the wisdom of the ancients and in particular the learning of Hellas. Nevertheless, so far as the mastery of discourse was concerned, the primary emphasis fell on the Latin rather than on the Greek tongue. As the educators themselves sometimes acknowledged, their own position in relation to the Latin language was roughly comparable to that of the ancient Romans in regard to the language of Greece.

In the temptation of Athens, Milton surely had the humanist educational program partly in mind, but he nevertheless preserved historical decorum by stressing the Greek arts of discourse rather than the Latin. Not only were the Hellenic models usually superior in quality, but they were precisely the models that the principal Roman poets and orators had been studying and imitating and that would form a substantial part of the curriculum in the schools of the Roman empire. Yet there were also tactical reasons for presenting the classical wisdom of antiquity entirely in a Greek setting, and for restricting the visionary *mise-en-scène* to Athens. The hero of the poem has already refused the imperial authority of Rome just as he had previously rejected the military might of Parthia, and it would be inappropriate to introduce yet another Roman temptation at this point. Each of these visionary tableaux profits by comparison and contrast with the others; and the visual perspective, offering an actual view of the "enticing object" (as in the temptation of Eve), confers greater persuasive force, definition, and concentration on the rhetorical appeals that complement the "rhetoric of vision." Moreover, in centering this temptation on Athens, Milton focuses his vision largely, though not entirely, on its schools and academies. Satan's arguments and Christ's rebuttals are relevant to the English schools and universities of the poet's own day.

In the context of Renaissance humanism, Satan's offer is all the more plausible since it apparently involves drinking from the proverbial fountainheads of eloquence and wisdom. This had long been a conventional argument in favor of classical studies and on behalf of the Latin language in comparison with the student's mother tongue, the language of his nation and his own contemporaries. Significantly, Christ rejects the classical language and literature for those of his own national heritage, preferring the prophets and poets of Israel. In replying to Satan's offer, he combines two arguments frequently applied in different contexts during the Renaissance: the claims of one's native language in comparison with those of the classical tongues, and the importance of mastery of the Hebrew language for an accurate interpretation of the Old Testament. On the former issue the humanists themselves had been divided. Erasmus, for instance, had scorned the vernacular. Milton himself, after some inner debate, had deliberately chosen English rather than Latin as the vehicle for his major poetry. As for the second issue, the defense of Hebrew studies had, long before, been a principal issue in the Reuchlin controversy, which had aligned many northern humanists and Reformers against the defenders of scholastic methods and the conservative establishment in German universities and in the church. That much of the content of Greek philosophy and poetry had been originally derived from Hebrew sources was also a commonplace of the period.[2]

The principle underlying much of the educational program of the humanists—a return to the sources of knowledge, bypassing a later and corrupt tradition—also underlies Milton's treatment of the temptation of Athens. Christ has gone beyond the Latin literature primarily studied in humanist schools to the Greek sources behind them; from those to Hebrew learning, the source of Greek wisdom; and beyond this to God himself as the ultimate fountain of light and of sacred utterance.[3]

The paradoxes and ironies of a situation in which the father of lies refers the divine Logos to the schools of Hellas for instruction—the true fountain of light to false springs and contaminated waters—would not have been lost on Milton's early readers. And perhaps for some of them the ironies would have been enhanced by the poet's adaptation of a Renaissance commonplace: the topic of restoration. In some respects Renaissance conceptions of clas-

2. *Cf.* Saint Augustine, *On Christian Doctrine*, trans. D. W. Robertson, Jr. (Indianapolis, 1958), 64, on this point: In answer to the claims of Platonists that Christ had learned all his lessons from the works of Plato, Saint Ambrose had shown that Plato himself "had probably been introduced to our literature by Jeremias." Pythagoras himself "did not live before the literature of the Hebrew nation. . . . Thus from a consideration of times it becomes more credible that the Platonists took from our literature whatever they said that is good and truthful than that Our Lord Jesus Christ learned from them."

3. *Cf.* Milton's discussion of the "procreant cause" in his *Ars Logica;* see also John M. Steadman, *Milton's Epic Characters: Image and Idol* (Chapel Hill, 1968), 146–58.

sical antiquity as a lost golden age, exemplary for its wisdom and eloquence and for its moral and political virtues, were a secular counterpart of the image of Eden and a lost perfection. The one was to be retrieved by returning to the classical fountains of knowledge and discourse; the other by a return to the *philosophia Christi* and the regeneration of the spirit. In both instances the ideal of the return was described in terms of the imagery of rebirth, renovation, and revival: an apocatastasis of secular or divine wisdom; the restoration of classical learning or the spiritual restoration of man.[4]

One of the principal objections that Milton's hero raises against the classical philosophers is that they were ignorant of themselves and of God, of the creation of the world, and of their fallen condition: "and how man fell / Degraded by himself, on grace depending" (*PR*, IV, 311–12). Hence as teachers they can only mislead, falling short of true wisdom and offering instead "her false resemblance . . . , / An empty cloud." The *eruditio* of the Greeks is deficient, therefore, and its arts of discourse are likewise defective; its poetry "Thin sown with aught of profit or delight," and its orators inferior to the Hebrew prophets as teachers. Thus in both aspects of the philosophy-and-eloquence criterion they are found wanting.[5]

4. Woodward, *Studies in Education*, 6.

5. On the ideal combination of wisdom-and-eloquence or philosophy-and-rhetoric in European tradition, see Joseph Anthony Mazzeo, "St. Augustine's Rhetoric of Silence: Truth vs. Eloquence and Things vs. Signs," in *Renaissance and Seventeenth-Century Studies* (New York, 1964), 1–28; Marcia Lillian Colish, *The Mirror of Language: A Study in the Medieval Theory of Knowledge* (New Haven, 1928); Jerrold E. Seigel, *Rhetoric and Philosophy in Renaissance Humanism: The Union of Eloquence and Wisdom, Petrarch to Valla* (Princeton, 1968); Richard McKeon, "Poetry and Philosophy in the Twelfth Century: The Renaissance of Rhetoric," *Modern Philology*, XLIII (1946), 217–34; McKeon, "Rhetoric in the Middle Ages," *Speculum*, XVII (1942), 1–32; John M. Steadman, *The Lamb and the Elephant: Ideal Imitation and the Context of Renaissance Allegory* (San Marino, Calif., 1974), 126, 181, and *passim*. In his prolusion "Learning Makes Men Happier Than Does Ignorance," Milton asserts that "it behoves an aspirant to true, and not to merely specious eloquence, to be instructed and perfected in an all-around foundation in all the arts and in every science" (*Complete Poems and Major Prose*, ed. Merritt Y. Hughes [New York, 1957], 622). In *On Christian Doctrine*, Saint Augustine raised the question of whether, "since by means of the art of rhetoric both truth and falsehood are urged," the defenders of truth should not be left unarmed against the eloquence of liars. "While the faculty of eloquence, which is of great value in urging either evil or justice, is in itself indifferent, why should it not be obtained for the uses of the good in the service of truth if the evil usurp it for the winning of perverse and

The views expressed in this scene differ substantially from those Milton had advanced years earlier in his tractate *Of Education*. There he had treated classical learning as one means of overcoming the effects of the fall of man—a point of view shared by Francis Bacon. "The end . . . of learning is to repair the ruins of our first parents by regaining to know God aright, and out of that knowledge to love him, to imitate him, to be like him, as we may the nearest by possessing our souls of true virtue, which being united to the heavenly grace of faith makes up the highest perfection." Yet in seeking this end, one must acquire "the knowledge of God and things invisible" largely by "orderly conning over the visible and inferior creature," and for this a mastery of the learned languages was necessary. "And seeing every nation affords not experience and tradition enough for all kind of learning, therefore we are chiefly taught the languages of those people who have at any time been most industrious after wisdom; so that language is but the instrument conveying to us things useful to be known."[6]

The course of study outlined in Milton's treatise comprised

---

vain causes in defense of iniquity and error?" Insisting on the superiority of wisdom to eloquence, he quoted Cicero's opinion that "wisdom without eloquence is of small benefit to states; but eloquence without wisdom is often extremely injurious and profits no one." The man who "can dispute or speak wisely, even though he cannot do so eloquently" may benefit his hearers less than if he could also speak eloquently. But "he who is foolish and abounds in eloquence is the more to be avoided the more he delights his auditor." If the Gentiles who taught the principles of eloquence nevertheless acknowledged its inferiority to wisdom, "being ignorant of that true wisdom which descends supernal from the Father of Lights, how much more ought we, who are the sons and ministers of this wisdom, to think in no other way? For a man speaks more or less wisely to the extent that he has become more or less proficient in the Holy Scriptures." The Scripture does not say, "the multitude of the eloquent," but "the multitude of the wise is the welfare of the whole world." Nevertheless, there are men out of the church "who treat the Scriptures not only wisely but eloquently" and in accordance with decorum. For there is a special kind of eloquence "fitting for men most worthy of the highest authority and clearly inspired by God. Our authors speak with eloquence of this kind, nor does any other kind become them." Our authors "have used our eloquence in such a way through another eloquence of their own that it seems neither lacking . . . nor ostentatious in them." The speaker's words "seem not to have been sought by the speaker but to have been joined to the things spoken about as if spontaneously, like wisdom coming from her house (that is, from the breast of the wise man) followed by eloquence as if she were an inseparable servant who was not called" (*On Christian Doctrine*, 118–24, *cf.* 128–32).

6. Milton, *Complete Poems and Major Prose*, 631.

the encyclopedia of arts and sciences, including agriculture, rational philosophy, mathematics, and such practical arts as fortifications, architecture, and "enginery." Although these studies "in nature and mathematics" were to be supplemented by the "helpful experiences" of persons in various practical vocations ("hunters, fowlers" and "architects, engineers, . . . anatomists"), and though the students were expected to learn Italian "at any odd hour," the authors studied were for the most part Greek and Latin writers. The curriculum was thus almost entirely classical.

The Christ of *Paradise Regained* appeals to both of these *topoi* in rejecting classical learning, but it is significant that in this instance his native literary tradition is the tradition of revealed truth. True eloquence and wisdom, he replies, belong not to the schools and literature of Greece but to *Hebraica veritas*. Moreover, Greece is not the true fountainhead of either wisdom or eloquence; it has acquired its learning, its arts and sciences from the Hebrew tradition:

> Or if I would delight my private hours
> With Music or with Poem, where so soon
> As in our native Language can I find
> That solace? All our Law and Story strew'd
> With Hymns, our Psalms . . . declare
> That rather *Greece* from us these Arts deriv'd.
> (IV, 331–38)

Indeed, the true source of inspired utterance is to be found in Heaven; and as Milton's readers well knew, this source must be sought in and through Christ himself, the metaphorical well of "living water." As the incarnation of the Logos, the "Wisdom" and the "Word" of God, he is in a unique sense the source and archetype of both truth and eloquence:

> he who receives
> Light from above, from the fountain of light,
> No other doctrine needs, though granted true.
> (IV, 288–90)

An appeal to the wisdom of this world is appropriate, if not inevitable, in the context of the second temptation, centering as it does specifically on the kingdoms of the world. Even if the kingdom proposed is essentially that of the mind and will—an empire over one's self and a metaphorical empire over the hearts of other men through teaching and persuasion—the humanistic character of the studies that Satan proposes is in some respects suggestive not only of the extensive literature devoted to the education of a prince or a counselor or a magistrate or a courtier but also of the classical education actually received by the heirs of Renaissance rulers. Moreover, the nature of this curriculum conforms to historical decorum. In the first century, virtually any temptation centering on the learning of the Gentiles would naturally focus on Greece and, more specifically, on the schools of Athens. Again, the Greek language was better known in Palestine and other parts of the eastern Mediterranean than Latin. Nevertheless, in the narrowing of the wisdom of the Gentiles and the wisdom of this world specifically to the arts and sciences of Hellas, there were scriptural associations. More significantly, several of these texts not only juxtaposed the wisdom of this world with the wisdom of God but explicitly contrasted the wisdom of the Greeks with the preaching of the Word.

At Athens (Acts 17:16–34) Paul had conversed with "certain philosophers of the Epicureans, and of the Stoics," and preached on the Areopagus (a probable site for the oratory that the tempter urges Milton's Christ to hear); the apostle had also adapted quotations from Greek poetry to the exigencies of his sermon. In Romans (1:14) he had differentiated the "wise" Greeks from the "unwise" barbarians. In an extended passage in 1 Corinthians (1:17–3:20) he had explicitly contrasted the wisdom and eloquence of the world with the wisdom of God and the power of preaching. He had been divinely sent "to preach the gospel" but "not with wisdom of words. . . . For the preaching of the cross is to them that perish foolishness." God had "made foolish the wisdom of the world"; inasmuch as "the world by wisdom knew not God, it pleased God by the foolishness of preaching to save them that believe." The "Greeks seek after wisdom," and regard the doctrine of "Christ crucified" as folly. Again, "my speech and my preaching were not with enticing words of man's wisdom, but in demonstration of the Spirit and of power; That your faith should not stand in the wisdom of men, but in the power of God. . . . For the wisdom of this world is foolishness with God."[7]

7. *Cf.* also 2 Cor. 1:12; James 3:15–17. *Cf.* Saint Augustine (*On Christian Doctrine*, 6–14): "[A]ll truth is from Him who said, 'I am the truth.' . . . Wisdom Himself saw fit to make Himself congruous with such infirmity as ours and to set an example of living for us. . . . Since we do wisely when we come to Him, He was thought by proud men to do foolishly when He came to us. And since when we

In this confrontation between the incarnate "wisdom of God" and the "wisdom of this world" offered by its prince, there is an implicit contrast between the way that the hero's destiny and mission, the Crucifixion itself, must inevitably appear in the eyes of the world and in the sight of God himself. To the wise Greeks it must seem folly; and in offering Greek wisdom, Satan is proposing not only a false sapience which is folly in divine eyes but precisely the kind of wisdom that would regard the Crucifixion and the Gospel as ridiculous. Moreover, Satan's lures represent the sort of knowledge and eloquence—a "wisdom of words"—that Paul had rejected as incompatible with the preaching of the Gospel. In this context, the nature of Satan's offer, and Christ's arguments against it, would suggest that Milton was directing his poetic exemplum partly to the English church of his own time, to the issue of a learned ministry and to the question of the kind of education a clergyman should receive.

As Howard Schultz and other scholars have suggested, most of the secular baits that Satan proposes in the course of the kingdom sequence are relevant not only to the character and destiny of the hero of the poem and to the life of the warfaring Christian but also to specifically ecclesiastical issues.[8] Underlying the sequence of secular ends and means in the kingdom sequence is the sharp contrast between the celestial and worldly kingdoms, the heavenly and earthy Adam, and the incompatibility of worldly power, wealth, and wisdom with the nature and ends of the church. Many of the essential features in the temptation sequence are implicit in the Pauline emphasis on the antithesis between heavenly and worldly values and on the divine paradoxes implicit in the providential government of this world. "But God hath chosen the foolish things of the world to confound the wise; and God hath chosen the weak things of the world to confound the things which are mighty; And base things of the world, and things which are despised, hath God chosen, yea, and things which are not, to bring to nought things that are, That no flesh should glory in his presence" (1 Cor. 1:27–29).

In the context of the fall of man, conventional means of instruc-

---

come to Him we grow strong, He was thought to be weak when He came to us. . . . Thus in the Wisdom of God the world could not know God through wisdom. Why did He come when He was already here unless 'it pleased God, by the foolishness of preaching, to save them that believe'?"

8. Howard Schultz, *Milton and Forbidden Knowledge* (New York, 1955).

tion and persuasion are ridiculously inadequate. The external
means that Satan proposes cannot truly illuminate an understanding darkened by sin or redirect a will enslaved by human
passions and appetites. These must first be regenerated from
within, and this is uniquely the office of deity.

Another facet of the Satanic *paideia* is its balance between philosophy and the arts of discourse. In combining philosophical
studies with the study of poetry and oratory, it recalls an ideal
familiar to most of Milton's readers and cherished by the poet
himself: the union of wisdom and eloquence. Couched in various
terms—as an alliance between philosophy and rhetoric, between
reason and imagination, between dialectics and the arts of expression, between *res* and *verba,* or even as a medicinal syrup
mixing instruction with delight—this ideal had been supported
by writers as diverse as Plato and Cicero, Saint Augustine and
Francis Bacon. Moreover, it had become a commonplace in Renaissance arguments for the moral and intellectual benefits of
rhetoric and poetry. It was through such a union with the arts of
discourse that the teachings of philosophy could affect conduct,
engaging the will and the affections of persons unskilled in the
subtleties of logic. Conversely, the union with philosophy meant
that the poet or orator could base his art on a knowledge of the
truth. In rejecting the wisdom and eloquence of Athens, the hero
of Milton's epic is refusing precisely the kind of means that most
Renaissance humanists would have regarded as indispensable for
teaching and persuasion and for pursuit of the public good.

Notably absent from Milton's painting of the "School of Athens"
are the mathematical sciences, the mechanical arts, and natural
philosophy. These would have been less appropriate for the decorum of a king, but there were more cogent reasons for neglecting them. In the late seventeenth century the achievements of the
ancients in these fields had begun to pale in comparison with
recent discoveries by the moderns. In the age of the Royal Society
the natural sciences of ancient Greece would have seemed a pal-
try lure indeed—though it would have been possible to present
future scientific achievements, real or imaginary, through the medium of vision and prophecy. Primarily, however, the sciences
were sacrificed to Milton's desire to depict the union of philosophy and the arts of discourse. These were the disciplines principally concerned with ethical instruction and persuasion, and as

such they provided a secular counterpoint to the Messiah's role as prophet and teacher. He must teach and persuade not only by discourse but by his own example and by inner illumination.

Despite the understandable neglect of Baconian *topoi* in Milton's epic, there are conspicuous points of similarity and dissimilarity between the Baconian hero, Renaissance ideals of the philosopher and orator as hero, and the hero of *Paradise Regained*. The *magna instauratio,* the great instauration of learning, through a program of cooperative experiments primarily in the natural sciences and in avowed independence of the authors of antiquity, stands in striking contrast to the revival of learning through studying closely the history and oratory and poetry of the ancients and assimilating their philosophies and sciences. For many of the humanists, as W. H. Woodward observed, "Progress meant a restoration of a past perfection, not the evolution of a new idea."[9] For Bacon, on the other hand, the further advancement and progress of learning must result from significant (though not total) independence from the past, commitment to the future, and the discovery of new methods for achieving new and fresh discoveries.

In promising a secular dominion through the instauration of learning, Bacon proved more successful than the Satan of *Paradise Regained*. Asserting that "knowledge is power," he had predicted an empire over nature through the discovery and exploitation of her still mysterious laws and forces, regaining the original dominion that man had forfeited by his transgression and fall. Like Milton after him, he adapted the Pauline doctrine of the knowledge of God through nature to a secular scheme of learning. The *topos* of the book of nature and the argument based on the fall of man served the ends of a scheme of organized research directed essentially toward improving the material conditions of man's estate. In a sense Bacon sought not so much to regain a paradise lost as to achieve a new Atlantis. Again, even though Milton himself had represented the right knowledge of God as the true end of learning, the immediate goal of his pedagogical scheme was secular: to provide his students with the "complete and generous education" which would prepare them for performing "justly, skilfully, and magnanimously all the offices, both private and public, of peace and war."[10]

9. Woodward, *Studies in Education*, 6.
10. Milton, *Complete Poems and Major Prose*, 632.

Milton makes no serious effort in this temptation episode to grapple with the theological implications of the new science and the experimental philosophy. Satan does not offer the kind of empire over nature that Bacon had promised: a scientist's kingdom of this world. He does not (significantly) make even a passing reference to the technical and scientific achievements of the Alexandrian Greeks. In his eyes the mechanical arts would probably appear base, too low for the decorum of a hero. Nor does he refer to natural philosophy. Unlike our own age, he does not envisage the ideal of the scientist as Messiah, or identify the Messianic kingdom with the New Atlantis.

Instead, the worldly wisdom that the devil extols is essentially moral and political in its orientation; and to achieve these ends, it involves the study of philosophy and oratory, history and poetry. It is practical as well as contemplative—and envisions a mixed form of intellectual heroism. Christ must learn from the Gentiles, Satan suggests, the arts of government and the arts of persuasion—what and how to teach. The schools of Athens will provide the education appropriate for a prince and for a teacher. The Satanic emphasis falls, however, not on natural philosophy (and the devil praises Socrates specifically for bringing philosophy down from Heaven to earth), but on moral and political science: what makes a nation happy and keeps it so. The arts of refuting the sophists and persuading the people, the intellectual disciplines that he proposes, are methodologies inherited from the ancients, not the new methods that Bacon was endeavoring to persuade the moderns to accept. Instead of experiment and observation, the devil proposes the venerable techniques of deductive inference, dialectical dispute, and public rhetoric. Instead of "real" erudition as most of Milton's contemporaries conceived it, he offers verbal learning. Words rather than solid matter; shadow rather than substance.

CHAPTER 9

Paradoxes of Magnanimity: Heroic Action and Inaction in Samson Agonistes

SAMSON AGONISTES begins and ends with paradoxes—
and not the least among these is the paradox of activity in apparent inaction. The idol's holiday sacred to Dagon affords the hero "ease to the body some, none to the mind"; this temporary respite from "Laborious works" immediately exposes him to the more painful labors of thought. For the greater part of the drama his position appears to be static: he does not initiate any action, and despite his threats of violent destruction against two of his Philistine visitors, his only real activity appears to be that of the understanding and the will. Throughout the morning it is his strength of mind, not his physical power, that is being exercised, perfected, and put to the proof: "Labouring thy mind / More than the working day thy hands." It is only at his final departure from the scene, immediately before the catastrophe of the play, that he can tentatively predict that "This day will be remarkable in my life / By some great act, or of my days the last."

After this ordeal of enforced passivity, in which the hero reflects, argues, and suffers but does not *do*, his ultimate "great act" of divine vengeance acquires additional shock force by contrast. For the chorus it comes as a sudden revelation. For these at least, this epiphany of heroic virtue is a conclusive theophany; and Samson's *aristeia*, his noblest exploit, is also a signal act of God. It is largely through a strategy of seeming inaction—not only the inaction of the hero but, more significantly, the inactivity of the hero's Deity—that Milton makes the divine miracle that concludes his drama seem miraculous to its immediate witnesses, and perhaps to a remote audience. Although the reader has foreseen the outcome from the beginning, he may still experience vicariously the admiration and marvel that the chorus feel at this sudden reemergence of both hero and divinity out of obscurity. Of the hero himself:

> So virtue giv'n for lost,
> Deprest, and overthrow'n, as seem'd
>
> . . . .
>
> Revives, reflourishes, then vigorous most
> When most unactive deem'd.
>
> (ll. 1697–1705)

And of the hero's God:

> Oft he seems to hide his face,
> But unexpectedly returns
> And to his faithful Champion hath in place
> Bore witness gloriously.[1]
>
> (ll. 1749–52)

Nevertheless, this contrast between the final act of violent destruction and the long period of apparent inactivity that had preceded it has sometimes proved embarrassing to critics of Milton's drama, raising doubts as to its central emphasis as well as to the coherence of its plot. Is not this tragedy of savage massacre— concluding with the slaughter of an entire social class, "Lords, Ladies, Captains, Counsellors, or Priests" of "each *Philistian* City round"—essentially a drama of the mind? Does not the plot, the "disposition of the fable," concern itself primarily with internal events, with the agons of the soul? Is not this "imitation of an action" preeminently a *mimesis* of character and thought? These are familiar issues in Milton criticism, and in reconsidering them, I should like to reexamine, in order, the problem of heroic models in *Samson Agonistes*, the question of decorum in character and in literary genre, and finally the interrelationship between character and action.[2]

In Milton's tragic protagonist there remain a few, but significant, traces of the heroic prankster of the Book of Judges; we shall ex-

1. These and all other passages from *Samson Agonistes* are quoted from John Milton, *Complete Poems and Major Prose*, ed. Merritt Y. Hughes (New York, 1957).
2. Among recent studies of *Samson Agonistes*, see William Riley Parker, *Milton's Debt to Greek Tragedy in "Samson Agonistes"* (Baltimore, 1937); F. Michael

amine these later. No less significant for Milton's characterization of his hero, however, is the New Testament conception of Samson as a "hero of faith." Central to the drama is the paradox of the enslaved deliverer, a paragon of divine strength undone by his human weakness. And much of the irony with which Milton develops both plot and character hinges upon the apparent frustration of a divine promise, the uncertainty of a divine prediction, the questionable benefit of a divine gift. In this tragedy, as in Milton's epics and several of his dramatic sketches, the unfulfilled oracle provokes a crisis of faith—an ordeal of doubt and despair, windy joys and abortive hopes—that is finally resolved by the catastrophe of the play, with the Deity's timely return to vindicate

---

Krouse, *Milton's Samson and the Christian Tradition* (Princeton, 1947); Arnold Stein, *Heroic Knowledge: An Interpretation of "Paradise Regained" and "Samson Agonistes"* (Minneapolis, 1957); Mary Ann Nevins Radzinowicz, *Toward "Samson Agonistes": The Growth of Milton's Mind* (Princeton, 1979); Anthony Low, *The Blaze of Noon: A Reading of "Samson Agonistes"* (New York, 1974); John S. Lawry, *The Shadow of Heaven: Matter and Stance in Milton's Poetry* (Ithaca, N.Y., 1968), 346–97; Joseph Anthony Wittreich, Jr. (ed.), *Calm of Mind: Tercentenary Essays on "Paradise Regained" and "Samson Agonistes" in Honor of John S. Diekhoff* (Cleveland, 1971); Balachandra Rajan (ed.), *The Prison and the Pinnacle: Tercentenary Essays on "Paradise Regained" and "Samson Agonistes"* (Toronto, 1972); Galbraith M. Crump (ed.), *Twentieth-Century Interpretations of "Samson Agonistes"* (Englewood Cliffs, N.J., 1968); A. S. P. Woodhouse, "Tragic Effect in *Samson Agonistes*," *University of Toronto Quarterly*, XXVIII (1959), 205–22; Martin E. Mueller, "*Pathos* and *Katharsis* in *Samson Agonistes*," *ELH*, XXXI (1964), 156–74; French Fogle, "The Actions of *Samson Agonistes*," in Max F. Schulz (ed.), *Essays in American and English Literature Presented to Bruce Robert McElderry, Jr.* (Athens, Ohio, 1967), 177–96; Thomas Kranidas, "Dalila's Role in *Samson Agonistes*," *Studies in English Literature*, VI (1966), 125–37; Charles Mitchell, "Dalila's Return: The Importance of Pardon," *College English*, XXVI (1965), 614–20; James Dale, "*Samson Agonistes* as Pre-Christian Tragedy," *Humanities Association Review*, XXVII (1976), 377–88; and the following essays in James D. Simmonds (ed.), *Milton Studies*: Jackie DiSalvo, "'The Lord's Battells': *Samson Agonistes* and the Puritan Revolution," IV (1972), 39–62; Carole S. Kessner, "Milton's Hebraic Herculean Hero," VI (1974), 243–58; John B. Mason, "Multiple Perspectives in *Samson Agonistes*: Critical Attitudes Toward Dalila," X (1977), 23–33; C. A. Patrides, "The Comic Dimension in Greek Tragedy and *Samson Agonistes*," X (1977), 3–21; Helen Damico, "Duality in Dramatic Vision: A Structural Analysis of *Samson Agonistes*, XII (1978), 91–116; Anthony Low, "The Phoenix and the Sun in *Samson Agonistes*," XIV (1980), 219–31; Mary Ann Radzinowicz, "The Distinctive Tragedy of *Samson Agonistes*," XVII (1983), 249–80; John T. Shawcross, "The Genres of *Paradise Regain'd* and *Samson Agonistes*: The Wisdom of Their Joint Publication," XVII (1983), 225–48; John Mulryan, "The Heroic Tradition of Milton's *Samson Agonistes*," XVIII (1983), 217–34. For discussion of Milton's concept of decorum, see Thomas Kranidas, *The Fierce Equation: A Study of Milton's Decorum* (The Hague, 1965).

his champion, and simultaneously vindicate his own oracle and his own name. The long period marked by divine delay and the apparent dereliction of the hero serves not only to exercise the latter's faith and patience (and those of his fellow Danites) but also to epitomize the process of inward renewal or renovation as Reformed theologians conceived it.

The action of the poem thus reflects the cardinal importance of faith (*fides*) or trust (*fiducia*) in Milton's moral theology. Regarding faith as the form or essence of good works and identifying its object as the divine promise, he not only exhibits in Samson's ordeal the close interrelationship between the trial of faith and heroic patience but also heightens his image of heroic trust by juxtaposing it with its contraries or opposites: carnal reliance and overweening presumption, doubt and despair, distrust of God and trust in idols.[3] The outcome of the drama, in turn, serves by "true experience from this great event" to confirm the faith of the visiting Danites (and presumably to strengthen that of Milton's contemporaries still awaiting deliverance from Philistian yoke). This final action, in turn, hinges on the dual and complementary fidelities of the hero and his Deity: the accomplishment of a kind of implicit covenant between both agents. The exploit of faith that concludes the drama depends, in the final analysis, upon a mutual fulfillment of trust; as Samson obediently submits to the guidance of the Spirit, the Deity unexpectedly returns to bear open witness to his faithful champion, demonstrably "favouring and assisting to the end."

As a heroic image, Milton's Samson meets two of the complementary and sometimes contradictory demands that Renaissance critics imposed on the epic poet and the tragic dramatist: that the heroic exemplar be at once unique and universal—raised above the ordinary condition of mankind by extraordinary valor and virtue or else cast beneath the ordinary human condition by extraordinary sufferings—yet, all the same, sufficiently human to serve as an example for lesser men. At one extreme the hero is virtually a demigod, though perhaps a fallen one; at the other extreme he is Everyman.

Like the miraculous strength that enables him to duel entire armies single-handed, winning the kind of victories that only he-

roes of romance are accustomed to achieve, the magnitude of
Samson's failure sets him apart from other men; yet in the eyes of
the chorus this makes him an exceptionally forceful exemplar
of the human condition:

> O mirror of our fickle state,
> Since man on earth unparallel'd!
> The rarer thy example stands,
> By how much from the top of wondrous glory
> Strongest of mortal men,
> To lowest pitch of abject fortune thou art fall'n.
> For him I reckon not in high estate
> Whom long descent of birth
> Or the sphere of fortune raises;
> But thee whose strength while virtue was her mate,
> Might have subdu'd the Earth,
> Universally crown'd with highest praises.
>
> (ll. 164–75)

> As signal now in low dejected state,
> As erst in highest, behold him where he lies.
>
> (ll. 338–39)

Although these are valid observations, especially in the light of
literary and iconographical tradition, in the context of Milton's
tragedy they are only half-truths. As the poet's emphasis shifts
from the loss of virtue and divine favor to their renewal, Samson
becomes an exemplar of "plain Heroic magnitude of mind," a
type of the regenerated elect, and an image of heroic faith. As the
drama progresses the figure of the protagonist temporarily reveals affinities with a wider spectrum of heroic types and prototypes; and the plot itself suggests a series of shifting but significant relationships with several conventional types or models of
tragedy. In varying degrees the play evokes disparate and even
antithetical paradigms: the simple tragedy of suffering and the
complex tragedy involving a reversal contrary to intent; the tragedy portraying a single outcome, fortunate or unfortunate, for the
protagonist and the tragedy depicting contrary endings, good
or evil, for either side; the tragedy portraying the hero's defeat
through vice or folly and the heroic drama celebrating triumphant
virtue; the tragedy of sin and punishment and the victorious ago-
nies of the martyr.

In the same way, Samson himself combines a variety of heroic
norms; and in Milton's tragic hero critics have found allusions to

classical, biblical, and contemporary models.[4] Samson has been compared with Hercules and Christ, or with Ajax and Prometheus, but also with suffering Job, the blind Oedipus and the blind Milton. He has also been regarded as a symbol of the British Reformation and a representative of the English nation after the defeat of the Good Old Cause. In this inaction the paragon of physical might demonstrates unexpected strength of mind; and in his final outburst of violence the fierce destroyer becomes also, in a degree, the self-sacrificing martyr. The minister of divine justice simultaneously accomplishes his own personal revenge.

Because of this complexity of allusion, Milton is able to combine several tragic models, playing one paradigm against the others and thereby enhancing both irony and suspense. Initially Samson is seen as the victim of one catastrophe; at the end of the play he appears, contrary to expectation, as the heroic agent and tragic victim of yet another catastrophe. For the greater part of the drama his plight is interpreted by friends and enemies alike as the ignominious end of a glorious career rather than as the prelude to the hero's last and greatest exploit. At the outset he is seen as the victim of a *de casibus* tragedy; and the motifs associated with this model persist well into the middle of the play, up to the sequence of visits by the Philistine antagonists.[5] One encounters them in the initial choral ode ("O change beyond report, thought, or belief!"), in Manoa's initial lament:

> O miserable change! is this the man
> That invincible *Samson*, far renown'd,
> The dread of *Israel's* foes . . .
>
> . . . .
> Select and Sacred, Glorious for a while,
> The miracle of men; then in an hour
> Ensnar'd, assaulted, overcome, led bound,
> Thy Foes' derision, Captive, Poor, and Blind,
> Into a Dungeon thrust, to work with Slaves?
>
> (ll. 340–67)

and in the choral ode immediately following Manoa's first exit:

---

4. See the discussion of these views in Parker, *Milton's Debt.*

5. For Boccaccio's *De casibus virorum illustrium* and the notion of tragedy as "a fall from greatness," see Madeleine Doran, *Endeavors of Art: A Study of Form in Elizabethan Drama* (Madison, Wis., 1964), 104–28, 345; Willard Farnham, *The Medieval Heritage of Elizabethan Tragedy* (Berkeley, 1936).

> But such as thou hast solemnly elected
> With gifts and graces eminently adorn'd
> To some great work, thy glory,
> And people's safety, which in part they effect:
> Yet toward these, thus dignifi'd, thou oft,
> Amidst thir highth of noon,
> Changest thy countenance and thy hand, with no regard
> Of highest favours past
> From thee on them, or them to thee of service.
>   Nor only doest degrade them, or remit
> To life obscur'd, which were a fair dismission,
> But throw'st them lower than thou didst exalt them high,
> Unseemly falls in human eye.
>
> (ll. 678–90)

Although *Samson Agonistes* presupposes the conventional "fall of an illustrious man" characteristic of the *de casibus* type, it follows in fact an altogether different model; the catastrophe of Milton's drama is notable rather for the unexpected triumph of the tragic hero and the sudden downfall of his enemies. Although the initial scenes explore the moral, political, and religious implications of his unseemly and untimely fall, the primary emphasis is placed rather on his lapse from virtue and divine favor than on the reversal in his external fortunes. Samson's tragic fall belongs to the past, however, and the model that seems to underlie the greater part of the play—from the blind hero's first complaint to the crowning ignominy of the Philistine summons to the Dagonalia—recalls that of the tragedy of suffering. During the first episodes his own reflections and the endeavors of his father and his friends to console him merely intensify his torment, which achieves its most powerful expression in the *threnos* immediately prior to Dalila's entrance. Afflicted by his own thoughts, by "faintings, swoonings of despair, / And sense of Heav'ns desertion," he can only pray for speedy death as his only cure. This is his spiritual nadir ("Hopeless are all my evils, all remediless"); and his would-be comforters can only respond by acknowledging the inutility of all written "Consolatories" unless the sufferer experiences some inner and supernal consolation:

> Unless he feel within
> Some source of consolation from above;
> Secret refreshings, that repair his strength,
> And fainting spirits uphold.
>
> (ll. 663–66)

In a dramatic context—and particularly at this point in the development of the tragic fable—the concluding prayer in this choral ode ("Behold him in this state calamitous, and turn / His labours, for thou canst, to peaceful end") is suggestive; the word *turn* might, not infrequently, refer to a dramatic *peripeteia* or reversal. The prayer of the Danites on this occasion eventually receives a divine response, though this is not precisely the answer that they might have anticipated and though it occurs in a manner contrary to their own expectation. The catastrophe of the play turns out to be far from peaceful; yet the hero's violent end does indeed bring an irreversible peace to himself, and "peace and consolation" to his fellow countrymen. Nevertheless there is a more immediate reversal, which is apparent rather in Samson's sufferings and his labors of the mind than in external actions. This ordeal too is far from peaceful, subjecting him to further trials of faith and patience as he confronts his Philistine adversaries, but it points indirectly toward internal peace. In the course of his ordeal he regains his sense of confidence, consecration, and divine favor.

Despite the essentially static nature of the "tragedy of suffering," a series of reversals do occur, and the most forceful examples spring essentially from operations of the Spirit itself.[6]

6. The predominantly static pattern of the tragedy of suffering can also be found in the tragedies of Seneca. Observing that his "reversals are slight," Doran quotes Harsh's judgment of the "normal pattern of Seneca's plays": "'The situation is very bad at the beginning, and it rapidly becomes much worse.'" See Doran, *Endeavors of Art,* 410; Philip Whaley Harsh, *A Handbook of Classical Drama* (Stanford, 1944), 410. Among the plausible but deliberately misleading impressions that Milton fosters in his drama is that Samson's fate may follow a similar pattern: from bad to worse. The hero's miseries, bitter enough at the opening of the drama, are intensified by the consolatory visits of his friends. He is confronted with formidable moral and physical perils through the blandishments or insults of his enemies. The summons to the Philistine theater is a supreme ignominy: a climax to the potentially humiliating (though in fact revitalizing) encounters with his treacherous wife and the gloating Philistine champion. Moreover, there are reiterated hints and suggestions that Samson's sufferings and despair may drive him to suicide: the fate of Sophocles' Ajax. When the chorus see in Samson's fall a "mirror of our fickle state," they are echoing a commonplace of the *de casibus* tradition; and it is significant that *A Mirror for Magistrates* had been conceived as a sequel to Boccaccio's work. According to William Baldwin: "How he [God] hath plaged evil rulers from time to time in other nations, you may see gathered in Bochas' book intituled *The Fall of Princes,* translated into English by Lydgate. How he hath dealt

First, there is Samson's rapid and unexpected moral recovery; as he successively defies his Philistine antagonists, there is an impressive, though gradual, alteration in the attitudes that both he and the chorus assume toward his heroic identity and toward his ordained mission as divine champion. After his challenge to Harapha, the chorus can at last foresee a heroic role for Samson either as a public deliverer triumphing by force or as his own deliverer triumphing through patience. Second, there is the sudden reversal of moral purpose as Samson alters his "absolute denial" and defiance of the Philistine lords and instead obeys the "rousing motions" of the Spirit. Finally, there is the catastrophic action itself, the sudden doom that he inflicts on his Philistine masters contrary to their intent. The "tragedy of suffering," which had hitherto seemed to be the dominant model for Milton's plot, thus proves inadequate; despite initial appearances, and contrary to initial expectations, he has actually followed the complex model, which involves *peripeteias* in action as well as in character: "the changes of that which is call'd fortune from without" as well as "the wily suttleties and refluxes of man's thoughts from within."[7]

The most significant factor in Milton's characterization of Samson (and hence the crucial concept for heroic decorum) is the hero's dedication as a Nazarite, a person "separate to God" and endowed not only with a divinely appointed mission but also with the "Heav'n-gifted strength" and the divine favor and guidance necessary to accomplish it. As he himself asserts in answer to the accusations of the Philistine giant, he is not a "private" person

---

with some of our countrymen, your ancestors, for sundry vices not yet left, this book named *A Mirror for Magistrates* can shew. . . . For here as in a looking glass you shall see (if any vice be in you) how the like hath been punished in other heretofore." And again: "Whan the printer had purposed with himself to print Lydgate's book of *The Fall of Princes*, . . . he was counsailed . . . to procure to have the story continued from whereas Bochas left unto this present time, chiefly of such as Fortune had dallied with here in this iland; which might be as a mirror for all men as well noble as others, to shew the slippery deceits of the wavering lady and the due reward of all kind of vices" (quoted in Hyder E. Rollins and Herschel Baker [eds.], *The Renaissance in England: Non-Dramatic Prose and Verse of the Sixteenth Century* [Boston, 1954], 270–71). See also Lily Bess Campbell, *Tudor Conceptions of History and Tragedy in "The Mirrour for Magistrates"* (Berkeley, 1936).

7. Milton, *The Reason of Church-Government*; see James Holly Hanford and James G. Taaffe, *A Milton Handbook* (5th ed.; New York, 1970), 307.

but rather a *publica persona* (as Milton's contemporaries might have expressed it) "With strength sufficient and command from Heav'n / To free my Country"—and much of the moral action in the drama centers on the use or abuse of this "Consecrated gift / Of strength" and on the contrasting decorums of hero and slave. At the beginning of the play Samson is alienated from his heroic mission and hence from his heroic identity; this self-alienation inevitably affects the roles of all those who surround him, friends and enemies alike. Not only is the deliverer himself enslaved, but his heroic virtue has been confounded with its logical contrary, with brutishness or *feritas*.[8] The Nazarite's consecrated strength has been "Put to the labour of a Beast," and "The glory late of *Israel*" has become its "grief." Thus the character of the hero has become a self-contradiction, a moral paradox or oxymoron. In a lesser degree the offices of wife, father, and antagonist exhibit similar contradictions.

At their first glimpse of the stricken hero, the chorus of visiting Danites find it impossible to identify the blind slave—seemingly a derelict "past hope, abandon'd, / And by himself given over"— with "That Heroic, that Renown'd, / Irresistible *Samson*" who had once triumphed so gloriously at Ramath Lechi. Yet before the catastrophe of the tragedy, the same chorus are able to perceive in the same fallen hero the signs of true heroic virtue and to predict that he may even yet become illustrious either for active valor (as formerly) or for patience, the truest fortitude:

> Either of these is in thy lot,
> *Samson*, with might endu'd
> Above the Sons of men; but sight bereav'd
> May chance to number thee with those
> Whom Patience finally must crown.
> (ll. 1292–96)

And at the end of the drama, the aged Manoa will recapitulate the heroic motif, declaring that "*Samson* hath quit himself / Like *Samson*, and heroicly hath finish'd / A life Heroic."

In this instance the problem of heroic decorum appears inseparable from the delineation of heroic magnanimity, and both are inalienably linked with the hero's identity as a "person separate

8. For *feritas* or brutishness as the contrary of heroic virtue in Aristotle's *Nicomachean Ethics* and in Renaissance tradition, see Steadman, *Milton's Epic Characters*, 24–32.

to God." The question of what actions or situations are worthy or unworthy of a hero becomes central to his relationships with those about him.[9] For the chorus and for Manoa, his base condition casts doubt on the justice of God's ways with men. In the eyes of his fellows his fall appears unseemly; and in his father's view his condition is not only unworthy of Samson himself but signally unworthy of his God:

> Alas! methinks whom God hath chosen once
> To worthiest deeds, if he through frailty err,
> He should not so o'erwhelm, and as a thrall
> Subject him to so foul indignities,
> Be it but for honour's sake of former deeds.
>
> (ll. 368–72)

Samson himself regards the indignities of his servile condition as less ignominious and less base than his former subservience to Dalila:

> But foul effeminacy held me yok't
> Her Bond-slave; O indignity, O blot
> To honour and Religion! servile mind
> Rewarded well with servile punishment!
> The base degree to which I now am fall'n,
> These rags, this grinding, is not yet so base
> As was my former servitude, ignoble,
> Unmanly, ignominous, infamous,
> True slavery, and that blindness worse than this,
> That saw not how degenerately I serv'd.
>
> (ll. 410–19)

He subsequently endures the indignities that Harapha heaps upon him as evils justly inflicted by God; but when the Philistine lords summon him to a crowning indignity that directly challenges his identity as a Nazarite, he rejects their command with a ringing assertion of moral freedom reminiscent of the Lady's defiance in *Comus* ("thou canst not touch the freedom of my mind"):

> Can they think me so broken, so debas'd
> With corporal servitude, that my mind ever
> Will condescend to such absurd commands?

9. A "regard to our own dignity, rightly understood" is an essential part of Milton's definition of magnanimity in *De Doctrina Christiana*, Bk. II, Chap. 9. Patrick Cullen regards both *Samson Agonistes* and *Paradise Regained* as "brief heroic poems with the common subject of a hero coming to knowledge of his identity through temptation" (Cullen, *Infernal Triad: The Flesh, the World, and the Devil in Spenser and Milton* [Princeton, 1974], 126).

> Although their drudge, to be thir fool or jester,
> And in my midst of sorrow and heart-grief
> To show them feats, and play before thir god,
> The worst of all indignities, yet on me
> Join'd with extreme contempt? I will not come.
>
> (ll. 1335–42)

Or again:

> Shall I abuse this Consecrated gift
> Of strength, again returning with my hair
> After my great transgression, so requite
> Favour renew'd, and add a greater Sin
> By prostituting holy things to Idols;
> A *Nazarite* in place abominable
> Vaunting my strength in honour to thir *Dagon?*
>
> (ll. 1354–60)

Even though he subsequently reverses this decision, he still persists in his determination

> Nothing to do, be sure, that may dishonour
> Our Law, or stain my vow of *Nazarite.*
>
> (ll. 1385–86)

> Nothing dishonourable, impure, unworthy
> Our God, our Law, my Nation, or myself.
>
> (ll. 1424–25)

Samson's breach of faith with his God has resulted not only in self-alienation but in an inversion of domestic and public relationships. Seemingly altogether "In power of others, never in my own," he is apparently dependent on the ministrations of those to whom he should minister, susceptible to the commands of those whom he himself should command, and vulnerable to the violence of those whom he should overcome. His disability has reversed the standard relationships between parent and child. As the chorus explicitly recognize, the old and weak must now nurse the young and strong; contrary to normal practice and expectation, the aged father must now provide for the powerful son:

> Fathers are wont to lay up for thir Sons,
> Thou for thy Son art bent to lay out all;
> Sons wont to nurse thir Parents in old age,
> Thou in old age car'st how to nurse thy Son,
> Made older than thy age through eye-sight lost.
>
> (ll. 1485–89)

Manoa himself is compelled to undertake the hero's ransom—an ironic inversion of Samson's own mission—and there is an element of the unseemly as well as the pathetic in the spectacle of the aged man bustling about the streets of Gaza endeavoring to deliver the enslaved deliverer.

Dalila in turn has not only broken her marriage faith, thus destroying the form or essence of wedlock by wedlock treachery, but has also inverted the traditional relationship between husband and wife by "female usurpation." Contrary to biblical injunctions reserving "superior rights to the husband" and forbidding "a woman . . . to usurp authority over the man," Dalila has usurped her husband's roles in the family as well as in the state.[10] The offer of freedom that she makes to Samson underscores his failures in economics as well as in politics, as the lord of the family as well as the deliverer of his people. Having already assumed his divinely appointed role as national savior, she now usurps his divinely sanctioned office as domestic despot, offering him liberty and ease under conditions that must compel him to accept her as both mistress and deliverer. In marriages untainted by domestic treason, the nursing care that she proposes would befit the "Character of a Faithful Wife" just as the similar offer by Manoa becomes the "Character of a Good Father"—but in this instance normal patterns of behavior have been inverted both by her breach of faith and by Samson's violation of his Nazarite vows. The uniform of a sister of mercy and the mantle of Florence Nightingale fit grotesquely on this Philistine Mata Hari; and, understandably, Samson scorns to "live uxorious to [her] will / In perfect thraldom."

The scenes with Harapha and the Philistine officer also involve role reversals, heightening the tension between the contrary decorums of hero and slave. The fallen hero who had once dueled entire armies single-handed (and who will shortly overwhelm the entire Philistine aristocracy) no longer seems a "worthy match" in a duel. No honor could be gained, and much honor could be lost, by fighting him; and the giant champion scorns his challenge to combat. In the following scene the summons of the Philistine officer brings into open conflict the opposition between divine law and human law (the law of the Hebrew people and that of the

10. See Milton, *Complete Poems and Major Prose*, 992–1005, for Milton's discussion of marriage and divorce in *De Doctrina Christiana*. Milton observes that in the Hebrew the same word signifies "both husband and lord."

Philistine state) and a more fundamental opposition between the commands of Scripture and the "intimate impulse" of the Spirit. Raising the issue of magnanimity as well as duty—what the hero owes to his own dignity, what (if anything) to his masters, and what he owes to God—this confrontation scene brings into diametrical opposition two contrasting patterns of servitude (obedience to the Philistine state versus obedience to God), only to bring them into apparent, though ironic, reconciliation at the end. Samson departs with the Philistine officer apparently as an obedient slave of the state yielding to its irresistible commands, but actually as a servant of the God of Israel obeying a divine impulse and accomplishing God's uncontrollable intent.

For the greater part of this scene the moral struggle hinges primarily on the paradoxes of magnanimity: first on Samson's initial refusal to stoop to an action unworthy of himself, to violate his duties as a Hebrew and his vows as Nazarite, or to compromise his own conscience and internal peace; but second, on his willingness to sacrifice the external aspects of heroic decorum and personal dignity and to subject himself to public humiliation in obedience to the divine will. It is important for Milton that Samson demonstrate his true "Heroic magnitude of mind" before he leaves the scene for his climactic exploit. Yet it is also important that one recognize this exploit as a crowning victory won in and through a supreme indignity. In contrast to Harapha, who disdained to risk compromising his honor for the sake of Dagon, Samson endures public disgrace in order to vindicate the honor of his own God.

Like the paradox of liberty in bondage and vision in blindness, Samson's final triumph involves an act of glory achieved through an act of shame. In this drama of paradoxes the hero's *aristeia* is a supreme oxymoron, a deed of devout impiety. In this instance, as in his marriage choices, obedience to the commands of the Spirit seems to entail overt disobedience to the written law, and the fulfillment of his mission as Nazarite to involve the violation of his Nazarite vows.

Even apart from the effects of his transgression on his own role and on those of the persons about him, the nature of Samson's peculiar brand of heroism involves him, again and again, in apparent violations of the normal decorums associated with both domestic and public offices. His special relationship with his Deity dominates all other personal ties, and all human relationships are in varying degrees compromised by his vocation as Nazarite. Set apart from other men by his miraculous strength, by his vows, and by the qualities that make him preeminently a hero of faith, he is in the fullest sense an extraordinary hero whose actions can be justified only by divine dispensation. A person "separate to God" and thus set apart by his holiness, Samson becomes increasingly isolated from his fellows, as the dictates of the Spirit lead him outward and onward beyond conventional relationships as son or husband or warrior, beyond the advice and consolation of friends, and beyond the guidance of the Scriptures themselves.

In the preface to *Samson Agonistes*, Milton insists on "verisimilitude and decorum" in the disposition of the fable and denounces "the Poet's error of intermixing Comic stuff with Tragic sadness and gravity; or introducing trivial and vulgar persons." He had expressed a similar preoccupation with decorum much earlier in his career. In *The Reason of Church-Government* he had attacked the "libidinous and ignorant Poetasters, who having scars ever heard of that which is the main consistence of a true poem, the choys of such persons as they ought to introduce, and what is morall and decent to each one, doe for the most part lap up vitious principles in sweet pils to be swallow'd down." And in *Of Education* he had hailed decorum as "the grand masterpiece to observe," condemning "our common rhymers and play-writers" as "despicable creatures."[11]

In spite of this reiterated emphasis on decorum in genre, critics have sometimes dismissed Samson's principal antagonists as alien intruders on the tragic stage. As types of the courtesan and the braggart soldier, Dalila and Harapha would befit the sock rather than the buskin. They belong, it has been argued, to the tradition of the meretrix and the *miles gloriosus* of classical and Renaissance comedy.[12]

Under the circumstances it would be difficult to see either of these mortal enemies—equally dangerous in their lures and in their threats—as comic figures, though there may be comic over-

11. Hanford and Taaffe, *Milton Handbook*, 307–308; Milton, *Complete Poems and Major Prose*, 637.

12. See Allan H. Gilbert, "Is *Samson Agonistes* Unfinished?" *Philological Quarterly*, XXVIII (1949), 98–106; Daniel C. Boughner, "Milton's Harapha and Renaissance Comedy," *ELH*, XI (1944), 297–306.

tones in their discomfiture and in the sarcastic comments of the chorus. As he strips their pretenses from them, Samson succeeds in making both of them appear not only vicious but ridiculous. Moreover, he does so by bringing into sharp dramatic focus the conflicts between their offices (whether domestic or public) and their actual behavior, or between their real motives and the motives they profess. Both are, in a sense, self-contradictions; each is exposed as a kind of ethical oxymoron.

As elsewhere in the same drama, it is the abuse of an office or function or the inutility of an instrument that makes it seem ridiculous. Before his downfall Samson had made the martial strength of his enemies look absurd, when unarmed he

> Ran on embattled Armies clad in Iron,
> And weaponless himself,
> Made Arms ridiculous, useless the forgery
> Of brazen shield and spear, the hammer'd Cuirass,
> *Chalybean* temper'd steel, and frock of mail
> Adamantean Proof.
>
> (ll. 129–34)

In the confrontation with Harapha, there is a recapitulation of this motif, even though the victory must be moral rather than physical. Sarcastically inventorying the giant's "gorgeous arms," challenging him to a duel that the Philistine dare not accept, and concluding with heroic billingsgate ("baffl'd coward," "bulk without spirit vast"), the blind Nazarite successfully exposes this redoubtable enemy also to ridicule.

In exposing Dalila's pretensions to conjugal love and benevolence as disguised malice and dismissing her as a supreme example of infidelity, Samson succeeds, in part at least, in turning the tables on the

> deceitful Concubine who shore me
> Like a tame Wether, all my precious fleece,
> Then turn'd me out ridiculous, despoil'd,
> Shav'n, and disarm'd among my enemies.
>
> (ll. 537–40)

Even more than the giant champion who contradicts his office by declining judicial combat, Dalila is a self-contradiction. The "Wife" is also the "Traitress"; and in emphasizing the disparity between office and *ethos*, between the decorum of a wife and mercenary infidelity, Samson has exposed both her motives and her arguments as meretricious. Although he stops short of branding her with harlotry, the allusions that both of them make to her future fame are suggestive. As most of Milton's readers were well aware, future generations would not only traduce her name with "the blot / Of falsehood most unconjugal" but would usually regard her as a meretrix like the harlot of Gaza (Judges 16:1). Indeed, in *The Reason of Church-Government*, Milton had likened "the state and person of a king" to "that mighty Nazarite Samson," who "laying down his head among the strumpet flatteries of prelates" is shorn of "those bright and weighty tresses of his laws and just prerogatives."[13] And in *Paradise Lost* he compares the fate of Adam and Eve to that of the Nazarite betrayed by a harlot:

> So rose the *Danite* strong
> *Herculean Samson* from the Harlot-lap
> Of *Philistean Dalilah*, and wak'd
> Shorn of his strength, They destitute and bare
> Of all thir virtue.
>
> (*PL*, IX, 1059–63)

Significantly both Samson and his father apply the term *ridiculous* specifically to the abuse of his God-given strength, either in violation of divine law or through idleness. In the Nazarite's eyes, to vaunt his "strength in honour to thir *Dagon*" is "vile, contemptible, ridiculous / What act more execrably unclean, profane?" (ll. 1361–62). Manoa, in turn, maintains that God would not have permitted Samson's

> strength again to grow up with his hair
> Garrison'd round about him like a Camp
> Of faithful Soldiery, were not his purpose
> To use him further yet in some great service,
> Not to sit idle with so great a gift
> *Useless, and thence ridiculous* about him.
>
> (ll. 1496–1501; italics mine)

It is essentially in their relationships with Samson that Dalila and Harapha tend to approximate the types of the cunning harlot and the cowardly braggart; these recognizable dramatic roles are not their proper roles but represent instead a moral verdict, an assessment of character. In both instances, moreover, this is associated with a violation of the persona's proper office and role. Milton has taken pains to transform Dalila from the harlot of liter-

---

13. Milton, *Complete Poems and Major Prose*, 688.

ary tradition into Samson's legal wife; but this elevation makes her betrayal all the more heinous, as it is now a breach of marriage faith. Her wedlock treachery makes her essentially, if not literally, a harlot; for, in Milton's view, the fornication that provides just grounds for divorce "signifies, not so much adultery, as the constant enmity, faithlessness, and disobedience of the wife, arising from the manifest and palpable alienation of the mind, rather than of the body." Like the concubine in Judges 19:2, Dalila has played the harlot "by refractory behaviour towards her husband."[14] In this context the meretrix label that critics have applied to her is appropriate, though not in the usual sense of the word, and its applicability is enhanced by her techniques of enticement and seduction, her affinities with Circe and the Sirens (often allegorized as types of the meretrix), by the mercenary motives underlying her breach of marriage faith, and not least by the meretricious arguments whereby she endeavors to justify herself and obtain reconciliation with Samson.

In seeking forgiveness and reconciliation, Dalila reverts to the character and office of wife, which she had seemingly forfeited forever. Significantly she appeals to the form or essence of marriage not only as the motive for her coming but also as the true motivation for her betrayal. In Milton's opinion "the prime end and form of marriage . . . is not the nuptial bed, but conjugal love, and mutual assistance through life." Pleading "conjugal affection" as her motive for visiting Samson and offering domestic help and solace, Dalila appears to be reaffirming "the *essential form* of marriage"; and in maintaining that she had acted in obedience to "Love's law" in betraying her husband, she is, in effect, arguing that her apparent breach of marriage faith was paradoxically an act of marital fidelity. Yet, as Samson perceives, the true motive for her visit was "malice not repentance," just as the true motive for her treachery had been "weakness to resist / Philistian gold." Their marriage is now "virtually dissolved," since its essential form has been dissolved; in Samson's view "thou and I long since are twain," and nothing remains except to pronounce the decree of divorce.[15]

14. *Ibid.*, 992–1005.
15. See *ibid.*, 1001–1004. Milton argues that "if the essential form be dissolved, it follows that the marriage itself is virtually dissolved" and that nothing could be "more natural, or more agreeable to the original institution, than that the bond which had been formed by love, and the hope of mutual assistance through life,

In Harapha's instance, reminiscences of the braggart soldier of classical and Renaissance comedy are less significant than analogies with the insolent and boastful warriors of classical and Renaissance epic, with types of violence in classical tragedy, and with the character attributed to the Old Testament giants by biblical commentators: men of might and renown and "bold emprise," tyrants and oppressors, the world's first nobility.[16] Samson cows his powerful adversary, to be sure, and his "Giantship" departs crestfallen. But the kind of threat that he represents, a type reminiscent of older generations of giants, is appropriately summed up by the chorus in its denunciation of "the mighty of the Earth, th' oppressor, / The brute and boist'rous force of violent men" who support "Tyrannic power" but persecute "The righteous and all such as honour Truth." If his boasts and threats remind one too strongly of comic warriors like Parolles and Braggadocchio, one should also recall the epic boasts and insults of Homeric heroes and the *vana gloriatio* (as Calvin terms it) of Harapha's giant son Goliath, his contempt for his opponent's trivial weapons, and his threat to "give thy flesh unto the fowls of the air, and to the beasts of the field."

Among the principal traits in Milton's characterization of this figure are Harapha's obsession with fame and martial glory, the technicalities of the duello, and the formalities of the code of honor. He is the conventional aristocratic warrior "writ large"— an inflation (or conflation) of conventional models of secular heroism. Whereas Harapha's victories must depend on conventional weapons and martial skills, Samson's triumphs result from the direct gift of God, his miraculous strength. It is significant that, just as "*Israel's* Governors, and Heads of Tribes" did not acknowledge "those great acts which God had done / Singly by me against their Conquerors," the Philistine giant cannot recognize them as the direct effects of a divine miracle, and can only dismiss them as wonders wrought by magic. In analyzing this confrontation scene, D. C. Allen has justly placed primary emphasis not on Harapha's moral weakness but on Samson's moral force

---

and honourable motives, should be dissolved by hatred and implacable enmity, and disgraceful conduct on either side."

16. On the character attributed to the biblical giants by exegetical tradition, see John M. Steadman, *Milton and the Renaissance Hero* (Oxford, 1967), and *Milton's Epic Characters, passim*.

and the mysterious power that could reduce a powerful warrior to cowardice.[17]

In both instances the question of moral and dramatic decorum brings the intrinsic absurdity of the character into sharper focus. Neither the national heroine nor the giant champion is properly a comic person; both have significant prototypes in classical tragedy; but the analogy with stock figures of comedy is by no means irrelevant. It emphasizes the inherent absurdity of certain conventional but secular ideals of heroism, and it enhances the poet's image of Samson's powers of judgment and insight as the blind Nazarite strips their pretensions from both figures, exposing the underlying moral reality as vicious and self-defeating: self-contradictory and therefore ridiculous.

Samson's visitors pursue ends of their own choosing, yet unwittingly further a divine intent still concealed from them. Their own designs are consistently thwarted, and their visits conclude with results almost diametrically contrary to those they had purposed. The chorus of Danites endeavor to console Samson but can only exacerbate his misery. Manoa comes to ransom him and bring him "Home to thy country," but remains to escort only his shattered body "Home to his Father's house." Dalila, who had formerly sought to make him "mine and Love's prisoner" and who now attempts to reaffirm their marriage ties, is dismissed with a sentence of divorce and a reaffirmation of Samson's moral independence. Harapha, who comes to survey his enemy and to boast of the honors he would have wrested from him "by mortal duel," goads him into reasserting his lost identity as divine champion, into issuing a formal challenge that the giant dare not accept, and into hurling insults and "dishonors" that Harapha dare not avenge. This series of reversals contrary to expectation or intent leads inevitably to other, more dramatic reversals that further accentuate the differences between divine providence and human purposes, God's uncontrollable intent and the ends of mankind. Driven by a spirit of frenzy, the Philistine lords summon their own destroyer. The future destroyer, still unaware of the divine will, first defies their command, only to reverse his decision at the

17. Don Cameron Allen, *The Harmonious Vision: Studies in Milton's Poetry* (Baltimore, 1954), 71–94. See also the discussion by Merritt Y. Hughes in Milton, *Complete Poems and Major Prose*, 531–48.

prompting of the Spirit. In the final scenes the vague surmises of Manoa and the chorus and the progressive stages of the messenger's report cause dramatic alternations between expectation and doubt, hope and fear, passionate grief and ultimate calm of mind.

Underlying this sequence of visitations is a logical succession as well as an emotional and moral progression toward the fulfillment of Samson's destiny and toward his countrymen's acquiescence in his fate: "All is best, though we oft doubt, . . . / And ever best seen in the close." The dramatic irony that pervades the poem depends on epistemological and teleological contrasts: the infinite disparity between the designs of God and those of mankind. It is essential to the poet's dramatic strategy that the full significance of Samson's ordeal should be concealed from all the dramatis personae and that the dramatic action should seem to point elsewhere than toward the catastrophe. In a drama centered (as *Samson Agonistes* is centered) on a trial of faith both for the protagonist and for the chorus of doubting yet expectant countrymen, one would not look for a plot structure consisting merely of a concatenation of external incidents. On the contrary, one would expect rather the kind of fable that Milton has given us: a plot that adapts the dramatic crisis to the demands of a theology of crisis; a plot that hinges on an unfulfilled oracle but leaves the fulfillment in a state of suspense until the last scene in the play; a plot that itself provides a test of faith until the final "acquist / Of true experience" from the one "great event" in a drama of heroic activity in inaction.

This ordeal of faith and patience depends not only on Samson's unfulfilled mission and God's unfulfilled promise but more notably on the apparent absence of God. Samson's father and fellow Danites fear that Samson has been abandoned by his Deity ("With God not parted from him, as was fear'd"), and the final verses of the chorus emphasize the unpredictability of the *deus absconditus* who often "seems to hide his face, / But unexpectedly returns." As a tragic dramatist, Milton must make the catastrophe appear almost totally "unexpected" when it occurs, yet also make it seem probable or necessary in retrospect. Although the theme of the Dagonalia is introduced early in the action, none of the personae voice the slightest suspicion that Samson's own presence at the pagan festival will be required. This crucial information—known only to the Deity and to the reader—is kept carefully hidden from the agents in the drama, and the summons of the Philistine officer comes as a totally unexpected blow to the hero and his companions. This is the first overt action that could lead directly to the preordained though unforeseen catastrophe, and it is immediately countered by Samson's "absolute denial to come." The catastrophe now seems more remote than ever, as the hero unwittingly closes the one way that would lead to victory. At this point he experiences the "rousing motions" that persuade him to change his purpose and accompany the officer to the scene of the catastrophe.

Samson's initial refusal constitutes a "delaying action" (as seventeenth-century critics would have called it), and the direct prompting of the Spirit clearly facilitates and hastens the outcome. Both of these events occur so late in the play, however, that they hardly suffice to answer Samuel Johnson's notorious objections to Milton's tragic plot: that it "has a beginning and an end which Aristotle himself could not have disapproved" but lacks a middle, "since nothing passes between the first act and the last, that either hastens or delays the death of Samson." [18]
These strictures by a lesser dramatist may seem manifest "indignities" to Milton's shade, but they nevertheless possess the merit of focusing attention on the "economy, or disposition" of his fable and, in particular, on the relationship between its violent catastrophe and the long section of apparent inactivity that, devoted largely to the labors of the mind, constitutes the missing middle of the play.
As this central portion of the drama is entirely the poet's own invention, his emphasis on character and thought, rather than on external events as the more significant preliminaries to the catastrophe, would seem to represent a well-considered choice. Moreover, according to the line of argument developed in Aristotle's *Poetics*, it should permit the poet to achieve a more sudden and more powerful *peripeteia*. When this final, and paradoxical, reversal does occur, its capacity to arouse passion and admiration, and thus to induce the tragic catharsis of pity and fear, is enhanced by its suddenness. By Aristotle's definition *peripeteia* is "the shift of

18. For criticism of Johnson's views, see M. E. Grenander, "*Samson's Middle: Aristotle and Dr. Johnson,*" *University of Toronto Quarterly,* XXIV (1955), 377–89; Milton, *Complete Poems and Major Prose,* 531–48.

the action towards the opposite pole . . . in accordance with probability or necessity"; and in commenting on this passage, a recent critic has observed that "peripety, though it represents . . . the whole 'shift' of the play, should be concentrated in a single scene; for it belongs to its nature to be 'marvelous,' that is, unexpected, sudden." [19] By delaying the divine impulses that immediately precipitate the catastrophe—the "rousing spirits" on Samson's part and the "spirit of phrenzy" on the part of the Philistine lords—Milton succeeds in making the operations of divine Providence and its contrary strategies toward the elect and the reprobate appear miraculous but also probable and necessary; inscrutable but also wise and just.

In Milton's source, the Book of Judges, barely nine verses (16:23–31) are devoted to the action that the poet has chosen to imitate, and these are principally concerned either with the occasion for the catastrophe or with the catastrophe itself: the Philistines' sacrifice to Dagon in thanksgiving for delivering into their hands "our enemy, and the destroyer of our country"; their sudden decision, at the height of their merrymaking, to summon Samson to "make sport for us"; his successive prayers to God for strength, revenge, and death; and his interment "in the burying place of Manoah, his father." The hero's meditations and his confrontations with successive visitors are Milton's own additions to the story, as are the contrasts and analogies that he develops in these scenes: the labors of the mind as a mode of inner deliverance from servile labor and external oppression, but also as a foil for the active valor of the standard heroic exemplar, the na-

19. Gerald F. Else, *Aristotle's Poetics* (Cambridge, Mass., 1967), 342, 345. Observing that "Peripety and recognition . . . are *special* varieties or structural forms of the tragic 'change,' the shapes it may take when the plot is complex," Else regards the former as "an *unexpected* yet *logical* shift in the events of the play from happiness to unhappiness or the reverse." He argues, "In a complex plot, unlike a simple one, the change is not visible for a while. . . . The notion of 'reversal of fortune' is inherent in all tragedy, as Aristotle sees it, not merely in complex tragedies. On the other hand the notion of a *sudden* reversal, which touches off the catastrophe, is inherent in *para ten doxan,* which implies that our expectation must have time to expand in one direction before the action 'swings' to the other." Unlike many other critics, "who make the reversal of the hero's intention or expectation the essence of peripety," Else maintains that the expectation is our own rather than the expectation of the hero (343–45). For the paradoxical nature of the tragic peripeteia, see 323, 346–47; for further discussion of Milton's plot in the light of Renaissance conceptions of peripeteia, see John M. Steadman, *Epic and Tragic Structure in "Paradise Lost"* (Chicago, 1967).

tional deliverer; the trial of faith and patience as a necessary precondition for heroic action; the traditional ideal of heroic virtue as a balance between two modes of superlative fortitude, strength of mind and strength of body; the moral logic underlying the Nazarite's spiritual ordeal and preparing him emotionally and spiritually for his final and greatest act. Other significant aspects of the central and concluding scenes have been developed out of hints in this passage or from earlier allusions in the biblical account of Samson.

Of Samson's visitors only the Philistine officer would seem to have been suggested by the biblical narrative of Dagon's feast, and only he would seem to hasten or delay the catastrophe (Judges 16:25: "And they called for Samson out of the prison house, and he made sport for them"). Harapha is an intruder into the Samson legend, an anachronism transferred from references to "the giant" (*ha raphah*) of Gath who had sired Goliath and other gigantic progeny (2 Sam. 21:22; 1 Chron. 20:8). The brief reference in Judges (16:16) to Samson's burial at the burying place of his father might well suggest that the aged Manoa is now dead. Dalila has disappeared from the biblical account after betraying Samson. Finally, the Danite messenger and the "friends and neighbours . . . From *Eshtaol* and *Zora's* fruitful Vale" are present not in response to Scripture but in compliance with the conventions of Attic drama and perhaps with the precedent set by Job's comforters. Milton's scriptural source left him maximum freedom of invention in conceiving and in structuring the central episodes in his plot. In the sequence of these episodes, in their thematic content, in the identity and character of the persons introduced, and in their effect on the character (or "moral purpose") of the protagonist and his fitness for his final act of deliverance, they are faithful to an underlying moral logic that leads inexorably, though not apparently, to the preconceived end.

For many of Milton's contemporaries, there would have been a familiar critical term for this section of his tragedy. Transferred from the criticism of Terentian comedy to tragic theory, the word *epitasis* usually denoted the middle section of the plot, characterized by increasing tension or suspense and culminating in a moment of highest strain shortly before the catastrophe. (The word literally signifies "a stretching," as of strings, and derives from a verb *epiteino* meaning "to stretch" or "tighten," or "to increase in

PACIFIC UNIVERSITY LIBRARY
FOREST GROVE, OREGON

intensity.")[20] During the Renaissance, as T. W. Baldwin has demonstrated, this and other technical concepts associated with the
critical tradition of Evanthius and Donatus had been assimilated
into the tradition of Aristotelian and Horatian poetics. The terms
summa epitasis, extrema epitasis, and *catastasis* designated the point
of highest tension.[21]

In his own plans for a tragedy Milton refers twice to the epitasis, and in both cases, it is his own invention, his own innovation on his biblical sources.[22] In "Abias Thersaeus" (that is, "Abi-
jah of Good Faith" or "of Good Confidence," 1 Kings 14) the
epitasis centers on the vain endeavors of the sick child's mother to
frustrate the prophecy concerning his imminent death, while in
"Moabitides or Phineas" (Numbers 25) it consists in a dispute
over a point of law. In both of these dramatic sketches, Milton's
allusions to the epitasis demonstrate his preoccupation with
problems of structure and in particular with the middle of his
play. Significantly, if one reexamines the language of the chorus at
a moment of exceptional dramatic tension, one may detect a similar concern in *Samson Agonistes*:

> Consider, *Samson*; matters now are strain'd
> Up to the highth, whether to hold or break;
> He's gone, and who knows how he may report
> Thy words by adding fuel to the flame?
> Expect another message more imperious,
> More Lordly thund'ring than thou well wilt bear.
> (ll. 1348–53)

The phrase "matters now are strain'd / Up to the highth" is a
literal English rendering of *summa epitasis,* a term that Milton
surely encountered in his own copy of Stiblinus' edition of
Euripides; and it occurs appropriately at the critical moment

20. *An Intermediate Greek-English Lexicon Founded upon the Seventh Edition of
Liddell and Scott's Greek-English Lexicon* (Oxford, 1968), s.v. *epitasis, epiteino.*

21. T. W. Baldwin, *Shakspere's Five-Act Structure* (Urbana, 1963), 285–305.
Among the divisions of tragedy Minturno distinguished "the protasis, which
being as it were the proposition of affairs explains part of the play, prepares the
peril"; then "the epitasis, where the action, being developed, is thrown into perturbation, or increases the peril, or brings on some evil"; and finally, "the catastrophe, where as if by the conversion of affairs, the outcome of the argument is
unfolded, whether the fortune is changed for the better, or as almost always happens, for the worse" (291).

22. See John M. Steadman, "Milton's 'Summa Epitasis': The Middle of *Samson
Agonistes*," *Modern Language Review*, LXIX (1974), 730–44.

when the ethical patterns exhibited in the previous scenes with Dalila and Harapha seem to demand that Samson persist in his "absolute denial to come" to the pagan festival.[23] As a supreme assertion of heroic magnanimity and moral freedom and a re-affirmation of his identity as a Nazarite consecrated to the service of God, this open defiance of the authority of the Philistine state is a logical climax to his earlier defiance of the treasonous wife and the insolent champion; and it is also a fitting and probable conclusion to the process of moral regeneration and recovery that had distinguished his role in both encounters. In progressive confrontation with himself, his friends, and his enemies, Samson has at last found himself again, and the moral logic underlying the central portion of the drama seems to require that he continue to act in character and refuse the summons. It is at this point, however, immediately following the "highest epitasis" or moment of supreme tension, that a higher wisdom intervenes and instantaneously reverses the situation, steering the action to an end divinely proposed but hitherto concealed from Philistines and Danites alike.

Like the destruction that the Philistines madly bring upon themselves, this moral reversal on Samson's part is not only sudden, unexpected, and contrary to intent; it is also the result of direct intervention by an inscrutable and unpredictable divinity who insists on accomplishing his own ends at his own times and places and by his own chosen instruments. The seemingly absent God returns as *deus ex machina* at precisely the moment of highest dramatic tension. At this point—the *summa epitasis,* or moment of highest strain—the moral, political, and religious conflicts in the drama have simultaneously reached a point of crisis. The opposition between the commands of God and man seems unresolvable, and it appears that the hero must single-handedly withstand the violent constraint or violent retribution of the Philistine state. His companions can foresee no conceivable solution. "How thou wilt here come off surmounts my reach." At this point the dilemma is resolved by divine guidance and divine dispensation; and it is the summons of a higher master, not the command of the idolatrous lords (though this too has been divinely prompted), that brings the hero to the scene of the catastrophe.

Far more than any sequence of external events, Samson's moral

23. See Baldwin, *Shakspere's Five-Act Structure,* 298.

ordeal is, in the final analysis, the clearest and most convincing preparation (or *parasceve*) for the catastrophe. In retrospect the reversal in the Philistine theater is not merely sudden and unexpected but also probable and necessary. Thematically it is necessary (and dramatically it is probable), for it represents the fulfillment of the incomplete oracle that had initially provoked the crisis of doubt. It answers the further doubts concerning Samson's eccentric marriage choices and their seeming violation of divine law. It resolves the more painful misgivings concerning divine justice in subjecting him to sufferings "Too grievous for the trespass or omission." It both illustrates and vindicates divine Providence; and without compromising dramatic decorum by theological subtleties or patent anachronisms, it effectively represents in epitome Reformation doctrines concerning the contrary strategies whereby divine Providence governs the regenerate and unregenerate. Throughout the drama the seemingly estranged and inactive divinity has been significantly present and operative: much like a skillful theatrical manager providing for the time, place, actors, audience, *mise-en-scène,* and other details of a scheduled stage performance. Although his activity becomes apparent only "in the close," the hidden God has scrupulously prepared both the external and internal causes of the catastrophe, arranging the occasion but also perfecting his champion ("The Image" of his "strength, and mighty minister") in the internal virtue essential for Samson's final act of divine vengeance.

In this drama of the Spirit, the principal actor is the *deus absconditus* himself, and he is active in the hero's apparent inaction as well as in his final great act. Promising victory and ordaining Samson's vocation as Nazarite, he has commissioned and consecrated the hero from the womb for his divine mission of deliverance. Against seemingly impossible odds he has converted Samson's disastrous second marriage, like the first, into a signal occasion for glorifying his champion and delivering his people. Regenerating and strengthening the hero both morally and physically, he has intervened directly to bring him to the scene of ultimate victory and endowed him with the power and the guidance of the Spirit. In the catastrophe of the plot, in Samson's sudden burst of activity, executing his "errand on the wicked," with "winged expedition / Swift as the lightning glance," the reader may easily recognize the proverbial arrows of divine judgment. But in the middle of the play, the epitasis, where the hidden deity tests and perfects the instrument of his intent in apparent inactivity, one may also, perhaps, recognize a process comparable to the stringing of Odysseus' bow. In the hero's seeming inaction the seemingly absent divinity has strung and tightened the bow of his revenge. And in the final scenes we see him guiding and directing the hero's aim.

In this poem of multiple paradoxes the reversal is itself a paradox—occurring logically yet also *parà tèn dóxan*. The contradictions of divine Providence and heroic magnanimity, developed in seeming inactivity, are conclusively (and paradoxically) resolved in the tragic action itself.

In the middle sections of this heroic drama the Danite triumphs over his Philistine adversaries, and over himself, primarily through patience and right reason: through dialectical combat and through suffering. In the final section of the tragedy he faces the organized might of the Philistine church and state, and overcomes it by violence. Milton has thus united the ideals of the suffering, the contemplative, and the active hero. In the final paragraphs of this chapter I shall reconsider briefly Samson's relationship to the heroic or pseudoheroic models exemplified by his Philistine visitors and in his final *aristeia* in the Philistine theater.

As critics have long recognized, Milton's drama offers suggestive parallels with the Old Testament tragedy (or epic) of Job: the initial visitation of sympathetic friends, whose efforts to console the afflicted hero ironically increase his torments; the theme of divine justice; the dialectical method, juxtaposing argument and counterargument; the fusion of the concepts of spiritual warfare and temptation; the image of the suffering hero, triumphing through patience and faith; the apparent abandonment of the hero by his God through the greater part of the drama, followed by the Deity's sudden, unexpected return to vindicate his champion. But there are also significant differences. Although both men are heroes of faith, Job is a righteous man whose sufferings are directly attributable to Satanic agency, not to his own transgressions. Samson, on the other hand, is a fallen sinner, one who has brought his own tragic plight upon himself. He is the victim not only of Philistine malice but of his own pride, uxoriousness, and misplaced confidence. His predicament is essentially the plight of fallen mankind.

As a victorious hero of faith and as a tragic hero who sins and repents, Milton's Samson serves as an exemplar of the regenerate elect: the spiritual warrior contending against ghostly or fleshly foes in the arena or theater of this world. Although the theological substructure of this poem is not obtrusive—violating neither the decorum of an Old Testament setting nor the aesthetic demands of a dramatic model partly derived from pagan Athens—the moral and psychological pattern underlying Samson's ordeal (and, in large part, the labyrinthine musings of his sympathetic countrymen) closely interweaves doctrines and concepts of vital importance for Puritan religious experience and for Milton's moral theology. The paradigm of Christian warfare is implicit not only in Samson's struggles with his own conscience and in his ordeal of contrition and doubt but also in his moral and dialectical encounters with Dalila and Harapha. In the central sections of the drama, the protagonist is successively confronted by adversaries who themselves embody heroic paradigms and who serve as foils for his own peculiar kind of heroism. They are distorted mirror images of himself—profoundly different yet also disturbingly similar—and in facing them he is compelled to confront his own past, to recognize and revalue various facets of his own heroic image.

His first Philistine visitor, the comely idolatress, has usurped her husband's mission and heroic identity, delivering her people from a fierce destroyer and thereby glorifying her national deity. It is this action, meritorious in the eyes of her priests, that has directly led not only to Samson's blindness and enslavement but also to the Dagonalia itself, the festival of thanksgiving that provides the occasion (or "procatarctic cause") for the action of the play. As a benefactress of her religion and her state, she may plausibly (if meretriciously) compare her role to that of Jael, and for Milton's readers this allusion might well suggest a further analogy with the later example of Judith. Achieving through her own charms and guile a victory that Philistine armies could not achieve, she has succeeded, like Samson, in making arms appear ridiculous. Even more than Harapha, the giant warrior, she is in a sense the real champion of her nation, and in her triumph over a national enemy one may recognize not only matrimonial treason but an ironic inversion of a favorite Miltonic *topos*: the "unresistible *might* of *Weaknesse*." If she is wanting in *virtù feminile*, she may still hope for renown as an illustrious example of *virtù donnesca*.

In Harapha, in turn, several critics have recognized Samson's alter ego, or Jungian shadow. As Philistine champion he is Samson's counterpart, and in his boasts of strength and prowess he may remind the reader of an earlier, more immature Samson— the "Samson Hybristes" who had strutted "like a petty God," proud of his might and renown and unaware of the fatal weaknesses in his own character. It is significant that, in deploring his former pride, Samson compares his own exploits with those of the ancient giants ("acts indeed heroic, far beyond / The Sons of *Anak*") and that Harapha cites the same parallel in boasting of his famous ancestry ("of stock renown'd / as *Og* or *Anak* and the *Emims* old").[24]

In both instances, of course, the heroic image is flawed, and the resemblance to recognized heroic types is ambiguous and equivocal. Although Dalila has apparently delivered her people from a fierce destroyer, she has actually, though unwittingly, brought about their violent destruction at his hands. Inasmuch as her own action has promoted the Dagonalia, she has literally set the stage for her own ruin and the wholesale massacre of her countrymen. Unlike Jael, with whom she invites comparison, she is not only guilty of marital treason but also precipitates the ruin of her nation.

The Philistine giant, too, is sharply differentiated from Samson not only in his attitude toward "carnal reliance" on "glorious arms" and his obsession with "glory of prowess" but also in the minimal degree of trust he places in his national deity. Unlike Samson, he is far more concerned with preserving his own honor than with fighting for the honor of his god. His boasts of prowess and noble ancestry, along with his trust in armaments, provide an impressive contrast to Samson's heroism of faith and an impressive analogy with familiar pagan stereotypes of heroic virtue: with Harapha's own son Goliath and earlier generations of biblical giants and with the warriors of the Greek heroic age.

In these exchanges with Dalila and Harapha, Samson not only confronts heroic images that reflect and distort his own image or else bring his own extraordinary mode of heroism into clearer focus by opposition and contrast. He is also facing two of the major temptations that traditionally confront the *miles Christianus*. In John Downame's *Christian Warfare*, the spiritual

24. See the discussion of the biblical giants in Steadman, *Milton's Epic Characters*, 177–93.

combatant overcomes both the lures and the threats of the world, successively defying its promises of pleasure and its menaces of violence. On the title page of Downame's book these complementary and antithetical temptations are symbolized by two contrasting images of the world—the first a seductive woman ("*In* Harlots habit") entitled *"Mundus adulans"*; the second a male figure entitled *"Mundus saeviens"* and accompanied by instruments of violence and persecution.[25] In the course of his spiritual combat the warfaring (or wayfaring) Christian must meet and defeat both of these formidable adversaries, and Milton significantly preserves this pattern in *Samson Agonistes* as well as in *Paradise Regained*. In both works the temptation of carnal or secular pleasure is complemented by the threat of worldly or fleshly violence.

The victories that Samson scores over both of these Philistine antagonists are essentially moral and dialectical victories. They do not alter his situation or his condition, but they successfully manifest his own constancy and magnitude of mind, and they point obliquely to the violent and overt "change of fortune" that will conclude the play, the scene in which he will triumph over the entire Philistine aristocracy by sheer physical strength after first having triumphed over himself, exercising his strength of mind. These dramatic victories also enhance Samson's heroic status in the eyes of the audience by giving him at the very least an ethical and eristic triumph over the faithless wife who had usurped his office as national deliverer and over the insolent warrior who as national champion (the counterpart of his own former role) has scorned him as no longer a worthy antagonist. Ethically they mark the progressive stages of his reviving virtue, a reassertion of the characteristic *thymos* of the warrior and a reaffirmation of his identity as Nazarite, as he overcomes his own self-doubts and despair and rededicates himself to his divinely appointed office as the champion of Jehovah. They lend probability and verisimilitude to the following scene in which he will directly challenge the power and authority of the Philistine state, defying its summons as contrary to his own personal dignity and to the principles of his religion. Finally, they foreshadow the final consummation of his predestined office as an extraordinary minister of his God: as divine instrument, champion, and executioner. The catastrophe of the drama is also a heroic epiphany.

25. See *ibid.*, 92–94.

The theological schema underlying the catastrophe as well as the reflections of the chorus on its significance is the contrasting strategy of divine Providence toward the elect and the reprobate as the hidden Deity steers the contrary purposes of the hero and his adversaries toward a single end: the fulfillment of a single "uncontrollable intent." In this concluding scene Milton has effectively combined classical conceptions of the tragic *peripeteia* as a reversal "contrary to expectation or intent" with Reformation doctrines concerning the divine decrees and the providential government of mankind.

When one turns, however, from general dramatic or heroic models to specific analogues, the problem of ascertaining their relevance becomes more difficult. In its savage conclusion, conceived and executed by an offended divinity, *Samson Agonistes* may recall Euripides' fiercely atavistic tragedy *The Bacchae*; here an outraged Dionysos afflicts the blaspheming monarch and his family with sudden madness (*atē*), an insane folly that spurs him on to a gory death at the hands of his nearest relatives. Similarly, in the *Odyssey*, a divinely sent madness seizes the lordly and insolent suitors at the drunken feast as they taunt the unrecognized Odysseus and invite their own destruction. The tension between the law of the gods and that of the state underlies the central dramatic conflict in Sophocles' *Antigone*; and in Samson's longing for death and preoccupation with his ignominious failure, readers might find a suggestive parallel with Sophocles' Ajax, brooding on his public disgrace and contemplating suicide. The analogy with Job might seem significant, though the differences between the two sufferers are even more pronounced. Samson is preoccupied with his own guilt, Job with his righteousness; and one is preeminently an exemplar of active fortitude, the latter of the fortitude of patience. Nevertheless, both figures display exemplary faith ("Though he slay me yet will I trust in him." [Job 13:15]); both are visited by comforters whose consolations intensify their suffering; both prompt doubts and misgivings concerning divine justice and Providence; and both are, in the end, vindicated by the Deity himself, suddenly returning to bear witness to his servant.

The analogy with Hercules as an exemplar of strength is traditional, and this comparison is implicit in the chorus' allusion to the Atlas myth ("and loaded so; / Like whom the Gentiles feign to bear up Heav'n"). Moreover, this analogy involves further points of comparison, linking as well as differentiating Hebraic and Hellenic traditions. For Renaissance mythographers, Herakles served both as a supreme example of heroic virtue yet also as a signal instance of sensual folly. In Cesare Ripa's *Iconologia* four emblems of Heroic Virtue are based on the exploits of this hero while a fifth emblem (significant for Samson's complaint concerning "impotence of mind, in body strong") portrays Hercules as an image of "Virtue of Mind and Body"—that is, "corporal virtue" and "magnanimity and strength of mind." [26]

On the other hand, Samson's "effeminate" bondage to Dalila parallels Hercules' ignominious subjection to Omphale and to Iole as well as the victims of Alcina, Armida, Acrasia, and other enchantresses of Renaissance epic and romance. In Dalila the temptations to ignoble ease and the perils of gynecocracy (or woman sovereignty) are made more formidable by paganism. She belongs to a tradition that includes biblical, classical, and Renaissance prototypes and that effectively unites the images of the sorceress, the concubine, the Amazon, and the idolatress. In yielding to her, Samson has suffered a moral defeat comparable to that of Hercules and Rogero and Rinaldo; and in rejecting her

26. In Cesare Ripa's *Iconologia* an image of "Virtue of Mind and Body" depicts Hercules guiding two beasts linked together and signifying respectively "corporal virtue" (or strength) and "magnanimity and strength of mind" (Steadman, *Milton's Epic Characters*, 17). Samson himself refers repeatedly to the disproportion between his physical strength and his powers of mind: "O impotence of mind, in body strong!" (*SA*, l. 52):

> Immeasurable strength they might behold
> In me, of wisdom nothing more than mean;
> This with the other should, at least, have pair'd,
> These two proportion'd ill drove me transverse.
> (*SA*, ll. 206–209)

The chorus similarly refer to the union (and subsequent disjunction) of strength and virtue: "But thee whose strength, while virtue was her mate, / Might have subdu'd the Earth" (*SA*, ll. 173–74). It is appropriate that for the greater part of the drama Samson's labors and trials should be those of the mind, exercising and perfecting him in "plain Heroic magnitude of mind." For the greater part of the play the emphasis falls on the trial of his strength of mind and the inner fortitude of patience, as the preliminary of the trial of physical strength in the Philistine theater. In the catastrophe the two qualities associated in Ripa's icon, hitherto disjoined, are once again united; heroic magnanimity (strength of mind) and celestial vigor (miraculous physical strength) combine to quell the oppressors. See Eugene M. Waith, *The Herculean Hero in Marlowe, Chapman, Shakespeare, and Dryden* (New York, 1962) for discussion of Ripa's icons and their significance for Renaissance English drama.

offer of domestic ease and the pleasures of less noble senses than sight, he recapitulates a pattern already well established in heroic poetry. Like Spenser before him, Milton adapts the pattern of the alienated hero—enslaved by passion and "effeminately vanquish't," but recalled to his identity as a warrior and to his public duty through the agency of reason, and often with the assistance of divine grace—to the theological schema of repentance and regeneration.

Less convincing are analogies between Samson and Christ. Although this comparison is traditional in Christian exegesis, there is little in Milton's drama to suggest that its protagonist should be regarded as a type of the Messiah or that the reader should look beyond the heroic acts of the Old Testament Nazarite to the "deeds / Above Heroic" of the New Testament Nazarene. It is true that Samson's temptation ordeal shows affinities with that of the Christ of *Paradise Regained,* especially in the hero's preoccupation with his divinely appointed mission and his constancy against both the lures and the threats of his antagonist. Moreover, both are in a sense examples of the "suffering servant" and the "saving victim." Both undergo voluntary death in order to accomplish the deliverance of others, and both achieve glory through humiliation and obedience. Furthermore, in both instances the act of deliverance is conditional; the responsibility for seizing "hold on this occasion" rests with other individuals, each endowed with free will to accept or reject a salvation freely offered. Nevertheless, in their paramount acts of deliverance it is the contrast between them that is most striking. The one triumphs through inflicting violence, the other through suffering violence. Of the two alternative modes of heroism differentiated by the chorus— "invincible might" and patience, "the exercise / Of Saints"—the first belongs properly to the Nazarite, the second to the Nazarene. Although Milton regards the latter as the "great pattern" of fortitude and though he subjects the former to a twofold "trial of . . . fortitude," that of the mind and of physical strength, they achieve victory through diverse kinds of fortitude. Samson excels as a fierce destroyer; and though he resembles the martyr in his self-sacrifice, he ultimately triumphs through sheer force, rather than through the martyr's "unresistible *might* of *Weaknesse.*"

If one insists on looking for Christian typology in *Samson Agonistes* (beyond the type of the *miles Christianus*), the more significant parallel would appear to be not the first but the Second

Advent—the Last Judgment rather than the Passion and Crucifixion. In Samson's role as image and minister of divine strength and
executor of divine justice, inflicting violent destruction on the
reprobate but delivering the elect, one may observe suggestive
analogies with the role of the Son in *Paradise Lost*, not only at the
Last Judgment, but also in the climactic battle of the angelic war.
(In this context it may be significant that Milton, in discussing his
own conceptions of the nature and scope of drama, twice alludes
to Paraeus' conception of the Apocalypse as a tragedy, and
that these references occur as early as *The Reason of Church-
Government* and as late as the preface to *Samson Agonistes*.) A similar pattern underlies the dichotomy of providential destruction
and salvation elsewhere in Milton's works: the ruin of Sodom and
the rescue of Lot in Milton's early dramatic plans; the contrary
fates of the "Sojourners of *Goshen*" and Pharaoh's "*Memphian*
Chivalry"; the first destruction of the world by the Deluge and the
extraordinary salvation of Noah. These signal instances of divine
judgment were frequently interpreted as types of the Last Judgment, and it is not improbable that Milton may have expected
his audience to draw eschatological inferences (as well as other,
more immediate conclusions) from the debacle of the Philistine
aristocracy.

Analogies between Samson and Milton himself are even less
satisfactory. When Milton first considered writing a tragedy on
the theme of the Dagonalia, he was neither blind nor captive nor
disgraced. Even at a much later date, when his personal afflictions
would indeed make his plight roughly analogous to Samson's, the
crucial parallel—a preoccupation with personal sin and failure—
would be notably absent. Writing of his own loss of sight, he
insists that "Not blindness but the inability to endure blindness is
a source of misery." He is "conscious of nothing, or of no deed,
either recent or remote, whose wickedness could justly occasion
or invite upon me this supreme misfortune." Samson has lost his
eyesight by betraying a sacred trust and compromising his mission to deliver his nation; Milton, on the contrary, has voluntarily
sacrificed his eyesight to his duties to "free my country" and "to
free the church." Although Milton (like Andrew Marvell) surely
recognized parallels between Samson's plight and his own condition and though he sometimes employed similar images and *topoi*
in describing them, there is little justification for identifying him
with his own tragic hero, and still less warrant for transforming

Samson's Philistine antagonists into surrogates for Mary Powell and Salmasius: the Royalist wife who had deserted the poet and the Royalist defender who had been Milton's most formidable antagonist as defender of the English people.

More plausible are those readings which regard Samson rather as a representative of the English nation than as a surrogate for the poet himself and which associate his fate with that of the Good Old Cause. If the poem does indeed belong among "those Dramatick constitutions" that are truly "doctrinal and exemplary to a Nation," it would be plausible to stress Samson's political significance as well as his moral significance and to see him not only as an exemplar of the regenerated individual, the Christian warrior, but also as a type of a regenerated England. Although the actual date of composition remains uncertain, and analogies between the dramatic situation in *Samson Agonistes* and the political situation of post-Restoration England must necessarily remain tentative and hypothetical, there is ample justification for such conjectures. Although we do not know when Milton actually wrote his tragedy, we do know when he published it. More than any of us, he was fully aware of its contemporary political relevance; and he might plausibly expect his original audience, Englishmen living in the year 1671, to interpret it in the light of the Commonwealth failure, and the conditions prevailing in the English church and state at the time of its publication.

Index

PACIFIC UNIVERSITY LIBRARY
FOREST GROVE. OREGON